The Royal Navy and the Mediterranean Convoys

A Naval Staff History

**With a preface by
Malcolm Llewellyn-Jones**

Whitehall History Publishing
in association with
Routledge

Routledge
Taylor & Francis Group

LONDON AND NEW YORK

First published 2007
by Routledge
2 Park Square, Milton Park, Abingdon, Oxon OX14 4RN

Simultaneously published in the USA and Canada
by Routledge
711 Third Avenue, New York, NY 10017

Routledge is an imprint of the Taylor & Francis Group, an informa business

© 2007 Crown Copyright

Typeset in Times New Roman by
Keystroke, 28 High Street, Tettenhall, Wolverhampton

British Library Cataloguing in Publication Data
A catalogue record for this book is available from the British Library

Library of Congress Cataloging in Publication Data
A catalog record for this book has been applied for
First issued in paperback 2014
ISBN 13: 978-0-415-86459-6 (pbk)
ISBN13 978-0-415-39095-8 (hbk)

Published on behalf of the Whitehall History Publishing Consortium.
Applications to reproduce Crown copyright protected material in this publication
should be submitted in writing to:
HMSO, Copyright Unit, St Clements House, 2-16 Colegate, Norwich NR3 1BQ.
Fax: 01603 723000.
E-mail: copyright@hmso.gov.uk

The Royal Navy and the Mediterranean Convoys

Naval Staff Histories

Series Editor: Malcolm Llewellyn-Jones

ISSN: 1471-0757

Naval Staff Histories were produced after the Second World War in order to provide as full an account of the various actions and operations as was possible at the time. In some cases the Histories were based on earlier Battle Summaries written much sooner after the event, and designed to provide more immediate assessments.

The Evacuation from Dunkirk: Operation 'Dynamo', 26 May–4 June 1940
With a preface by W. J. R. Gardner.

Naval Operations of the Campaign in Norway, April–June 1940
With a preface by David Brown

The Royal Navy and the Mediterranean, Vol. I: September 1939–October 1940
With an introduction by David Brown

The Royal Navy and the Mediterranean, Vol. II: November 1940–December 1941
With an introduction by David Brown

German Capital Ships and Raiders in World War II:
    Vol I. From Graf Spee to Bismarck, 1939–1941
    Vol. II. From Scharnhorst to Tirpitz, 1942–1944
With an introduction by Eric Grove

The Royal Navy and the Palestine Patrol
Ninian Stewart

The Royal Navy and the Arctic Convoys: A Naval Staff History
With a preface by Malcolm Llewellyn-Jones

The Royal Navy and the Mediterranean Convoys: A Naval Staff History
With a preface by Malcolm Llewellyn-Jones

Contents

Foreword

Admiral Sir Jonathon Band, KCB, ADC, First Sea Lord and Chief of Naval Staff

Convoys in the Second World War have been largely associated with attacks by U-boats but, as this Naval Staff History of the Mediterranean Convoys to Malta shows, these sailed in the face of multiple threats from the air and surface, as well as from underwater enemies. By and large, these attacks were mastered by the determination and tactical expertise of the Royal Navy and the steadfast courage of the Allied merchant marine, even when the odds were heavily stacked against them. The account presented here deals with the naval side of these Mediterranean convoys. As the History and the new Preface make clear, the convoys were critical to the ultimate survival of that island and, though our hold on the island was at times fragile, its defence and re-supply were major factors in the defeat of Axis forces in the Mediterranean. This is disputed by some historians, but was readily acknowledged by the enemy at the time. The provision of the necessary aircraft carriers, battleships, cruisers and destroyers to escort these small but vital convoys placed a heavy strain on British resources. It was, however, a commitment that – albeit, sometimes, by a narrow margin – the Royal Navy was able to meet, because of the inherent flexibility of seapower, which allowed the necessary ships to be concentrated from other stations, often hundreds of miles away, and then readily re-deployed. Thus many ships were sequentially used in Mediterranean and then Arctic convoys.

The Western Alliance has, for many years now, enjoyed almost complete control over the World's oceans. It is easy to forget how fragile this command can be, even when threatened by weak asymmetric threats. Who can predict whether another maritime power might possess, in the not too far future, the global reach to threaten this hegemony? It is therefore easy to take for granted that the oceans can be used for our own purposes: to transport armies and supplies at will. British military campaigns ashore are supplied overwhelmingly by sea. When this Staff History was written, these lessons were in the forefront of most naval officers' minds. Sixty years on, it is perhaps time for a gentle reminder that our hegemony may not automatically remain intact and that we may, once more, have to fight supplies through to a future battlezone. The History shows how the Royal Navy was able to plan and execute the complex tactical operations required to see the Mediterranean convoys through to their destination, without (for the most part) unacceptable losses – at least by the standards of their day. These operations also demonstrated that, against a multitude of threats, the age-old strategy of 'convoy and escort' succeeded in simultaneously protecting trade and inflicting heavy loss on the enemy. Even taking into account the great changes in naval technology, convoys remained vital for the survival of the United Kingdom – a lesson we forget at our peril! The security of the High Seas and maritime trade remain as important as ever. As for this Staff History, it is now fifty years old, but the account, written with the echoes of the events still ringing in the author's ears, retains an immediacy and candour that the casual reader and academic researcher alike will not find in other secondary accounts.

Preface to the Published Edition[1]

Battle Summary 18, *Mediterranean Convoys, 1941*, and Battle Summary No. 32, *Malta Convoys, 1942*, were both completed by Commander J. Owen of the Historical Section and issued in 1944 and 1945.[2] These Battle Summaries were revised and combined after the war by Pitcairn-Jones and issued in 1957 as *Selected Convoys (Mediterranean), 1941–1942*. By this time, Pitcairn-Jones had access to the full records (some of them highly classified), including those captured from German and Italian forces. The Staff History was thus produced as a Confidential study for use within the Royal Navy.[3] Although long since declassified, it is published for the first time here in this volume, where it is deliberately reproduced in facsimile and with no attempt at revision. It will be seen that this Staff History, in common with the whole series, was narrowly focussed on the naval aspects of the Mediterranean Convoys to Malta. This Preface, however, is new and is intended to provide additional context for the operations described in the Staff History and, in particular, to emphasise the value of the continuing resistance of Malta to the Mediterranean theatre generally.

What did The Mediterranean Convoys Achieve?

The Admiralty's Historical Section were under no illusion as to the importance of Malta to British strategy in the Mediterranean. In a lecture they prepared the Historical Section concluded that:

> When the history of the war comes to be written, it will be generally recognised that the maintenance of Malta, as a base for offensive operations, was the 'Corner Stone' on which the whole strategy of the war in the Mediterranean has been built. The success of its air and submarine offensive in the last months of 1941, and from July onwards of 1942, played a decisive part in those Military successes in Libya and North Africa which have culminated in the tremendous victory in Tunisia. Malta's contribution to the destruction of the Axis air strength alone is impressive: 1,000 enemy aircraft have been shot down by the fighters and A/A gunfire of the Island. . . .[4]

During the war, however, it had not always seemed so certain. After Italy entered the war and with France defeated, it was realised that Mediterranean through-convoys would have to be abandoned and that Malta would be too vulnerable to act as a Fleet main base. However, there was no plan to abandon Malta entirely, for its strategic position athwart Italian (and later German) lines of communication to North Africa meant that it could be used as a base for sea and air offensive operations.[5] This was realised by the enemy too, and the neutralisation of the island was one of *Luftwaffe*'s objectives when Fliegerkorps X was despatched to Sicily in January 1941. Thereafter the whole Mediterranean situation, of which Malta was frequently the focus, caused the Germans to constantly reinforce the theatre at the end of 1941, even at the expense of air support on the Russian front.[6]

However, the struggle was not as one-sided as this might suggest, for the ability of Malta to play a significant part in the interdiction of the enemy's supply routes, and even to guarantee its own survival were, for a long time, in the balance during 1941–42. The decision in April 1942, for example, to abandon the sailing of a planned re-supply convoy prompted the Governor of Malta to signal London that:

> . . . our situation is so grave that it is my duty to restate [it] in the clearest possible terms. The decision materially reduces our chances of survival not because of any failure of morale or fighting efficiency but because it is impossible to carry on without food and ammunition. . . . The position with regard to these is as follows:–
> (A) Flour. We have enough to last until the later half of May. . . .
> (B) A/A Ammunition...we have slightly over a month's supply. . . .[7]

Even in the following September, after the arrival of the 'Pedestal' convoy (the last dealt with in the Staff History) the position had imperceptibly improved. After listing the items of essential stores to be carried in a single ship totalling 8,000 tons (of which just over 40% was to be flour), the Governor again signalled in the starkest of terms that:

> Only absolutely essential articles of food and fuel are included with small allocation of civil and service stores. Object would be to put off target date until early January.[8]

The Governor's 'target date' was the date by which Malta would be forced to surrender unless the essential supplies were received.[9] Malta's ability to act as an offensive base remained on a knife-edge and, in the circumstances, it is remarkable that her strike forces achieved so much.

During 1942 the Royal Navy was heavily committed in the Atlantic combating the U-boats. Resources were also consumed in vain attempts to stem the Japanese advance in the Far East and, of course, in supporting the Russians via the Arctic Convoys. The desperate shortage of heavy ships (particularly aircraft carriers) made the adequate protection for Mediterranean convoys problematic. As a result, Malta's critical situation often had to be allayed by the use of submarines to ferry stores and fuel to the island. Thus three trips were made in 1940, 39 in 1941, and at least 50 during 1942.[10] The carriage of stores by air was a by-product of the transfer of aircraft to Malta for reconnaissance and strike operations, though in early 1942 the Air Ministry agreed to 24 Squadron, equipped with long-range Hudsons, to be used for regular flights to Malta carrying passengers and small quantities of high value cargo, such as medical and electronic supplies. When aircraft carriers were available, fighter aircraft could be ferried to Malta and, by this means, about 700 Hurricanes and Spitfires were delivered.[11] The security these aircraft gave Malta allowed the island to become a progressively more effective base for strikes against enemy shipping. Their convoys were trying to supply the Axis armies in North Africa, whose ultimate objective was the capture of the Middle East oil fields.

During 1942 the *Luftwaffe* increased its commitment to the Mediterranean theatre by some 50%, until they were maintaining over 1,000 aircraft. This contrasted markedly with the steady decline in the *Luftwaffe* on the Russian front, where their strength fell from

4,800 to 3,950 aircraft during 1942, and thereafter to less than 1,800 aircraft.[12] In both theatres the Germans were at last meeting numerically superior opponents, with the consequent increase in aircraft wastage, and never enough aircraft to undertake all the operations needed to support German positions. In mid June 1942, for example, the Eighth Army began a well-ordered retreat from Gazala. This could have been turned into a rout if the *Luftwaffe* had been able to attack the exposed columns, but the enemy's air forces were instead concentrated against the 'Harpoon' and 'Vigorous' convoys making their way to Malta. The Panzer Army was thus forced to advance into Egypt without adequate air support, while the enemy aircraft lost in the convoys battles reduced their strength for future operations. The switch of bomber force bases caused considerable disorganisation, and the intensity of the anti-convoy operations also markedly effected subsequent aircraft serviceability. The cycle was repeated in August against the 'Pedestal' convoy.[13] On the Allied side, the arrival of two ships in the 'Harpoon' convoy allowed Malta to resume offensive operations, which prompted urgent discussions between senior Axis Commanders. The German General Staff were informed:

> The situation of the British Army demands that successes gained so far be exploited as far as possible. In spite of this, it must be taken into consideration that the supply problem offers difficulties. The air base of Malta has resumed offensive operations. The Tripoli route must be temporarily abandoned and the route to harbours in Cyrenaica is also endangered. It is planned to neutralise Malta again, employing formations to be transferred from Germany. This, however, requires time, during which a critical period cannot be avoided.[14]

The third Axis air 'blitz' was launched against Malta in July, but by then Malta's fighter defences had been augmented to such a degree that the enemy's assault was defeated. The enemy were also in no doubt over the effects the Malta garrison was having on their naval operations. Admiral Weichold, for example, revealed the inter-relationship between the Allied convoy operations and the enemy's ability to transport and protect supplies to the Panzer Army in North Africa. During the June convoys operations the Italian Fleet had expended 15,000 tons of fuel and this left them with insufficient reserves to maintain their extensive convoy protection commitments. This in turn caused a further drop in the rate of delivery of supplies to North Africa. Although some of the shortfalls were:

> ... made good by the windfall obtained with the capture of Tobruk, this was no substitute for a controlled and successful supply programme, and in fact it merely helped to conceal the real extent of the supply crisis of the Panzer Army. Later, when fully revealed by the pressure of events, the shortage of supplies became one of the most important factors in the failure of the Panzer Army, at El Alamein.[15]

Perhaps no better appreciation of the value of Malta, bought at such high cost, can be found than in this unwitting testimony from the enemy.

A contemporary assessment was made by the Director of Naval Operational Research of the effect of the Malta striking forces. The study reviewed the period from the 'Torch' landings in November 1942 to May 1943, when the campaign ended and the Mediterranean was reopened for through convoys. It was based, in part, on '... captured enemy documents and other sources ...' and concluded that:

... 26% of the [enemy's] supplies sailing have been sunk or turned back through damage. During November [1942] there were no sinkings, in December 31% was sunk and in January and February 23% and 21%, after that sinkings rose to 37% in March, 45% in April and 78% in May.[16]

The principal means of sinking Axis shipping were aircraft and submarines operating from several bases in the Mediterranean, although roughly half of the air strikes and half of the enemy shipping sunk were by aircraft flying from Malta.[17] This was as a direct outcome of a gradual accrual of strength by the Malta garrison, especially after the arrival of the 'Harpoon' convoy in June 1942.[18] Thus, the Axis forces were constantly beset by their lack of an assured supply route across the short stretch of the Mediterranean that lay between Italy and North Africa. In addition to their attempts to send supplies by sea '... about 40,000 tons arrived by air. Nearly all of this was transported in Ju 52's carrying 2 tons each, or Me 323's carrying 10 tons.'[19] Smaller proportions were carried by other Italian aircraft, but the whole enterprise was hugely inefficient. But even with all these exertions, the Axis army in North Africa was deprived of half of their supplies and, more significantly, two-thirds of their oil.[20] Meanwhile, the British managed, by and large, to maintain and even expand their army in North Africa via the long sea routes round the Cape.

Continuing Relevance of the Naval Staff Histories

In parallel with the *Mediterranean Convoys* study Admiralty issued *The Defeat of the Enemy Attack on Shipping* which focussed mainly (but not exclusively) on the Atlantic U-boat campaign.[21] The volume covering the *Arctic Convoys, 1941–1945* had been issued three years earlier, and together with the other two volumes, provided detailed analyses of all the main convoy operations during the war. Of course, much has changed since the Second World War: the technological promises of that earlier era have become realities and the politico-strategic environment has altered out of all recognition. In the late 1980s, some professional experts thought that convoys were much less valuable as a means of protecting shipping, because the improvements in ocean surveillance systems meant that more 'offensive' anti-submarine operations could be contemplated. Moreover, dispersion and deception were seen as the principal counters to both the submarine and aircraft capable of firing long-range missiles, for the enemy would be less sure of identifying their principal target. In any case, if they were to fire, it would be from well outside any convoy's traditional defensive perimeter.[22] This is, surely, a misreading of the *Mediterranean Convoys* and the other Staff Histories, for the shape of multi-threat future operations as conceived at the beginning of the Cold War, bore a great resemblance to the convoy and fleet actions in the Mediterranean, the Arctic and the Pacific. The histories of these campaigns showed how attack-at-source and other offensive operations had directly effected the defence of shipping. Indeed, for those contemplating a nuclear attack-at-source strategy launched from the Mediterranean, and later the Arctic, these histories provided direct information of these operational areas.[23]

The *Mediterranean Convoys* volume confirmed the value of convoy in the defence of shipping against air and submarine attack, and demonstrated the necessity of aircraft carriers '... for fighter protection and fighter direction ... against shore-based air attack.'[24] This was a lesson reinforced during the 1982 Falklands War. Aircraft carriers and other fleet units also played an indirect part in the success of the convoys, by neutralising the enemy's surface fleet in actions such as the Fleet Air Arm attack at Taranto and the Battle of Matapan.[25] The *Mediterranean Convoys* volume also confirmed another lesson: that complex operations could be mounted by ships drawn from widely separated theatres at short notice. An example was HMS *Ashanti*, a Home Fleet ship, who took part in the Arctic PQ17 convoy, followed by the Mediterranean 'Pedestal' operations and then went back to the Arctic for convoy PQ18. One of *Ashanti*'s officers was the future Chief of the Defence Staff, Admiral of the Fleet Lord Lewin.[26] These operations made a distinct impression on Lewin which stayed with him for many years. When he was asked, just after *Sheffield* was sunk at the beginning of the 1982 Falklands campaign, whether further heavy losses of ships would result in the abandonment of the operation, he reminded '. . . the War Cabinet that in 1942 Operation 'Pedestal' had lost two-thirds of the merchant ships involved. . . .' He might have added that an aircraft carrier, a cruiser, an anti-aircraft ship and a destroyer were also lost, with others damaged, but, Lewin emphatically assured the War Cabinet, the Royal Navy '. . . had still saved Malta.'[27]

As an example of pure history, this Staff History provides a fascinating and detailed account of important events during the Second World War with an authority which is seldom possible elsewhere. Their value is enhanced when it is realised that these histories were written by a professional historian, Pitcairn-Jones, a man of considerable naval experience and technical knowledge, who had access to an impressive range of primary sources, including Ultra intelligence material and the personal testimony of many individuals involved in the events depicted. Given that the history was written 'in-house', it is surprisingly balanced in its treatment of, what were sometimes, controversial events and this, surely, is an example to be followed. Furthermore, this Staff History takes a positive view of the Malta convoys. Many subsequent histories have dwelt on the cost of these operations and concluded that they were therefore wasteful of effort. The Staff History, on the other hand, while not belittling the setbacks and losses, emphasises the achievements, as well as the detrimental effect on Axis operations, by the continued British possession of Malta. While the strategic and operational environment in which the Royal Navy now operates is vastly different to that depicted in *Mediterranean Convoys*, the History restates the vital necessity for detailed operational planning if success is to be assured. Also that the courage and determination of both the military and merchant sailors, and the airmen was essential to fight through their convoys, more often that not against heavy odds. The history shows that aggressive action could reap benefits – in the psychological as well as the material arenas – and that high technology was not the only determinate of success. The Naval Staff in the 1950s read and commented on the drafts and found that the narrative chimed well with their experiences of the Mediterranean Convoys.

Dr. Malcolm Llewellyn-Jones
Naval Historical Branch
1 December 2004

1 The author would like to thank those who helped variously with encouragement, criticism and unearthing records during the preparation of this Preface, especially Michael Whitby (Department of History and Heritage, Ottawa), Peter Nash (King's College, London), Kate Tildesley and Mac McAloon (both of the Naval Historical Branch).

2 'Historical Section of TSD – Review of Narrator Posts,' Roger M. Bellairs, 11 November 1949, T.27309, NHB. Owen does not appear in the list of narrators in 1949. 'Extra Pay Allowance,' Rear Admiral Roger M. Bellairs, HSL.261 29 December 1949, in, 'Personnel and Administration, 1 June 1948 to 31 December 1949,' TSD/HS, NHB.

3 The original can be found in the National Archive at the Public Record Office (hereafter PRO): 'Selected Convoys (Mediterranean), 1941–42, Battle Summary Nos. 18 and 32,' 1957, PRO ADM 234/336, and in both the Naval Historical Branch and Admiralty Library.

4   'Malta, Lecture,' n.d., in, 'Lectures,' Folder No. 7, NHB.

5   *ibid.*

6   Air Ministry, Pamphlet No. 248: *The Rise and Fall of the German Air Force (1933 to 1945)* (Issued by the Air Ministry (A.C.A.S.[I]), 1948), pp. 129 and 133.

7   Governor and C-in-C, Malta, to Admiralty for Chiefs of Staff, Hush Message, 1320/20 April 1942, 'Hush Signals, April to June 1942,' Microfilm, NHB, p. 289.

8   Governor Malta to Admiralty, Hush Message 1430B/27 September 1942, 'Hush Signals, August to October 1942,' Microfilm, NHB, p. 162.

9   The author is especially indebted to Arnold Hague for drawing his attention to this aspect of the campaign and the Hush Signals series.

10 Arnold Hague, *The Supply of Malta, 1940–1942* (unpublished paper, May 1995), pp. 73–80.

11 *ibid*, p. 64.

12 Much of the drain of aircraft from the Russian front was, of course, due to the increasing effectiveness of the direct attack on Germany first by RAF Bomber Command and later by the USAAF Air Forces based in Britain and the Mediterranean. Air Ministry, Pamphlet No. 248: *The Rise and Fall of the German Air Force (1933 to 1945)* (Issued by the Air Ministry (A.C.A.S.[I]), 1948), pp. 219–221.

13 'Operation "Pedestal": Enquiry from Commander L.J. Pitcairn-Jones,' Mervyn Mills, Air Historical Branch, 10 December 1955, in, 'Selected Convoys: Mediterranean, 1941–42, Revised Battle Summaries, Nos. 18, 32,' Folder, NHB.

14 Quoted in, 'The June Convoys to Malta (Operations "Harpoon" and "Vigorous"): Enquiry from Commander L.J. Pitcairn-Jones, RN,' [Squadron Leader Mervyn Mills, 24 January 1956], in, 'Selected Convoys: Mediterranean, 1941–42, Revised Battle Summaries, Nos. 18, 32,' Folder, NHB.

15 *ibid.*

16 'Enemy Supplies to Tunisia,' [E.C. Bullard], CAOR, May 1943, 'Lectures,' Folder No. 7, NHB.

17 *ibid.*

18 'The June Convoys to Malta (Operations "Harpoon" and "Vigorous"): Enquiry from Commander L.J. Pitcairn-Jones, RN,' [Squadron Leader Mervyn Mills, 24 January 1956], in, 'Selected Convoys: Mediterranean, 1941–42, Revised Battle Summaries, Nos. 18, 32,' Folder, NHB.

19 'Enemy Supplies to Tunisia,' *op cit.*

20 Richard Overy, *Why the Allies Won*, paperback edn. (London: Pimlico, 1996), p. 52.

21 'Naval Staff History: Defeat of the Enemy Attack on Shipping 1939–1945: A Study of Policy and Operations: Volume 1A, Text and Appendices,' CB 3304(1A), 1957, PRO ADM 239/415 and 'Naval Staff History: Defeat of the Enemy Attack on Shipping 1939–1945: A Study of Policy and Operations: Volume 1B, Plans and Tables,' CB 3304(1A), 1957, PRO ADM 239/416. (See also PRO ADM 234/578 and PRO ADM 234/579.) These books have been published in a single volume: Eric J. Grove (ed.), *The Defeat of the Enemy Attack on Shipping, 1939–1945*, revised edn. (Aldershot: Ashgate for The Navy Records Society, 1997).

22 Geoffrey Till, *Air Power and the Royal Navy, 1914–1945, A Historical Survey* (London: Jane's, 1979), pp. 143–145.

23 For more detail see Michael A. Palmer, *Origins of the Maritime Strategy: The Development of American Naval Strategy, 1945–55* (Annapolis: Naval Institute Press, 1990); Eric J. Grove, *Vanguard to Trident: British Naval Policy since World War II* (London: The Bodley Head, 1987).

24 'Selected Convoys (Mediterranean), 1941–42, Battle Summary Nos. 18 and 32,' 1957, PRO ADM 234/336, Section 74.

25 'Selected Operations (Mediterranean), 1940, (Battle Summaries Nos. 2, 8, 9 & 10),' Historical Section, BR 1736(6), 1957, and 'The Battle of Cape Matapan,' Historical Section, BR 1736(35), 1950, NHB.

26 Ashanti was part of the escort for the Home Fleet. Richard Hill, *Lewin of Greenwich: The Authorised Biography of Admiral of the Fleet Lord Lewin* (London: Cassell, 2000), pp. 39–50.

27 Richard Hill, *Lewin of Greenwich: The Authorised Biography of Admiral of the Fleet Lord Lewin* (London: Cassell, 2000), p. 370; 'Selected Convoys (Mediterranean), 1941–42, Battle Summary Nos. 18 and 32,' 1957, PRO ADM 234/336, Appendix N.

Appendix to the preface

Abbreviations used in the preface

CB	Confidential Book(s)
C-in-C or CinC	Commander-in-Chief
HMS	Her Majesty's Ship
PRO	Public Record Office (now the National Archive)
RAF	Royal Air Force
TSD	Tactical and Staff Duties (Division) (Admiralty)

A Note on Sources

The documentary sources used in *Mediterranean Convoys* are referenced by the original file structure used within the Admiralty. For researchers who wish to explore these further a translation of these references into the Public Record Office (now the National Archive) numbering has been provided below.

Sources for Mediterranean Convoys

In the listings below, 'N/T' stands for 'No Trace'. This does not necessarily indicate that the document concerned has been destroyed but that it has proved impossible to identify the current National Archive designation of the record.

Original Ref	*Current National Archive Ref*
Admiralty Historical Section War Diary	ADM 199/2195–2326
CinC Mediterranean: War Diary	ADM 199/414–415 (1941),
	ADM 199/650–651 (1942)
Vice Admiral, Malta: War Diary	ADM 199/413 (1941), ADM 199/424 (1942)
Reports of Proceedings, etc., contained in the following Record Office cases and dockets:–	

Operation 'Excess'

WH 7603, 7363: FO, Force 'H'	ADM 199/656
WH 7721, 8122: CinC Mediterranean	ADM 199/797
WH 8088, 8091: Submarines	ADM 199/1150, ADM 199/1153
A. 0655/41: HMS *Illustrious*	N/T

Operation 'Substance'

WH 7604, 7745, Force 'H'	ADM 199/657, ADM 704 & 705
WH 7745, CinC Mediterranean	ADM 199/830
WH 8027, 8028, 8030, 8092, 8093:	ADM 199/1119, N/T, ADM 199/1154,
Submarines	ADM 199/1155

Operation 'Halberd'

WH 7746: FO, Force 'H'; Home Fleet	ADM 199/831
WH 8020, 8027, 8089, 8091, 8092:	ADM 199/1116, ADM 199/1119,
Submarines	ADM 199/1151, ADM 199/1153,
	ADM 199/1154

Operation MG 1

WH 8287: CinC Mediterranean	N/T
WH 8202, 8212: Submarines	ADM 199/1218 & 1219, ADM 199/1224
WH 7758: Naval Air Squadrons	ADM 199/844

Operation 'Harpoon'

WH 8285; SO Force 'T'; VA Malta;	N/T
various ship's reports	
M.10/27/55: Loss of HMS *Bedouin*	N/T
WH 8373: HMS *Welshman*	N/Y
WH 8281: Submarines	N/T
WH 7758: Naval Air Squadrons	ADM 199/844

Operation 'Vigorous'

WH 8286: CinC, Mediterranean	ADM 199/1244
WH 8202, 8213: Submarines	ADM 199/1219, 199/1225

Operation 'Pedestal'

WH 8267, 8268, 8269: SO Force 'F';	199/1240 & 1241, 199/1242, 199/
VA Malta; various ship's reports	
WH 8210, 8213: Submarines	ADM 199/1222 & 1225
M.014103/42: HMS *Pathfinder*	N/T

Various ships' logs (as necessary)	ADM 53
Italian Official Naval History, Second World War	
Naval Staff History, *Mediterranean, Vol. II*	ADM 186/801
Naval Staff History, *Submarines, Vol. II*	ADM 234/381
Naval Staff History, Battle Summary No. 22, *Arctic Convoys*	ADM 234/340
Naval Staff History, *Development of British Naval Aviation, Vols. I and II*	ADM 383 & 384

Air Ministry Pamphlet No. 248, *The Rise
and Fall of the German Air Force*
War Vessels and Aircraft, British and   ADM 239/70 & 72
Foreign
Navy Lists
Pink Lists   ADM 187
The Second world War, The Right Hon.
W.S. Churchill, OM, PC, CH, MP
A Sailor's Odyssey, Admiral of the Fleet
viscount Cunningham of Hyndhope,
KT, GCB, OM, DSO

B.R. 1736 (11)

NAVAL STAFF HISTORY

SECOND WORLD WAR

SELECTED CONVOYS

(MEDITERRANEAN), 1941-1942

BATTLE SUMMARIES Nos. 18 and 32

HISTORICAL SECTION

ADMIRALTY

A

Admiralty, S.W.1
31st December, 1957

H.S. 4/56

B.R. 1736(11), Naval Staff History, Second World War, *Selected Convoys (Mediterranean)*, 1957, having been approved by My Lords Commissioners of the Admiralty, is hereby promulgated.

B.R. 1736(11), dated 1944, and B.R. 1736(25), dated 1945, are hereby superseded and should be destroyed in accordance with the instructions contained in B.R.1.

By Command of Their Lordships,

J. S. Lang

FOREWORD

THE two Battle Summaries superseded by this volume were originally issued in 1944 and 1945, and were contained in two separate books. In the present volume they have been largely rewritten to include information from the opposing side and other sources not available at the time they were produced. They have also been amended in matters of detail, where such have proved in error. The Introduction and Chapters VII and VIII are entirely new.

Part I of the ensuing book contains the story of three convoys in 1941, when the arrival of German air forces to stiffen the Italians greatly complicated the problem. (This was formerly Battle Summary No. 18.)

Part II deals with the attempts to relieve Malta in the critical conditions of March, June and August, 1942 (former Battle Summary No. 32).

It must be remembered that all these events took place in the early days of radar. Few ships were fitted with sets other than for the detection of high-flying aircraft, and fewer still for fighter direction.

Plans illustrating the events described have been redrawn to include up-to-date information and will be found at the end of the volume, together with a reference chart of the Mediterranean Sea.

January 1956

Contents

Part I. Convoys in 1941

(*Battle Summary No. 18*)

CHAPTER I. OPERATION " EXCESS ", JANUARY 1941

CHAPTER II. OPERATION " SUBSTANCE ", JULY 1941

CHAPTER III. OPERATION " HALBERD ", SEPTEMBER 1941

CONTENTS

Part II. Convoys in 1942

(Battle Summary No. 32)

CHAPTER IV.   OPERATION " M.G.1 ", MARCH 1942

CHAPTER V.   OPERATION " HARPOON ", JUNE 1942

CHAPTER VI.   OPERATION " VIGOROUS ", JUNE 1942

CHAPTER VII.   OPERATION " PEDESTAL ", AUGUST 1942

CHAPTER VIII. COMMENT AND REFLECTIONS

Appendices

Figures in Text

ACTION IN THE GULF OF SIRTE, 22ND MARCH 1942

Plans

(at end of book)

Sources

Admiralty Historical Section War Diary
C.-in-C., Mediterranean: War Diary
Vice-Admiral, Malta: War Diary
Reports of proceedings, etc., contained in the following Record Office cases and dockets :—

Operation " Excess "

  W.H. 7603, 7363: F.O., Force " H "
  W.H. 7721, 8122: C.-in-C., Mediterranean
  W.H. 8088, 8091: Submarines
  A. 0655/41: H.M.S. *Illustrious*

Operation " Substance "

  W.H. 7604, 7745: F.O., Force " H "
  W.H. 7745: C.-in-C., Mediterranean
  W.H. 8027, 8028, 8030, 8092, 8093: Submarines

Operation " Halberd "

  W.H. 7746: F.O., Force " H "; Home Fleet
  W.H. 8020, 8027, 8089, 8091, 8092: Submarines

Operation M.G. 1

  W.H. 8287: C.-in-C., Mediterranean
  W.H. 8202, 8212: Submarines
  W.H. 7758: Naval Air Squadrons

Operation " Harpoon "

  W.H. 8285: S.O., Force " T "; V.A., Malta; various ships' reports
  M.10/27/55: Loss of H.M.S. *Bedouin*
  W.H. 8373: H.M.S. *Welshman*
  W.H. 8281: Submarines
  W.H. 7758: Naval Air Squadrons

Operation " Vigorous "

  W.H. 8286: C.-in-C., Mediterranean
  W.H. 8202, 8213: Submarines

Operation " Pedestal "

  W.H. 8267, 8268, 8269: S.O., Force " F "; V.A., Malta; various ships' reports
  W.H. 8210, 8213: Submarines
  M.014103/42: H.M.S. *Pathfinder*

Various ships' logs (as necessary)
Italian Official Naval History, Second World War
Naval Staff History, *Mediterranean, Vol. II*
Naval Staff History, *Submarines, Vol. II*
Naval Staff History, Battle Summary No. 22, *Arctic Convoys*
Naval Staff History, *Development of British Naval Aviation, Vols. I and II*
Air Ministry Pamphlet No. 248, *The Rise and Fall of the German Air Force*
War Vessels and Aircraft, British and Foreign
Navy Lists
Pink Lists
The Second World War, The Right Hon. W. S. Churchill, o.m., p.c., c.h., m.p.
A Sailor's Odyssey, Admiral of the Fleet Viscount Cunningham of Hyndhope, k.t.,
  g.c.b., o.m., d.s.o.

Abbreviations

A.A.	Anti-aircraft	N.I.D.	Naval Intelligence Division
A/C	aircraft	P.M.	Prime Minister
A/S	anti-submarine	R.A.	Rear-Admiral
A.S.V.	air-surface vessel (radar)	R.A.(A)	Rear-Admiral, Aircraft Carriers
C.-in-C.	Commander-in-Chief	R.A.F.	Royal Air Force
C.S.	Cruiser Squadron	R.F.A.	Royal Fleet Auxiliary
D. of S.T.	Director of Sea Transport	R.O.	Record Office (Admiralty)
E-boat	motor torpedo boat	R/T	radio-telephony
F.A.A.	Fleet Air Arm	S.O.O.	Staff Officer, Operations
H.A.	high angle (gunnery)	T.S.D.S.	two-speed destroyer sweep (minesweeping)
L.A.	low angle (gunnery)	U.K.	United Kingdom
M.S.	merchant ship	V.A.	Vice-Admiral
M/S	mine-sweeper/sweeping	V.H.F.	very high frequency
M.T.B.	motor torpedo boat	W/T	wireless telegraphy

INTRODUCTION

The passage of a convoy through narrow waters in the face of determined attacks by aircraft, submarines, surface craft and mining is one of the most hazardous and arduous operations of maritime warfare.

This was the problem which immediately confronted Great Britain on the declaration of war by Italy in June 1940.

It was at once apparent that the regular flow of slow merchant shipping through the Mediterranean was impracticable, and the bulk of supplies for Alexandria and the Middle East was diverted round the Cape of Good Hope. But occasions arose in which the urgency of the situation in the Middle East necessitated the running of fast convoys through the Mediterranean, and there was always Malta—at once the linchpin of British strategy and its " Achilles heel." Malta, within 60 miles from Sicily and roughly a thousand miles alike from Gibraltar and Alexandria, had to be kept supplied either from the east or from the west; and it was on the ability of the British Navy, with the help of the Air Force, to achieve this that the security of the island depended.

The problem had been much debated in the years prior to 1939, and investigations in which the R.A.F. took part had been held at the Royal Naval Staff College and elsewhere. Broadly speaking, the result of these pre-war investigations had been to confirm the R.A.F. in their view that enemy air power would render the undertaking impossible; while the Navy, though not convinced of the truth of this conclusion, was very well aware of the hazards such operations would involve.

Within a few days of the outbreak of war with Italy, Admiral Sir Andrew Cunningham put the matter to the test, and by the end of 1940 it was felt that the measure of the enemy had been taken. Brushes between Italian heavy ships and the Mediterranean Fleet in July[1] and Sir James Somerville's Force " H " in November[2] had led to the precipitate withdrawal of the enemy on each occasion, and the attacks of the Italian air force, though severe, had inflicted little damage and, together with submarine attacks, could be regarded as an acceptable war risk.

At the beginning of 1941, however, a " potent new factor " made itself felt. Strong German air forces were based in Sicily; and from then onwards operations in the Central Mediterranean became hazardous in the extreme. It was found possible, nevertheless, to maintain the supply of Malta throughout that year.

The beginning of 1942 saw a change greatly in favour of the enemy, which continued throughout the greater part of the year. In the first place, serious losses in capital ships in the late autumn of 1941[3] and the necessity to

---

[1] See N.S.H., *Battle Summary No. 8* and *Mediterranean, Vol. I.*
[2] See N.S.H., *Battle Summary No. 9* and *Mediterranean, Vol. II.*
[3] The *Barham* was sunk by a submarine on 25th November, 1941. In December the *Prince of Wales* and *Repulse* were sunk off Malaya, and the *Queen Elizabeth* and *Valiant* seriously damaged by Italian midget submarines at Alexandria.

form the Eastern Fleet on the outbreak of War with Japan had reduced the Mediterranean Fleet to a handful of cruisers and destroyers. The *Ark Royal*, too, had been sunk in November, leaving only the old carriers *Eagle* and *Argus* available to work with Force " H ".

Conditions in Malta itself and the events of the land campaign in Libya, too, rendered the supply of the island very much more difficult. In December 1941 air attacks on Malta were stepped up and continued to increase in severity till May 1942. Desperate though the island's needs, even if supplies could be got there, to land them during the heavy assaults from the air in April and May was out of the question, as was plainly shown by the fate of the ships which arrived towards the end of March. As for the fighting on land, the Germans and Italians advanced from Agheila to Gazala between 21st January and 7th February, thereby depriving the Fleet of the valuable advanced base of Benghazi and ships in the Central Mediterranean of the air cover which the Royal Air Force had provided from airfields in Cyrenaica; Tobruk fell a week after the convoy operations in mid-June, and by the end of that month the German and Italian forces had crossed into Egypt and were facing the British Army at El Alamein, less than 50 miles from Alexandria. There they stayed until the last week in October, when there began that great British advance which reached Tripoli in three months and went on to Tunis.

In these difficult circumstances, up to August six convoys—four from the east and two from the west—met with indifferent success. Two convoys from Egypt, one in January and one in March—the latter only to be virtually destroyed after arrival—reached Malta; but an attempt in February failed, and the fourth convoy in June was forced to turn back. Two convoys from the west, one in June (synchronised with the one from Egypt) and one in August, both sorely reduced by losses on the way, reached the island. After that the Home Fleet, from which the bulk of the escorts came, was fully occupied with the convoys to North Russia; several of the destroyers that escorted the August convoy in the Mediterranean went straight back to serve with the Arctic convoys in September.

Then came calls on the Home Fleet in connection with the landings in Algeria at the beginning of November, and it was not till the 20th of that month—the day the Army took Benghazi—that another convoy from Egypt arrived at Malta. The crisis was then passed and others followed in December.

Altogether 60 supply ships sailed for Malta under escort during the year: 30 arrived, 20 were lost and 10 had to turn back. An aircraft carrier, two cruisers, an A.A. ship and nine destroyers[1] were lost in these operations, whilst other warships were seriously damaged.

Apart from the regular convoys, the most pressing needs of Malta were supplied by submarines, which carried twenty small cargoes to the island during the year, and by the fast minelayers *Welshman* and *Manxman*, which made six passages sailing alone. Some 350 fighter aircraft arrived also, flown off from H.M. ships *Argus*, *Eagle* and *Furious* and from U.S.S. *Wasp*.

Chapters I, II and III[2] of the ensuing book describe the passages of three military convoys from Gibraltar in 1941. There were other similar operations during that year, but the three described have been chosen as illustrating the different sorts of opposition that had to be faced and overcome. In none of these operations did the convoys suffer attack from a hostile fleet, though on one occasion heavy ships approached within 50 miles or so. But the

---

[1] Besides the 8 destroyers mentioned as lost in the following account, the *Gurkha* was sunk by a submarine on 17th January, when with Convoy MW 8 from Egypt.

[2] *Battle Summary No. 11* (revised).

threat was always present, and attacks by submarines, torpedo-boats, and especially aircraft in varying forms threw a heavy strain on both warships and merchant ships.

Chapters IV to VII[1] deal with the convoys run in the worsened conditions of March, June and August, 1942. The losses and setbacks to these were mainly due to the enemy's strength in the air; but behind this was the great numerical superiority of the Italians in surface ships which, had they been more enterprising, could scarcely have failed to inflict material damage on more than one occasion, and, as things were, by its mere existence prevented the arrival of Convoy MW 11 from Egypt in June. The Italians always had three or four battleships ready for service and a considerable force of large cruisers and destroyers. The convoys in the western basin had the support of a battleship or two, lent from the North Atlantic or Home Fleet; but in the eastern basin cruisers and destroyers alone were available as escorts. How a weaker force outfaced material superiority, and also when it had to abandon the attempt, emerges from the story.

---

[1] *Battle Summary No. 32* (revised).

PART I. CONVOYS IN 1941

(Battle Summary No. 18)

CHAPTER I

Operation "Excess", January 1941

1

ON OCTOBER 28th, 1940, the Italians had crossed the Albanian frontier and invaded Greece, expecting an easy victory over the ill-equipped Greek army. Things did not go according to plan, however; the Italians failed in their thrusts, and in mid-November the Greeks, supported by the R.A.F., went over to the offensive. By 28th November they had driven the Italians back to within 50 miles of Durazzo; then severe winter weather held up the offensive, though the Greeks held their positions till early in April, when the Germans came to the rescue of their Allies.

From the naval point of view the Italian attack on Greece enabled our Mediterranean Fleet to use Suda Bay as a much-needed advanced base.

Naturally, assistance to the Greeks in every feasible form became one of our main concerns in the eastern Mediterranean, and in January 1941 an operation was staged to pass a military convoy named "Excess" from Gibraltar through the Mediterranean. It consisted of four ships, three for the Piraeus with stores for the Greek Army and one with stores for Malta—in all, 39,500 gross tons. Small as at first sight it might appear, the operation employed nearly all our naval strength in the Mediterranean, namely Force " H " from Gibraltar under Vice-Admiral Sir James Somerville and the bulk of the Mediterranean Fleet from Alexandria under Admiral Sir Andrew Cunningham. When the convoy reached the narrow waters between Sicily and Tunisia, the Gibraltar force turned back, leaving the transports to go on with a small escort to meet the Mediterranean ships beyond the Narrows. Admiral Cunningham took advantage of the occasion to ensure the passage of three subsidiary convoys (Operation MC. 4) between Egypt and Malta. These consisted of two ships from Alexandria to Malta (MW. 5½), two fast ships from Malta to Alexandria (ME.5½), and six slow ships from Malta to Port Said and Alexandria (ME.6). The first of these three convoys went to Malta during the passage of the fleet westward to meet Convoy " Excess ";

the other two left Malta as the fleet was returning, the fast ships joining Convoy " Excess " near Malta and keeping it company so far as their ways lay together, while the slow ships went eastward along a parallel route farther south.[1]

The most dangerous part of the voyage was that between Sardinia and Malta. There for a stretch of some 400 miles (26 hours at 15 knots) ships were exposed to attack from enemy air stations in Sardinia and Sicily, less than 150 miles away. Submarines and surface torpedo craft were a constant menace, and mines too were a possible danger. Attack by large surface ships was less likely, though potentially more dangerous, especially if the Italians attacked the convoy with battleships on one side and cruisers on the other, which Admiral Somerville thought possible.[2] They had no lack of forces for such an attack; for they had two or possibly three battleships and a dozen cruisers ready for service. To guard against this danger, Admiral Somerville asked for a third capital ship and some cruisers to strengthen Force " H ", which otherwise would have consisted only of the *Renown* and *Malaya*, the *Sheffield* and *Bonaventure* (a new type of anti-aircraft cruiser), the aircraft carrier *Ark Royal*, and a screen of 11 destroyers. Failing this addition, he proposed three counter-measures, first, a maximum concentration of submarines, suitably disposed in the western basin; secondly, the operation of an air striking force from Malta against the Italian fleet on critical days; and finally, a feint movement of heavy forces from the eastern Mediterranean towards the Narrows on the afternoon and night before the most critical day of the voyage. Admiral Cunningham thought the Italian superiority in cruisers did not greatly matter, provided the safe arrival of the convoy was the single purpose of the expedition, as difficulties in the service of convoys arose in his opinion chiefly from the handicap of a divided object. To meet the contingency, however, he detached two cruisers, the *Gloucester* and *Southampton*, to join Convoy " Excess " for the dangerous passage between Sardinia and Malta, which left him four cruisers and an old anti-aircraft ship to serve the other convoys. He also decided that, instead of making a " feint movement," he would join Convoy " Excess " himself, a few miles east of the Narrows (*i.e.*, 100 miles west of Malta), with the battleships *Warspite* and *Valiant*, the aircraft carrier *Illustrious*, and some destroyers.[3]

2

There were three critical stages in the passage from Sardinia to Malta, and the following were the escorts allotted to protect Convoy " Excess " in those areas.

SARDINIA TO THE NARROWS (130 MILES)

Capital ships, 2—*Renown* (Flag, Vice-Admiral Sir James Somerville), *Malaya*
Aircraft carrier, 1—*Ark Royal*
Cruisers, 4—*Sheffield, Bonaventure, Gloucester* (Flag Rear-Admiral Renouf), *Southampton*
Destroyers, 12 (including one from the Eastern Mediterranean)

THROUGH THE NARROWS (150 MILES)

Cruisers, 3—*Bonaventure, Gloucester, Southampton*
Destroyers, 5

---

[1] See Appendix A. There should have been another ship for Greece, the *Northern Prince*, but she drove on shore in a gale a few days before the convoy sailed from Gibraltar.
[2] See Appendices G and H.
[3] The battleship *Malaya* had joined Force " H " from the eastern Mediterranean towards the end of December 1940. Besides the ships employed with the convoys, there was another battleship (*Barham*) and another aircraft carrier (*Eagle*) with a destroyer screen in the eastern Mediterranean. These ships were earmarked for an attack on enemy shipping that was to start whilst the convoys were still at sea.

THE NARROWS TO MALTA (110 MILES)

Capital ships, 2—*Warspite* (Flag, Commander-in-Chief), *Valiant*
Aircraft carrier, 1—*Illustrious*
Cruisers, 3—*Bonaventure, Gloucester, Southampton*
Destroyers, 13

In addition, three submarines were stationed near Sardinia while Convoy "Excess" was passing that island—the *Pandora* off the east coast and the *Triumph* and *Upholder* to the southward, as shown in Plan 1.

For the protection of the Malta-Egypt convoys there remained available the cruisers *Orion* (Flag, Vice-Admiral Pridham-Wippell), *Perth, Ajax* and *York*; the anti-aircraft ship *Calcutta*; two destroyers and four corvettes.

The Royal Air Force also took part in the operation. Aircraft from Gibraltar furnished anti-submarine patrols while the convoy was passing through the Straits, and aircraft from Malta reconnoitred Italian ports, an area north and west of Sicily, and the Narrows. The reconnaissance was not, however, on a big scale, and Admiral Somerville reported that he was " obliged to rely solely on carrier reconnaissance for information of the presence of enemy surface vessels in the area south and east of Sardinia." He added that " the danger of surprise contacts with enemy surface forces will continue until existing shore-based reconnaissance can be augmented." The orders made no provision for the air striking force he had proposed, nor for protection by shore-based fighters, nor for attack upon the enemy's air stations during the passage of the convoys.

The operation was marked by the first appearance of German aircraft in large numbers in the Mediterranean. Admiral Cunningham reported afterwards that the enemy had probably some 400 or 500 German bombers[1] at Catania in Sicily and at African air stations, apart from the many Italian aircraft within reach of the convoys. Their air force operating from Sicily made a great effort to destroy the *Illustrious*; and the dive-bombing attack on her and the *Warspite* and *Valiant* was pressed home with grim determination.

3

Convoy " Excess ", consisting of four ships, left Gibraltar before dark in the evening of 6th January, escorted by the *Bonaventure* and four destroyers. At first they steered westward to mislead spies, turning back in the night in time to pass Europa Point after moonset and before daylight next morning; the ruse was successful though the *Bonaventure* reported that fishing craft and merchant ships must have seen the convoy going east again while the moon was still up. At dawn on the 7th, the *Bonaventure* parted company to return to Admiral Somerville, who sailed about that time with the rest of the ships which were to form the escort from Sardinia to the Narrows.

All that day the convoy followed the Spanish coast as if bound for a Spanish port; the wind was light, the sea was calm; that night the convoy crossed to the coast of Africa and steered eastward for the Narrows, keeping 30 miles or so off shore. January 7th was to be Day One of the operation. The Admiral had arranged to overtake the convoy and its four destroyers in the night of 7th–8th January, and then to keep some distance north and east of them until the morning of the 9th, in order to screen them from enemy aircraft, unless he had reason to believe that Italian ships were at sea to the west of

---

[1] This was an over-estimate. Flieger Corps X, based in Sicily, by mid-January 1941 comprised 120 long-range bombers, 150 dive-bombers, 40 twin-engined fighters and 20 reconnaissance aircraft.

Sardinia; in this case he would join the convoy with his whole force. In any case the convoy was to be joined by the *Bonaventure* in the morning of the 8th, and by the *Malaya* and two more destroyers in the evening.[1] As it turned out, air reconnaissance from Malta in the forenoon of the 8th located two or possibly three Italian battleships at Naples, three cruisers at Messina, and four cruisers at Taranto—the other cruisers were probably at Brindisi and Naples. When morning dawned on the 9th, the Admiral was ahead of the convoy with only the *Renown*, *Ark Royal*, *Sheffield* and five destroyers. At 0500,[2] in 37° 45′ N., 7° 15′ E., the *Ark Royal* flew off five Swordfish aircraft for Malta, some 350 miles away, all of which arrived safely. The Admiral then turned back to meet the convoy, joining it about 0900, roughly 120 miles south-west of Sardinia. The *Ark Royal* had seven reconnaissance aircraft, one anti-submarine and three fighters up. At 0918 an aircraft made an enemy report of two cruisers and two destroyers to the eastward. These ships turned out to be Force " B " under Rear-Admiral Renouf from the Mediterranean Fleet; and an hour later Admiral Renouf joined the convoy with the cruisers *Gloucester* and *Southampton* and a destroyer.[3]

Admiral Renouf had sailed from Alexandria at 1300 on 6th January with troops for Malta on board his cruisers. They arrived in the Grand Harbour at 0915 on the 8th, disembarked the troops, and sailed at 1345 in the afternoon. They passed Pantellaria that evening, sighting five mines 15 miles west of the island. The moon was bright and the weather fine. A signal station on the island had apparently challenged him. Apart from this minor incident there was nothing to suggest that the enemy knew anything of the operation until just before the junction of the three groups of ships. At 0900 on the 9th, however, an Italian aircraft closed Admiral Renouf's force, making off when fired at; another shadower, sighted about 1000, escaped from the *Ark Royal's* fighter patrol. At 1320, in 37° 38′ N., 8° 31′ E., by the *Gloucester's* reckoning, bombers appeared on the scene and made their attack.

The convoy of four ships was steaming at the time in two columns in line ahead, 1,500 yards apart, the *Gloucester* and *Malaya* leading the columns, with the *Bonaventure* and *Southampton* as sternmost ships and seven destroyers in the screen ahead. The *Renown* and *Ark Royal*, screened by the *Sheffield* and five destroyers, were stationed " in close support " on the convoy's port quarter. The mean line of advance was 088°, and the ships were zigzagging at 14 knots. The enemy consisted of ten Savoia bombers. The *Sheffield* detected them 43 miles off (the maximum working range of her radar), fine on the starboard bow, and they came in sight fourteen minutes later, flying down the starboard side of the convoy out of range at a height of about 11,000 ft. Twelve minutes later still, at 1346 having worked round broad on the bow, they began their attack, coming in from 145°, the bearing of the sun. All the ships opened a heavy fire, which Admiral Somerville considered much more accurate than on previous occasions. Admiral Renouf thought the barrage from the *Renown* and her consorts, bursting over the convoy, diverted the enemy from their original course. On the other hand, Captain Egerton of the *Bonaventure* remarked that most of the shells burst well below the aircraft. Eight aircraft dropped bombs, some of which fell near the *Gloucester* and *Malaya* but did no harm, while the rest fell clear. The other two bombers turned away during the approach, perhaps upset by the ship's fire, and a Fulmar from the *Ark Royal* shot them down; they crashed within sight of the *Malaya*, and three men of their crews were picked up. The other

---

[1] At 1630 on the 8th the convoy was some 30 miles south-westward of the *Renown*.

[2] Zone Time minus 2 is used throughout.

[3] Admiral Somerville remarked that the aircraft were aware that Force " B " would be encountered and that more care should have been taken in establishing identity.

fighters lost touch with the enemy in the clouds during the attack; except for one possibly shot down by the *Bonaventure*, the rest of the bombers got away.

Nothing more happened that afternoon, 9th January, though the fighter patrol reported sighting another party of Savoia aircraft from Cagliari half an hour after the attack. Nor was there even a hint of danger from the Italian fleet. The *Ark Royal* had had seven aircraft up all the forenoon, reconnoitring as far as the Skerki Bank and back to the south-east coast of Sardinia, and two aircraft left her at 1600 to search a hundred miles ahead of the convoy. They saw nothing; and a " nil " report had also come at midday from the Royal Air Force flying boat on patrol north and west of Sicily. At dusk, in 37° 42′ N., 9° 53′ E., some 30 miles westward of the Narrows and north of Bizerta, Admiral Somerville parted company to go back with Force " H " proper to Gibraltar, where he arrived on the 11th after an uneventful passage. Admiral Renouf in the *Gloucester* took the convoy on with the three cruisers and five destroyers of Forces " B " and " F ".[1]

4

They had a quiet night, passing Pantellaria after moonset and giving the island as wide a berth as possible, while keeping in deep water to lessen the danger of mines. But next morning—the 10th—at 0720, just as dawn broke, they encountered two Italian torpedo boats, the *Vega*[2] and *Circe*[2], some three miles off on the port beam, in about 36° 30′ N., 12° 10′ E., a dozen miles south and east of Pantellaria. The *Jaguar*, port wing ship in the screen, and the *Bonaventure*, stationed astern of the columns, sighted the strangers at the same time. Thinking they might be destroyers of Admiral Cunningham's force, which the convoy was due to meet, both British ships reported the enemy by signal to Admiral Renouf before attacking, and the *Bonaventure* challenged them. Then she fired a star shell, turned for the enemy at full speed, and engaged the right-hand ship of the pair. Admiral Renouf turned the convoy away from the danger, while the *Southampton*, *Jaguar* and *Hereward*, hauling out from their stations on the engaged side, made for the enemy. By the time they arrived the *Bonaventure* had shifted her attention to the other Italian (the *Vega*), which came towards her at full speed to attack. She fired her torpedoes, which the *Bonaventure* avoided; and between them the four British ships quickly stopped the enemy, but did not sink her, though the *Bonaventure* alone fired 600 rounds. In the end the *Hereward* torpedoed her, some forty minutes after the fight began. The first Italian had disappeared.[3]

5

At 0800, 10th January, Admiral Cunningham arrived on the scene with Force " A ", before the little fight was finished (see Appendix A). Half an hour later, when the Fleet had turned south-east again in the wake of the convoy, the destroyer *Gallant* in the screen had her bows blown off by a mine. The *Mohawk* took her in tow, and they steered for Malta, escorted by the *Bonaventure* and *Griffin*, which were joined later by Admiral Renouf with the *Gloucester* and *Southampton*. Two Italian torpedo aircraft attacked whilst the cripple was getting in tow, but the fire of the *Bonaventure* and *Mohawk* forced

---

[1] See Appendix A.

[2] 640 tons, three 4-in. guns, four 18-in. torpedo tubes.

[3] In this action and her previous action with a raider in the Atlantic on 25th December, 1940, the *Bonaventure* expended 75 per cent of her low-angle outfit of ammunition. On this occasion she had one man killed and four wounded.

them to drop their torpedoes at long range without effect. Between 1130 and 1800, as the two crawled along at five or six knots, with the escort zigzagging at 20 knots, they were attacked or threatened ten times by aircraft, nearly all German high-level bombers, which came in ones, twos or threes. Fortunately the *Bonaventure* always managed to give warning, and the ships' fire generally spoilt the attacks; for, though the enemy dropped their bombs in five out of the ten attempts, there was only one moment of real danger—at 1300, when three German dive-bombers succeeded in slightly damaging the *Southampton* by a near-miss. The *Gallant*, with the *Bonaventure*[1], *Mohawk* and *Griffin*, reached Malta safely the next forenoon (11th).

The ships with Admiral Cunningham had a similar experience on a larger scale. The enemy had good intelligence of the Admiral's movements, for their aircraft had found him on the 7th (the day he sailed from Alexandria) and again on the 9th, and finally in the morning of the 10th at 0930, an hour and a half after his joining Convoy "Excess". In the course of the afternoon, heavy dive-bombing attacks were pressed home with skill and determination, mainly directed against the *Illustrious*. They attacked chiefly with German dive-bombers, though there was one attempt by a pair of Italian torpedo aircraft and one by Italian high-level bombers. Had some of the dive-bombers attacked the convoy instead of the supporting men-of-war, said Admiral Cunningham, all four transports must inevitably have been sunk. As it was, out of 70 or 80 aircraft altogether engaged, only three high-level bombers attacked the convoy and without effect. On the other hand, the *Illustrious* was disabled, and her services were lost to the fleet for many months.

At noon the transports were steering south-eastward, zigzagging at 14 to 15 knots, with an escort of three destroyers—joined at 1320 by the *Calcutta* which arrived before the bombing of the convoy itself began. The *Warspite*, *Illustrious* and *Valiant* were steaming in line ahead on the convoy's starboard quarter, course 110°, zigzagging at 17 and later at 18 knots, with seven destroyers in the screen. The weather was clear, with high cloud; a fresh breeze was blowing from south-south-west, roughly at right-angles to the mean line of advance.[2]

The fleet was in 35° 59′ N., 13° 13′ E., some 55 miles west of Malta, when the battle began with an attack by two Savoia torpedo aircraft, which were detected six miles away on the starboard beam at 1220. They came in at a steady level, 150 feet above the water, and dropped their torpedoes about 2,500 yards from the battleships. They were sighted a minute before firing, and the ships received them with a barrage from long- and short-range guns, altering course to avoid the torpedoes, which passed astern of the rearmost ship, the *Valiant*. Five Fulmars from the *Illustrious* had been patrolling above the fleet, but one had returned on board, disabled while assisting to destroy a shadower some time before the attack; the other four fighters chased the torpedo planes as far as Linosa Island, about 20 miles to the westward, and claimed to have damaged both of them.

Directly after this attack, while the ships were re-forming the line, a strong force of aircraft was reported at 1235 coming from the northward some 30 miles away. The Fulmars, of course, were then a long way off, flying low, and with little ammunition left after their two engagements; indeed, two had fired all they had. They were ordered back over the fleet, and the *Illustrious* sent

---

[1] The *Bonaventure* was destined for Malta in any case, having embarked passengers from the *Northern Prince*, the transport that could not sail from Gibraltar with Convoy "Excess".
[2] The *Calcutta* had arrived off Malta that morning, the 10th, with Convoy MW.5½. She then joined ME.6, on its sailing, but was soon called away to join Convoy "Excess" presumably to replace the *Bonaventure*.

up four fresh aircraft besides reliefs for the anti-submarine patrol. This meant a turn of 100° to starboard into the wind to fly off; the enemy came in sight in the middle of the operation, which lasted about four minutes, and the ships opened fire. The fleet had just got back to the proper course of 110°, and the Admiral had made the signal to assume loose formation, when the new attack began. The enemy had assembled astern of their target " in two very loose and flexible formations " at a height of 12,000 feet.

6

They were Junkers dive-bombers, perhaps as many as 36, of which 18 to 24 attacked the *Illustrious* at 1240, while a dozen attacked the battleships and the screen. They came down in flights of three on different bearings, astern and on either beam, to release their bombs at heights of 1,500 to 800 ft.: " a very severe and brilliantly executed dive-bombing attack," said Captain Boyd of the *Illustrious*. The ships altered course continually, and, beginning with long-range controlled fire during the approach, shifted to barrage fire as the enemy dived to the attack. They shot down at least three aircraft, while the eight Fulmars shot down five more, at a cost of one British fighter; even the two that had no ammunition left made dummy attacks, and forced two Germans to turn away. But, as Captain Boyd pointed out, " at least twelve " fighters in the air would have been required to make any impression on the enemy, and double that number to keep them off. The *Illustrious* was seriously damaged. She was hit six times, mostly with armour-piercing bombs of 1,100 pounds. They wrecked the flight deck, destroyed nine aircraft on board, put half the 4·5-in. guns out of action, and did other damage, besides setting the ship on fire fore and aft and killing and wounding many of the ship's company. The *Warspite*, too, narrowly escaped serious injury, but got off with a split hawsepipe and damaged anchor.[1]

The ship being useless as a carrier and likely to become a drag on the fleet, Captain Boyd decided to make for Malta. The Commander-in-Chief gave her two destroyers for escort, one from his own screen and one from the convoy's, and she parted company accordingly. She had continual trouble with her steering gear, which at last broke down altogether, so that she had to steer with the engines, making only 17 to 18 knots speed, though on first leaving the fleet she had worked up to 26 knots. Meanwhile, those of her aircraft which were already in the air at the time of the attack flew to Malta, anti-submarine Swordfish as well as Fulmars—some of the fighters had a further turn of service later in the day.

A third attack came at 1330 that afternoon of 10th January. By this time the *Illustrious* was 10 miles north-eastward of the battleships; and owing to their manœuvres during the previous attacks, while the convoy was steaming steadily on, the battleships were nearly as far from the transports, which were themselves attacked at 1340 (see Plan 1). The enemy were high-level bombers, probably Italian, though there may have been some Germans among them. Seven of them attacked the *Illustrious*, and seven more the battleships, while three attacked the convoy. They were detected in good time, the *Valiant* being able to warn the *Illustrious* by signal before the latter sighted her assailants; and the ships received them with a heavy fire as they appeared at a height of 14,000 or 15,000 feet. Even the *Illustrious*, then turning in circles out of control, with only half her guns fit for service, was able to spoil

---

[1] Appendix B gives further details of the attack. The *Illustrious* had 13 officers and 113 men killed or missing, and 7 officers and 84 men wounded.

the enemy's aim. All the bombs fell wide. The *Calcutta*, which had arrived but a short time before the attack and was now stationed astern of the transports, hit and perhaps destroyed one bomber.

More serious in its results was a second dive-bombing attack upon the *Illustrious* at 1610. Again the *Valiant* detected the enemy and gave timely warning. There were 15 Junkers bombers, escorted by five fighters, but only nine dropped bombs, the others being kept at arm's length by the fire of the *Illustrious* and her two destroyers. Six aircraft attacked from astern and on either quarter, followed by three that attacked from the starboard beam. Captain Boyd said "this attack was neither so well synchronized nor so determined as that at 1240"; yet one bomb hit, and there were two near misses, resulting in more damage and loss of life. However, the ship was well under control by this time, able to alter course to avoid bombs, and with eight 4·5-in. guns and some pom-poms in action, though smoke and haze from a fire still burning in the hangar interfered with the aim of guns on the lee side. She and the *Jaguar* destroyed at least one enemy aircraft between them.[1]

A few minutes after the attack on the *Illustrious* the six aircraft she had driven off approached the battleships, but again retired on coming under fire. The turn of the battleships for a second dive-bombing attack came an hour later, at 1715, when 17 Germans attacked as before, except that they dropped their bombs at a greater height. The *Valiant* had detected them 50 miles away, so the ships were once more prepared; and they received the enemy in the same way, with controlled fire during the approach and a barrage as they spiralled down into the dive. No bombs hit, but splinters from near misses killed a man in the *Valiant*, and a bomb fell very near the *Janus* without exploding. The ships may have destroyed one aircraft by gunfire. Three Fulmars of the original patrol from the *Illustrious*, directed by wireless from the Valiant, came out from Malta and damaged three bombers returning from the attack.[2]

This turned out to be the end of the ordeal for Convoy "Excess" and its supporting ships of war, but not for the *Illustrious* which had one more encounter with the enemy before she reached Malta. About 1920, a little more than an hour after sunset and in moonlight, some aircraft approached from seaward, when she was only 5 miles from the entrance of the Grand Harbour. She had warning from Malta that aircraft were about, and she sighted two—probably torpedo planes. She and her escorting destoyers fired a blind barrage, on which the enemy disappeared. Directly afterwards, the *Hasty* got an Asdic contact and fired depth charges, but whether it was a submarine is uncertain. The *Illustrious* entered harbour about 2100, accompanied by the *Jaguar*, which had passengers to land. Further trials were in store for her in the thirteen days of hurried repairs that followed at a port within easy reach of the enemy's air power.[3]

7

In the meantime, after the mild attack at 1340 on the 10th, Convoy "Excess" went on its way unhindered, escorted by the *Calcutta* and a screen of destroyers.

---

[1] Captain Boyd remarked that there "may have been" some Hurricane fighters from Malta present during this attack.

[2] The *Janus* had joined the fleet screen only that afternoon, having come from Malta, where she had been docking.

[3] The *Illustrious* left Malta on 23rd January, arrived at Alexandria on the 25th, and later proceeded to Durban and on to Norfolk (U.S.A.) for repairs, which were completed on 29th November, 1941.

Its movements then became involved in those of the Malta-Egypt convoys, which were being run under cover of the main operation with the special support of Vice-Admiral Pridham-Wippell's four cruisers of Force " D ", the *Orion, Perth, Ajax* and *York*.   The first of these convoys, the two ships of MW.5½, had left Alexandria for Malta on 7th January, some hours after Admiral Cunningham sailed westward with Force " A " to meet Convoy " Excess ". Both ships had reached Malta without adventure in the morning of the 10th, escorted by the *Calcutta, Diamond* and *Defender*.   On arrival, the *Calcutta* joined the six slow ships bound for Port Said and Alexandria, Convoy ME.6, which had just sailed with four corvettes to go east by a route parallel to but south of that followed by Convoy " Excess ".   At the end of the searched channel they met Admiral Pridham-Wippell, who had been cruising north and east of the incoming convoy the night before, the 9th, and now took charge of ME.6; the *Calcutta* was ordered to join Convoy " Excess ", and arrived in time to defend it from the Italian bombers, as already described.   The last convoy, ME.5½, two fast ships bound for Alexandria, also left Malta in the morning of the 10th under escort of the *Diamond*,[1] they were to join Convoy " Excess " and proceed in company till they reached the point where the ships for Alexandria must turn southward to clear Crete, while Convoy " Excess " stood on for the Piraeus.   The two convoys met that afternoon; and the transport *Essex* left Convoy " Excess " to go to Malta, escorted by one destroyer, which rejoined the fleet after seeing her into harbour.

Admiral Pridham-Wippell stayed with the eastgoing Convoy ME.6 until dark on the 10th, and then went on with the *Orion* and *Perth* towards a rendezvous with the Commander-in-Chief appointed for next day.   But the battleships, owing to the air attacks in the afternoon, were considerably behind time and a long way astern of Convoy " Excess ", so Admiral Cunningham ordered Admiral Pridham-Wippell to go north of Convoy " Excess " for the night so as to be between the convoy and possible attack by Italian ships from Taranto or Brindisi.   Meanwhile, the battleships also kept to the northward, and gaining ground during the night arrived some 25 miles north of the convoy by daylight, the 11th, at which time Admiral Pridham-Wippell joined the Commander-in-Chief, who then kept both forces within a few miles of the convoy.

8

These arrangements for the protection of Convoy " Excess " left the six ships of Convoy ME.6 some 70 to 90 miles to the south and west of the battle fleet with only the *York*[2] and the four corvettes for escort.   In the forenoon of the 11th, therefore, the Commander-in-Chief sent his Walrus aircraft to Admiral Renouf, telling him to overtake and support the convoy with the *Gloucester, Southampton* and *Diamond* with which he was then steering for Suda Bay, having left the disabled *Gallant* off Malta some hours before.   The order reached Admiral Renouf a little after midday, and he shaped course accordingly, steaming at 24 knots against the convoy's 9 or 10 knots, and sending up his aircraft to find the convoy.   At 1522, when his ships were some 30 miles astern of it, in 34° 56′ N., 18° 19′ E., they were suddenly attacked by a dozen German dive-bombers.   Fortune was against them.   The attack

---

[1] The *Diamond* then joined the crippled *Gallant*, and later proceeded in company with Admiral Renouf's cruisers.

[2] The *Ajax* had parted company soon after joining on 10th January with orders to fuel at Suda Bay and then to join Rear-Admiral Rawlings, who was due to leave Alexandria on the 11th in the *Barham*, with the *Eagle, Wryneck* and four destroyers, for operations in the eastern Mediterranean.

came as an entire surprise, and, according to Captain Rowley of the *Gloucester*, "aircraft were not sighted until the whistle of the first bomb was heard". Six bombers attacked each cruiser, diving steeply from the direction of the sun and each releasing a 550-lb bomb at heights of 1,500 ft to 800 ft. The ships opened fire with 4-in. guns and below, increasing speed and altering course to avoid the attack; but two bombs, or perhaps three, hit the *Southampton*, exploding in " A " boiler-room and the gunroom flat and doing disastrous damage. The *Gloucester* too, was damaged by a bomb which hit her forward 6-in. director tower and penetrated five decks, fortunately without exploding; she was also hit by splinters from a couple of near misses. Half an hour later seven high-level bombers attacked, but the ships saw them and opened fire in good time, and the bombs fell wide. At about the same time a solitary aircraft dropped two bombs between the columns of the convoy, then in 34° 54' N., 19° 7' E.

Admiral Renouf had immediately reported the damage to the cruisers by signal to the Commander-in-Chief, who turned to the south-westward to close them, sending Admiral Pridham-Wippell ahead with his two cruisers and two destroyers. Before they arrived, however, Admiral Renouf reported that the *Southampton* must be abandoned and that he would sink her, so the battleships turned east again. The *Southampton* had caught fire badly on being hit. For a time the ship's company fought the fire successfully and kept the ship in action and under control: indeed, she steamed at 20 knots during the second air attack and for an hour longer. Then the fire spread; it was found impossible to flood certain magazines, and after striving nearly four hours to save the ship, officers and men had to give it up. Shortly before 1900 fresh fires were breaking out, water and fire-fighting appliances had failed, and the *Diamond* was ordered alongside to take off the crew.[1] As soon as this was accomplished, a torpedo was fired into her by the *Gloucester*, which, however, did not sink her. The *Diamond* then went alongside the *Gloucester* to transfer survivors; but at 2050 ships were seen approaching and she cast off, lest they were enemy. They proved to be Admiral Pridham-Wippell's force; the *Southampton* was sunk by three torpedoes from the *Orion* and the transfer of survivors was completed by 2220,[2] when course was shaped to rendezvous with the Commander-in-Chief next morning. Meanwhile, the ships for Alexandria had left Convoy " Excess " during the evening of 11th January, the *Calcutta* putting into Suda for oil, while the three ships of Convoy " Excess " with their destroyer screen stood on for the Piraeus, where they arrived safely next morning, the 12th of January.

9

On the morning of the 12th January, the *Orion, Perth, Gloucester* and the three destroyers joined the Commander-in-Chief at a rendezvous off the west end of Crete, meeting there also Rear-Admiral Rawlings with the *Barham, Eagle, Ajax* and their destroyer screen. Under the original plan, the fleet was then to have begun a series of attacks on the Italian shipping routes; but the disabling of the *Illustrious* put an end to the chief part of the plan, so Admiral Cunningham took the *Warspite, Valiant, Gloucester* and some destroyers straight back to Alexandria. Eventually bad weather prevented Admiral Rawlings

---

[1] " *Diamond* was most skilfully handled throughout and her assistance was invaluable, many more lives being saved than would otherwise have been possible."—Rear-Admiral Renouf's report.

[2] The *Gloucester* embarked 33 officers and 678 ratings, of whom 4 officers and 58 ratings were wounded: the *Diamond* retained 16 wounded ratings. The *Gloucester's* own casualties amounted to 1 officer and 8 ratings killed, and 10 officers and 13 ratings wounded.

from carrying out his share of this operation. Admiral Pridham-Wippell went to the Piraeus with the *Orion* and *Perth*, embarked some troops from ships of Convoy " Excess " there, and took them to Malta—a task the *Southampton* was to have done. Meanwhile, the six ships of Convoy ME.6, the last to reach port, arrived at their destinations on the 13th. A signal was received on 17th January from the Governor of Malta, expressing high appreciation of the work of the fleet and sympathy for the losses suffered in bringing much-needed aid to Malta.

Not a single ship of the 14 in the four convoys had been lost; but the fleet had had to pay a heavy price for their safety. German dive-bombers had appeared on the scene, presenting " a potent new factor " in the Mediterranean, where the fleet's unquestioned supremacy over the Italian airmen had hitherto enabled it to do its work without undue risk. From that day a heavy menace hung over the Sicilian route, and the voyage to Malta became one of perilous hazard.[1]

---

[1] See Appendix C.

CHAPTER II

Operation "Substance", July 1941

10

THE SPRING of 1941 saw great changes in favour of the Axis in the strategical situation in the eastern Mediterranean. In Libya German-Italian forces had launched an offensive which compelled General Wavell's army—depleted in order to send assistance to Greece—to relinquish all the ground gained in the winter with the exception of Tobruk, and carried the Axis forces as far as the Egyptian frontier town of Sollum. At the same time the Germans overran Yugoslavia, and the following month occupied Greece and Crete.

The Mediterranean Fleet suffered very heavy loss and damage in these operations, which offset its success in the Battle of Matapan in March. But more serious was the deterioration in the air situation, owing to the possession by the enemy of airfields in Cyrenaica and Libya and their denial to the British. Moreover, the enemy had gained Benghazi as a useful supply base for his armies in addition to Tripoli, while the Mediterranean Fleet had lost its valuable advanced base at Suda.

In the western Mediterranean there had been no great change in the situation, and it was therefore natural that when Malta's needs became compulsive the attempt to reinforce the island should be made from this direction.

Accordingly an operation known as " Substance " was planned to take place in July. The object was to take six storeships and a troopship, known as Convoy GM1, from Gibraltar to Malta and at the same time to protect the passage of seven other transports, Convoy MG1, going empty from Malta to the westward.

Admiral Somerville was to accompany the convoy from Gibraltar with his whole force as far as the Narrows between Sicily and Tunisia, as he had done in January; but this time Force " H " was to be strengthened considerably by ships that brought out the transports from home. Rear-Admiral Syfret, in the *Edinburgh*, was then to take the convoy through the Narrows to Malta with a detachment of cruisers and destroyers known as Force " X ".[1] Meanwhile, the empty transports from Malta, sailing on 23rd July, the day the east-going convoy reached the Narrows, were to pass through that area the same night, but by a different route. After parting with Admiral Syfret, the main body of Force " H " cruised south-west of Sardinia to await the return of Force " X " and to " endeavour to distract attention " from the empty ships on their passage westward, " but keeping if possible out of the range of shore-based fighters ". To support these operations, Admiral Cunningham arranged a diversion in the eastern Mediterranean by which he led the enemy to believe their ships would risk meeting the Mediterranean Fleet should they put to sea to attack the convoys.

Admiral Somerville had two capital ships, *Renown* and *Nelson*, the aircraft carrier *Ark Royal*, four cruisers, the *Edinburgh*, *Manchester*, *Arethusa* and *Hermione*, the minelayer *Manxman* (serving as a cruiser), and seventeen destroyers—including one employed to escort an oiler from which the destroyers of the fleet were to oil during the voyage. There were also eight submarines at sea, patrolling off Sardinia, Sicily and Naples during the critical days of the operation (see Plan 2). The convoy of empty transports had only one destroyer for escort.

As the Italians were believed to have five battleships fit for service (three of them at Taranto) and no fewer than ten cruisers divided between Taranto, Messina and Palermo, the empty transports ran considerable risk in going from Malta westward without a stronger escort. But there was no help for it. It was not possible to give them better protection without running the gauntlet of the Narrows twice or calling on the Mediterranean Fleet.

The Royal Air Force was able to give more help than in January. Aircraft from Gibraltar furnished anti-submarine patrols for the first two days of the passage east, and others reconnoitred areas between Sardinia and Africa, while aircraft from Malta reconnoitred between Sardinia and Sicily, besides watching the Italian ports. Malta also provided fighters to protect Force " X " and the convoy after the *Ark Royal* had left them. Fortunately, according to the latest intelligence, there were no longer any German aircraft in that part of the Mediterranean. The Italians had apparently some 50 torpedo aircraft and 150 bombers (of which 30 were dive-bombers), roughly half of each type being stationed in Sardinia and half in Sicily.

The transports bound for Malta and most of the other ships of war that joined Admiral Somerville for the occasion came from England with the *Nelson;* the rest, including Admiral Syfret's flagship the *Edinburgh*, were already at Gibraltar with Force " H ". In order to conceal the convoy's passage into the Mediterranean, it was arranged that as many ships as possible should go through the Strait of Gibraltar in the night of 20th–21st July, without entering harbour. Some ships had to fuel, however, and others had passengers to embark; for there were 5,000 troops going to Malta in the convoy, and part of these troops had to be divided among ships of the escort at Gibraltar. The ships that had to go into harbour were to leave the convoy in two groups in time to arrive on the 19th and 20th respectively; and the passengers were to remove into their new ships after dark on those days. The oiler *Brown Ranger*, too, with her escorting destroyer, was to leave Gibraltar in the night of the 20th–21st to join the convoy next morning. Admiral Somerville was to sail last, with the *Renown*, *Ark Royal*, *Hermione* and eight destroyers, leaving harbour in time to clear the Strait before dawn on the 21st.

---

[1] See Appendix D.

11

The six storeships entered the Mediterranean in the night of the 20th–21st as arranged, escorted by Admiral Syfret with the *Edinburgh*, *Nelson*, *Manxman* and five destroyers. The ships that left Gibraltar that night were held up by fog. The *Manchester*, *Arethusa* and the other three destroyers joined the convoy in the morning, as did the *Brown Ranger* and her escort; unfortunately the troopship *Leinster* ran on shore whilst turning out of Gibraltar Bay, and 1,000 troops thus missed their passage. Admiral Somerville overtook the convoy at midday,[1] the 21st; and having adjusted the destroyer screens with a view to economy of fuel, he stretched ahead and to the northward, so the fleet went east in two groups at varying distances apart, with Sunderland flying boats from Gibraltar giving anti-submarine protection to each group. Next day, the 22nd, Admiral Syfret's ten destroyers oiled at sea, two at a time, a task that took about ten hours, after which the oiler *Brown Ranger* went back to Gibraltar. An Italian aircraft seems to have reported the ships with Admiral Somerville in the morning, but did not apparently find the convoy, then nearly a hundred miles away to the south-westward. A little before midnight a submarine attacked the *Renown*, which was able to avoid the torpedoes through a timely warning from the *Nestor*.

12

Admiral Somerville joined the convoy again at 0800 on the 23rd, as the fleet was approaching the dangerous part of its voyage past Sardinia. The ships took up Cruising Disposition No. 16 (see Plan 3), with the *Renown*, *Ark Royal*, *Hermione* and their destroyers " formed as a flexible port column of the convoy with the object of providing anti-aircraft protection whilst still remaining free to manœuvre for flying ". The mean course was 090°, ships zigzagging, and the speed of advance 13½ knots. The sea was calm, the sky was clear, and a light breeze was blowing from the north-east.

Shadowing aircraft had already reported the position of the fleet that morning, and heavy attacks soon followed. The first came about 0945, a well-timed combination of nine high-level bombers and six or seven torpedo bombers approaching from the north-east. The *Ark Royal* had eleven fighters up, which met the bombers about 20 miles from the fleet, and shot down two for the loss of three Fulmars. The other seven bombers came on, working round the head of the screen of destroyers to attack the convoy from the starboard beam at a height of some 10,000 feet; their bombs fell harmlessly among the leading ships as they altered course to avoid the attack. The torpedo aircraft were more successful. They came from ahead out of the sun, flying low, and as the destroyers opened fire they divided into groups of two or three to attack the convoy on both sides. Two aircraft attacked the *Fearless*, stationed ahead in the screen, dropping their torpedoes at ranges of 1,500 and 800 yards from a height of 70 feet; the destroyer avoided the first torpedo, but was hit by the second, set on fire, and completely disabled. Other aircraft went on to press home their attacks on the convoy itself. One of them, dropping its torpedo between two transports, hit the *Manchester* as she was turning to regain her station after avoiding two torpedoes fired earlier; this time she reversed her helm once more, but without avail. The ships had opened a long-range controlled fire at the bombers; and they fired a barrage

---

[1] Zone Time minus 2 is used throughout this chapter.

with both long- and close-range guns against the torpedo aircraft, bringing down three of them.

The *Manchester* could use only one engine out of four, and as at first she could steam only 8 knots (she afterwards worked up to 12), the Admiral ordered her back to Gibraltar with the *Avon Vale* for escort. That evening, about 100 miles on the way to the westward, the two ships were attacked by three torpedo aircraft, but their guns kept the enemy at a safe distance. They reached Gibraltar on the 26th without further adventures except an abortive attack by a submarine on the 24th.[1]

The *Fearless*, however, was done for. By order of the Admiral, another destroyer torpedoed and sank her.

At 1010 on the 23rd, half an hour after the first engagement, five more bombers tried to attack the convoy, crossing this time from north to south. Five fighters from the *Ark Royal*, though unable to reach within 1,000 feet of the enemy, forced them to drop their bombs at a great height and mostly outside the screen. Again, about 1645, five torpedo bombers led by a seaplane came in from the northward; but three Fulmars caught them nearly 20 miles away, shot down two, and drove off the rest. Soon afterwards the fleet arrived off the entrance to the Skerki Channel. There the *Nelson* joined Admiral Somerville, the *Hermione* joined Admiral Syfret in place of the *Manchester*, and the destroyers took up their proper stations, six with Force "H" and eight with Force "X". At 1713 Admiral Somerville hauled round to the westward, while Admiral Syfret stood on, forming Cruising Disposition No. 17 (see Plan 4) for the passage through the Narrows. For an hour more, until the Royal Air Force Beaufighters arrived from Malta to relieve them, the *Ark Royal* kept Fulmars up to attend the convoy. When the Beaufighters did arrive, they did not identify themselves, apparently through lack of experience, and were engaged by gunfire from the fleet.

There was still nearly five hours to go before dark, and the convoy had to suffer yet further attacks from the air that day. Four torpedo bombers arrived from the eastward at 1900, flying low and working round from ahead to the starboard side of the convoy. They approached in pairs in line abreast, and kept the *Sikh* (on the starboard bow of the screen) between them and their target until nearly the moment for attack, thereby hampering the fire of other ships. They dropped their torpedoes at long range from a height of 50 feet, and nearly hit the *Hermione*, sternmost ship in the starboard column. To avoid the attack, each column of the convoy turned 90 degrees outwards; and the men-of-war opened barrage fire from all guns that would bear. The barrage fell short, but the fire from the cruisers, though it possibly endangered the destroyers as much as the enemy, probably caused the Italians to drop their torpedoes early, and may have brought down one aircraft.

This attack scattered the convoy, which took some time to re-form. At 1945, soon after the ships were again on their course and in station, about seven bombers appeared from ahead at a height of some 14,000 feet to attack the convoy on the port side. The convoy altered 40 degrees to port together by signal; and the escort opened a controlled fire—with some hesitation, for the Italian aircraft looked very like Beaufighters, several of which had lately joined, while others were expected. The bombing was reported as extremely accurate; several bombs fell near the *Edinburgh*, which was leading the port column, and a near-miss abreast a boiler-room disabled the *Firedrake*, the port destroyer of two that were sweeping ahead of the convoy. She could no longer steam, so Admiral Syfret ordered her back to Gibraltar in tow of the *Eridge*.

---

[1] The *Manchester* had 750 troops for Malta on board.

They had an anxious passage, being shadowed by aircraft continuously during daylight hours, but were not again attacked; on the 25th the *Firedrake* managed to raise steam in one boiler and slipped the tow; they entered harbour on the 27th.[1]

13

Soon after leaving the Skerki Channel in the evening of 23rd July, the convoy hauled up to the north-east towards the coast of Sicily, instead of standing on for Pantellaria, as Convoy " Excess " had done in January and as the enemy evidently expected it to do. The object of this " long and tortuous route," as Admiral Syfret called it, was to lessen the danger from mines; but it also saved the convoy from an air attack at dusk, which was his principal anxiety. The result was excellent. The Italians did not shadow the convoy after their attack at 1945, and therefore missed this alteration of course, which was made at 2000. An hour or so later, as it was growing dark, enemy aircraft searched diligently for the convoy along its old line of advance. Again, in the hour before midnight, the convoy several times sighted flares, some 20 miles off to the southward, which the Admiral supposed to be towed by aircraft in an attempt to find the convoy. As for mines, the only evidence of their presence was the parting of the *Foxhound*'s sweep apparently by a mine, soon after the turn southward into the known Italian convoy route to Tripoli a little after midnight.

The principal feature of the night took the form of attacks by Italian motor torpedo boats in the early hours of the 24th, while the convoy was passing Pantellaria. They seem to have made three distinct attacks, between 0250 and 0315, all from the port bow; and for twenty minutes more some of these craft were hovering about the convoy. Their number was uncertain, estimated at half a dozen all told, though some ships thought it was more; actually there were only two. Admiral Syfret considered the enemy did not expect the meeting, and did not attack resolutely. They were hard to see, but could be heard to start their engines, and gave themselves away by using high speed. " One felt," he said, " they would have achieved more success had they kept quiet whilst and after firing their torpedoes." Nevertheless, they succeeded in torpedoing the *Sydney Star*, the middle transport in the starboard column, though she reached Malta. They were thought to have lost one or perhaps two boats sunk by the fire of the escort, but actually none was sunk.

The *Cossack*, ahead of the port column, was the first to find the enemy. She detected three objects on the port bow by radar about 0245, and a few minutes later heard the starting of engines and saw two boats close on the port beam, one of which she lit up by searchlight and engaged with 4·7-in. and smaller guns. The *Edinburgh*, leading the port column, heard and sighted the same boat at about the same time; she turned towards the enemy, increased speed, and opened fire with pom-poms and Oerlikon guns. The *Manxman*, leading the starboard column, also sighted this boat; lit up by crossed searchlight beams from the *Edinburgh* and *Cossack*, she made " a perfect target," to be fired at " unseen ourselves and almost at leisure." Between them the three ships might have sunk this boat, but it was she that torpedoed the *Sydney Star*. Meanwhile, the other boat ran down between the screen of destroyers and the port column of transports, and was engaged by the *Farndale*, and by the *Arethusa* and *Hermione* in the rear of the convoy, and was probably damaged. In the second attack, at 0305, the *Foxhound* and *Cossack* apparently fired on a boat crossing from starboard to port, and the *Foxhound* tried to ram;

---

[1] The *Edinburgh* and *Firedrake* both sighted tracks of torpedoes during the air attack by the bombers, perhaps fired by a submarine.

then the *Edinburgh*, lighting the target with her searchlight, smothered it with fire from small guns at a range of 1,500 or 2,000 yards, and thought she had sunk it with a full broadside of 6-in. fire. At 0315 the *Edinburgh* again saw a boat on her port beam. The enemy went ahead, crossed the bows of the *Cossack*, which tried to ram, and eventually escaped past the convoy after firing a torpedo that nearly hit the *Cossack*.[1]

Commanders Stokes (*Sikh*) and Courage (*Maori*), whose destroyers were stationed abreast the columns thought that they would have been more useful ahead of the convoy, where there was more room to manoeuvre, and where they could hope to beat off such attacks before the enemy could fire torpedoes. As it was, Commander Courage in the *Maori* dared not fire lest he should hurt a friend, for the enemy was passing between his ship and the transports; and Commander Stokes in the *Sikh* was in the same station on the disengaged side. Admiral Syfret, however, considered that small torpedo craft might well pierce an extended screen, and that the *Maori* ought to have closed still nearer to the convoy to stop the enemy from passing inside her.

On being torpedoed, the *Sydney Star* had dropped astern and was found by the *Nestor*, which was stationed on the starboard beam of the convoy. Commander Rosenthal put his destroyer alongside the transport, took her troops and part of her crew on board, and persuaded her master to try to reach Malta. In an hour or so the two ships were under way, the transport making 12 knots despite serious leaks in her holds. Torpedo aircraft twice threatened attack between 0615 and 0650, the 24th, the second hour of daylight, so the *Nestor* called for help, on which Admiral Syfret sent back the *Hermione*, which had no passengers on board. At 1000, eight German dive-bombers and two high-level bombers attacked, their bombs falling close to the escorting ships; and the *Hermione* shot down one dive-bomber. This was the last attack they had to face. The three ships arrived at Malta early in the afternoon.[2]

14

The main body of the convoy went on its way unhindered after the attacks by motor boats, except for an attempt by three torpedo bombers about 0700, probably some of those which the *Nestor* and *Sydney Star* had seen. These aircraft dropped their torpedoes at a safe distance, however, when fired on by the destroyers in the screen ahead. According to the orders, Admiral Syfret was to leave the convoy at this stage of the voyage, if the situation as regards Italian surface forces were considered satisfactory, and go on to Malta with the cruisers and some of the destroyers. There they were to land passengers and stores, complete with fuel, and return to Admiral Somerville as soon as possible, while the remaining destroyers, keeping the transports company to Malta, were also to rejoin Force " H " as soon as they could. Admiral Syfret felt easy about the surface danger, as all the Italian ships were reported in harbour the day before; but he was anxious about the air. The Beaufighters at Malta had no previous experience of working with ships, and their tactics and their failure to identify themselves the evening before made the Admiral doubt their

---

[1] Captain Chapman remarked: " It was most noticeable from H.M.S. *Arethusa* that when destroyers ahead of the convoy exposed searchlights, the ships of the convoy stood out clearly in the silhouette, so much so that E-boats in a position to benefit would have been greatly assisted in finding and attacking targets. It was appreciated that waiting E-boats were probably ahead of the convoy, and for this reason it was decided not to expose a searchlight in H.M.S. *Arethusa*."

[2] The *Nestor* took nearly 500 people from the *Sydney Star*. She had already nearly 300 on board of her own ship's company and passengers.

ability to protect the convoy. "At one time", he said, "it appeared that all our efforts to get the convoy to Malta might be frustrated unless all cruisers and destroyers remained with the convoy to the end." However, it was urgently necessary to save time, and at 0745 the *Edinburgh, Arethusa* and *Manxman* left the convoy and pressed ahead at high speed to Malta, where they arrived at midday, the 24th July. The transports and destroyers arrived about four hours later, having been attacked once by a torpedo aircraft since the separation. All four cruisers sailed again in company the same evening, followed by five destroyers, which overtook the cruisers in the morning of the 25th—the sixth destroyer had to stay at Malta to make good defects. Instead of returning by the way they had come, both groups of ships kept south of Pantellaria and close along the African coast, and joined Admiral Somerville north-westward of Galita Island about 0800 on the 25th.

15

After parting with the convoy in the evening of the 23rd, Admiral Somerville had taken Force " H " westward at 18 knots until the afternoon of the 24th, going as far west as longitude 3° 30′ E. He then turned back to meet Admiral Syfret, first sending from the *Ark Royal* to Malta six Swordfish aircraft, which left the carrier in 37° 42′ N., 7° 17′ E., at 0100 on the 25th. After their junction, Forces " H " and " X " made the best of their way towards Gibraltar. Fighter patrols from the *Ark Royal* shot down a shadowing aircraft soon after the fleet shaped course westward, losing a Fulmar in doing so; but another shadower had already reported the fleet, and high-level bombers from the east and torpedo bombers from the north appeared about 1100. The *Ark Royal* had four fighters in the air, and sent up six more. They prevented the bombing attack, shooting down three aircraft out of eight at a cost of two Fulmars, while the ships watched the enemy jettison their bombs 15 miles away. The torpedo attack came to nothing too; for the enemy gave up their attempt and retired while still several miles from the fleet, though the fighters did not succeed in intercepting them. Two days later, 27th July, the fleet reached Gibraltar.

There remains to tell of the seven empty transports going from Malta to Gibraltar. Six sailed in the morning of the 23rd, escorted by the *Encounter*, but the seventh was held up for some hours through an accident when leaving harbour. At dusk, when a few miles east of Pantellaria, the six ships divided into pairs according to their speeds, and continued separately, keeping close along the shore of Tunisia. The *Encounter* at first escorted the middle pair, but joined the leading ships the following evening, the 24th, when past the Galita Bank. Italian aircraft, both bombers and torpedo bombers, attacked all these ships on the 24th to the southward of Sardinia, not far from where the *Fearless* and *Manchester* had been torpedoed the day before. They made their first attempt on the second pair of transports and the *Encounter*, four torpedo aircraft attacking at 1230 and four bombers at 1250; the bombs fell close, but no ships were hit. Next came the turn of the leading pair, which was attacked farther westward by two bombers that came singly at 1330 and 1400, the second nearly hitting the *Breconshire*. Finally, when the third pair of transports reached about the same position in the evening, it was attacked by torpedo bombers and the *Hoegh Hood* was damaged, though she arrived at Gibraltar within a few hours of her consort on the 27th, the same day as the fleet. The four faster ships had arrived the day before. The seventh ship, delayed at Malta, arrived on the 28th.

16

On the two critical days, 23rd and 24th July, the Mediterranean Fleet carried out the proposed diversion in the eastern Mediterranean. Admiral Cunningham had arranged that Vice-Admiral Pridham-Wippell should sail from Alexandria on the 23rd with two battleships and several cruisers and destroyers, and steer to the westward to suggest that he was bound for the central Mediterranean. The surface ships, however, were to turn east again after dark "with a view to the fleet's being lost by enemy reconnaissance", leaving two submarines to make a series of fictitious signals in the morning of the 24th from positions Admiral Pridham-Wippell might have reached had he continued westward. All went as intended: enemy aircraft shadowed the fleet in the afternoon and evening of the 23rd, as it was hoped they would, and the submarines made their signals. Admiral Cunningham said " nothing of interest occurred during the operation, but it is understood that the diversion was successful, and that the enemy was left with the impression that the Mediterranean Fleet was entering the central Mediterranean".

17

The transports all reached their destinations without hindrance from the Italian fleet. Admiral Somerville remarked that the enemy's inactivity may have been due to the work of the Allied submarines, which were patrolling in the zones shown in Plan 2 from the morning of 22nd July to the evening of the 26th. None of them sighted large ships of the enemy, but some made their presence known by attacking enemy convoys when going to their stations or during their patrol. For instance, the *Olympus* attacked a small convoy on the 21st on her way to her station; and although he had little hope of success Lieutenant-Commander Dymott " considered it worth firing at extreme range, as . . . a hit would have furthered my object"; and he attacked a merchant ship off Ischia on the 23rd.

As for the dangers the transports did encounter, Admiral Syfret drew certain conclusions about the attacks from the air:—

(i) " Shore-based fighters need careful training and a clear understanding of fleet requirements to enable them to work with the fleet."

(ii) " Italian high-level bombing is accurate, unless the formation is broken up by fighters."

(iii) " Italian torpedo bombers will not face determined barrage, and use torpedoes with a long- or medium-range setting."

Of the merchant ships he remarked: " That the operation was successfully carried out is due in no small measure to the behaviour of the merchant ships in convoy. Their manœuvring and general conduct was excellent, and caused me no anxiety whatever. I had complete confidence that orders given to them by me would be understood and promptly carried out. Their steadfast and resolute behaviour during air and E-boat attacks was most impressive and encouraging to us all."

CHAPTER III

Operation "Halberd," September 1941

18

OPERATION "HALBERD" was very like Operation "Substance" in July; but on this occasion part of the Italian fleet appeared at sea between Sardinia and Sicily. There were nine transports with troops and stores (Convoy G.M.2) to go to Malta and three empty ships (Convoy M.G.2) to come back to Gibraltar, and Admiral Somerville gave them protection with Force "H" on the same lines as before. Force "H" was greatly strengthened for the occasion, and had three capital ships—the *Nelson* (flag, Vice-Admiral Somerville), *Prince of Wales* (flag, Vice-Admiral Curteis) and *Rodney*, with the aircraft carrier *Ark Royal*, five cruisers, *Kenya* (flag, Rear-Admiral Burrough), *Edinburgh* (flag, Rear-Admiral Syfret), *Sheffield*, *Hermione*, *Euryalus*, and eighteen destroyers. On reaching the Narrows the east-going convoy went on to Malta with all the cruisers and half the destroyers (Force "X"), under Rear-Admiral Burrough, while the main body (Force "A") drew off to the westward to wait for Admiral Burrough's return and to distract the enemy's attention from the empty ships coming from Malta.[1] There were nine submarines off Sardinia, Sicily, and southern Italy in the stations shown on Plan 5 and aircraft of the Royal Air Force from Gibraltar and Malta provided anti-submarine patrols, reconnaissance and fighter protection.

Admiral Cunningham had supported Operation "Substance" in July by sending the Mediterranean Fleet to sea to show itself, and by having dummy signals made from submarines on its pretended track. His proposal in September appeared in the following signal he made to Admiral Somerville on the 22nd (1050B/22): "I do not intend to follow any hard and fast plan, but will keep Mediterranean Fleet at short notice from 0800 on Day Two [the 26th] with the idea of proceeding to sea and being observed steaming westward as soon as your forces are sighted by enemy; my intention is to prevent German air force turning west from Libya." With this in view he sailed from Alexandria on the 26th with the *Queen Elizabeth*, *Valiant*, *Barham*, and some cruisers and destroyers, returning to harbour next day. He did not

---

[1] Details of Forces "A" and "X" and the Convoys are shown in Appendix E. Only the *Nelson*, *Ark Royal*, *Hermione* and ten destroyers belonged to Force "H" proper.

sight any enemy aircraft, nor was there any sign that the enemy knew the fleet had gone to sea; accordingly, in the night of the 26th–27th signals were made by wireless to ensure that this diversion should have effect.

19

The transports from home went out escorted by the *Prince of Wales*, two cruisers, and some destroyers under Vice-Admiral Curteis, with the troops (about 2,600) divided among the transports and such men-of-war as were going to Malta. As they approached Gibraltar, the escorting ships took turns to go ahead into harbour to complete their fuel and rejoin, arriving and sailing again in the dark; and ships already at Gibraltar joined the convoy, which entered the Mediterranean in the night of 24th–25th September with the *Prince of Wales*, four cruisers, and seven destroyers. Meanwhile, Admiral Somerville had sailed from Gibraltar westward in the *Nelson* with a screen of destroyers before dark on the 24th. His flag was left on board the *Rodney* at Gibraltar, and farewell signals were openly exchanged between the two ships as if the *Nelson* were going home and the *Rodney* taking her place; but the Admiral turned east again in the night to overtake the convoy, while the *Rodney* sailed eastward likewise with the *Ark Royal*, *Hermione*, and the rest of the destroyers. " This ruse," said Admiral Somerville, " appears to have created the desired impression." Another opportunity to mystify and mislead enemy spies was given by the presence of some extra transports that accompanied the convoy from home; these ships were bound for Freetown, but they were sent into Gibraltar during the night of the 24th–25th September to show themselves next day in the hope of lulling suspicion had the convoy's passage through the Strait been detected.

The whole fleet assembled inside the Strait at 0900[1] on the 25th, and divided again into two groups to sail separately until the 27th, when they would join forces for the critical passage past Sardinia. Admiral Somerville, with the *Nelson*, *Ark Royal*, *Hermione* and six destroyers (Group I), stretched ahead of the convoy and went eastward along the African coast to give shadowing aircraft the impression that only " the usual " Force " H " was at sea.[2] His passage was uneventful on the 25th; but at 0932 next day the *Nelson* sighted a shadowing aircraft, flying very low 10 miles off to the south-east, which had not been detected by radar. Owing to a complete failure of radio-telephony in the fighter leader's aircraft, delay occurred in vectoring the fighters and no interception took place. An enemy report was intercepted at 0935, and this was re-broadcast by an Italian station twenty minutes later. At 1537 two aircraft were sighted low down to the eastward by the *Zulu*, *Nelson* and *Hermione*. They were thought to be Hudsons, but shortly afterwards an Italian enemy report went out. On the first occasion of sighting, Group I was in roughly 37° 30′ N., 4° 30′ E., some 250 miles south-westward of Cagliari; in the afternoon it was about 25 miles farther east. At this time the Admiral was steering to the westward to reduce his distance from the convoy, and did not turn east again till dusk.

Group II, under Admiral Curteis, with the convoy of nine transports, kept at first north-eastward along the coast of Spain, turning south-east on approaching the Balearic Islands—a track " through an area which experience

---

[1] Zone Time minus 2 is used throughout.
[2] " During the 26th," says an Italian account, " the English ships divided into various groups on different courses and adopted other methods to confound our reconnaissance. The enemy's ruses were successful—the Naval Staff was induced to think that the English force included only one, or at most two, battleships."

suggested was reasonably clear of merchant ships and civil aircraft." At 1700 on the 25th, in 36° 36′ N., 1° 58′ W., the *Sheffield*, *Duncan* and *Gurkha*, all in the screen ahead, attacked a submarine with depth-charges.[1]   On the 26th the twelve destroyers with the convoy oiled in pairs from the *Brown Ranger* as the destroyers with Admiral Syfret in July had done—the *Brown Ranger* had sailed from Gibraltar ahead of the convoy and returned there at dusk on 26th September after fulfilling her task.   That afternoon, an aircraft with Spanish colours appeared suddenly out of the clouds over Group II and was thought to have reported the convoy to the enemy.

20

Meanwhile the Italians had received early information of the departure of the British forces from Gibraltar.   The Naval Staff at first formed the opinion that the British were contemplating a landing at Pantellaria, or perhaps a bombarding operation against the Ligurian coast.   Accordingly, submarine patrols were redisposed and arrangements were made with the Air Force to intercept and attack.   The battleships *Littorio*, wearing the flag of the Commander-in-Chief, Admiral Iachino, and *Vittorio Veneto*, with the 6-in. cruisers *Abruzzi* and *Attendolo*, were ordered to proceed to Maddalena; and the 8-in. cruisers *Trento* (flag, Vice-Admiral Lombardi), *Trieste* and *Gorizia* were ordered to Spezia.

Later, when it appeared that the operation was not directed towards the Ligurian coast, these orders were modified, and at 0315, 27th September, Admiral Iachino received orders for the whole force to rendezvous 50 miles east of Cape Carbonera, Sardinia, at noon that day.

This concentration was duly effected, and Admiral Iachino then had with him two battleships, three 8-in. and two 6-in. cruisers and 14 destroyers. Believing at this time that the British force only consisted of one battleship (though reports suggested that another might be at sea), a carrier, two cruisers and five destroyers, he decided to seek action, and shaped course to the southward at 24 knots in order to intercept the British force.

21

To return to the British.

The two groups met again about 0800 on the 27th; and the fleet assumed Cruising Disposition No. 16A, with all three battleships formed on the convoy, yet free to move independently, and the *Ark Royal* with the cruisers *Euryalus* and *Hermione* following on the weather quarter (see Plan 7).   Whatever the enemy may have learnt through the air and submarine contacts of the previous two days, they soon knew all they needed to know; for their shadowing aircraft reported the fleet as the ships were taking their new stations in the morning, and at least once later in the forenoon.   The expected air attacks came in three phases between 1255 and 1405, all by Italian torpedo bombers, mainly of types BR.20 and S.79.   It was a calm, sunny day with patches of thundercloud at 1,000 feet and a very light breeze varying between south-west and west.   The ships were zigzagging, speed about 12 knots, mean line of advance 075°.   The mean position of the attacks was roughly 37° 45′ N., 9° E.—some 90 miles to the southward of Cagliari.

---

[1] It was thought at the time that damage might have been inflicted, but it is now known that this was not the case.

The first to attack were a dozen torpedo aircraft, of which a half reached the fleet, escorted by six CR.42 fighters. They were discovered to the north-east at 1255, on which the *Ark Royal's* patrol of eight Fulmars was ordered to intercept. The Fulmars met the enemy 10 miles from the fleet, the torpedo planes being low near the water with their escort 7,000 feet above them. The British fighters succeeded in shooting down one torpedo plane and driving off others without the Italian fighters interfering; but one Fulmar, separated from the rest in the clouds, met the Italian fighters, and was damaged in the encounter and eventually shot down by the *Prince of Wales* on its return to the fleet. Meanwhile, six torpedo planes persevered, attacking the fleet from the port side about 1300 and dropping their torpedoes at a range of 5,000 yards from the convoy at a height of 300 feet. The convoy and escorting ships made large turns towards the enemy and fired a barrage. No ship was hit, though the *Rodney, Lance* and *Isaac Sweers* had narrow escapes. On the other hand, the fleet shot down three enemy aircraft and the Fulmars yet another, which was retiring from its attack—making five all told in this phase.[1]

Towards the end of this engagement, seven more Fulmars were sent up by the *Ark Royal*, steaming fast down wind for the flying off and passing ahead of the *Nelson*. There were thus 14 fighters in the air to meet the next attack, which came from the starboard side of the fleet just before 1330; yet despite this unusually strong protection it was during this phase of the battle that the enemy gained their one success in daylight. Three aircraft, out of six or seven that attacked, pressed through the destroyers' barrage and made for the flagship. The first dropped its torpedo from a height of 200 feet, only 450 yards from the *Nelson*, fine on her starboard bow. She had turned towards the enemy to comb the torpedo tracks, steaming 18 knots or over, and had just steadied on a course when she saw the torpedo, too late to avoid it. It hit her on the port bow, limiting her speed eventually to 15 knots.[2] The aircraft was shot down by the *Prince of Wales* and *Sheffield* as it flew away. The second plane dropped its torpedo from a greater height and at twice the range, missing the *Nelson* by a hundred yards. The *Laforey* and other destroyers shot down the third plane as it passed over the screen. The rest of the enemy attacked the fleet from the starboard quarter; but the Fulmars intercepted them, spoilt their aim, and shot one down. On the other hand, one Fulmar was unfortunately shot down by the *Rodney*.

The third phase of the attack followed close on the heels of the second. About 1345 some 10 or 11 planes, flying very low, came in sight 10 miles away to the southward. Most of them retired on being fired at by the fleet, but three or four tried to work round to port ahead of the convoy, which made a large turn to port to meet the attack; the aircraft, diverted by the destroyers' fire, dropped their torpedoes outside the screen without effect, though the *Lightning* was narrowly missed by a torpedo fired at a range of 500 yards. Three of the aircraft that had originally turned away then came back from abaft the beam to attack the *Ark Royal;* none dropped torpedoes, and one was shot down by the *Ark Royal* and *Nelson* and another by Fulmars. At 1358 an aircraft outside the screen, right ahead of the *Nelson*, dropped a torpedo, which the *Cossack* was able to avoid with the help of her Asdic set. An Italian fighter " performing aerobatics " over the destroyers, evidently to make a diversion for the torpedo planes, was either shot down or failed to pull out of a dive.

---

[1] The *Rodney, Prince of Wales, Lively, Heythrop* and s.s. *Rowallan Castle* seem to have had the chief share in destroying the Italian aircraft shot down by the fleet.

[2] The hit was abreast 60 Station, 10 ft. below the waterline. Admiral Somerville remarked that *Nelson's* lack of anti-aircraft guns which will bear on fine bow bearings was possibly the cause of her being torpedoed; " she has not a single anti-aircraft gun which will train across the bow at low elevation."

Further attacks threatened as the afternoon wore on; but they came to nothing, the enemy being generally driven off by Fulmars a long way from the fleet. Out of 30 aircraft that attacked that day, only 18 got within firing range and gained one hit; six were shot down by the guns of the fleet, besides the four brought down by fighters. This was largely due to the disposition of the destroyers, which turned back most of the enemy, shooting down two, so that only four aircraft got past the screen and none reached a good position for a shot at the convoy. But it meant some risk to the destroyers; several reported being endangered by the fire of big ships and transports astern, and the *Oribi* had two men wounded by splinters of British shells.

22

The attack from the air was still going on when news came of the Italian fleet. According to the latest intelligence (an air report of 26th September from Malta), the Italians had three battleships, six cruisers and some destroyers at Taranto, and two battleships, one cruiser and some destroyers at Naples. Then, at 1404 on the 27th, Admiral Somerville received a report timed 1340/27, by a Royal Air Force aircraft scouting from Malta, that two battleships and eight destroyers were in 38° 20′ N., 10° 40′ E., steering 190° at 20 knots, which put them about 74 miles 070° from the *Nelson* at 1404. Twenty minutes later a further signal timed 1350 reported four cruisers and eight destroyers 15 miles west-south-west of the enemy battle fleet, and making the same course and speed.[1] The appearance of an enemy fleet to the eastward, on the route of the convoy, altered the whole situation. Admiral Somerville considered that the enemy, believing he had only one capital ship, intended either to meet him at the western end of the Narrows or to draw the British heavy ships north-east, so that the convoy should lie open to attack by lesser forces in the Narrows at dusk. He decided to make for the enemy at his best speed with his three battleships and a few destroyers, leaving his three large cruisers and the bulk of the flotilla with the convoy, while the *Ark Royal*, the two anti-aircraft cruisers and two destroyers were to keep near it; the carrier was to send up two aircraft at once to shadow the Italian fleet, and a striking force armed with torpedoes as soon as it could be got ready. This arrangement would place the battleships between the convoy and the enemy, and enable the latter to be brought to battle should they make for the convoy. At 1408, therefore, he ordered the *Ark Royal* to prepare a striking force and to fly off shadowing aircraft, and at 1417 he ordered the battleships to form on the *Nelson* which was already stretching ahead of the convoy.[2]

But it soon became apparent that the *Nelson's* injuries would prevent her going more than 15 knots, and the Admiral revised his plan. At 1446 he ordered Admiral Curteis, with the other two battleships, two cruisers and two destroyers, " to drive off the enemy," while the *Nelson* stayed with the convoy. Admiral Curteis proceeded accordingly at 27 knots, with the *Edinburgh* and *Sheffield* five miles ahead of the *Prince of Wales* and the *Rodney* following as fast as she could.

Actually, the enemy had altered course to 360° a quarter of an hour previously and was then steering directly away from the British. Though Admiral Iachino had received a signal from the Naval Staff giving him " freedom of manœuvre," his instructions permitted him to " engage only in conditions of decisive superiority ". But visibility was poor, being limited

---

[1] This second signal was received in the *Prince of Wales* about 1412.
[2] Appendix G shows Admiral Somerville's previous instructions. See also Plans 5 and 6

by mist to about 5 miles, and he was uncertain as to the position and composition of the British forces; he knew, however, that they included a carrier, and the fighter escort from Cagliari which he had requested had not turned up. In these circumstances he did not feel sure of his " decisive superiority " and at 1430 altered course towards Sardinia, hoping that the fighter protection would materialise and that air reconnaissance reports would soon clarify the situation.

It was not long before Admiral Curteis received news of this change of course.

At 1521 a report came from the Royal Air Force reconnaissance aircraft that the Italian battleships had turned to 360° at 1445[1]; and at 1530 another signal timed 1503 made their course 060° and put them several miles to the northward of their position as previously reported. This made it clear to Admiral Curteis that he could not hope to force an action. It was possible, however, that the enemy might still come down between the Skerki Bank and Marittimo, to raid the transports when it grew dark, or attack them from the westward, having decoyed the British squadron northward. In these circumstances, Admiral Curteis decided to " close the passage between Skerki and Marittimo, while keeping well placed to fall back on the convoy," and he proceeded accordingly. About 1700, however, he received orders from Admiral Somerville to rejoin the convoy, " just as I was reaching a position," he said, " from which I could cover a movement either to the eastwards or westwards without fear of the enemy's winning the race." An hour or so later his detachment returned to the fleet.

Admiral Somerville had recalled him because he believed the Italians had abandoned any idea of a fight and were retiring. Even if the *Ark Royal's* aircraft succeeded in reducing the enemy's speed, he thought it too late for Admiral Curteis to gain touch before dark, when a " successful issue was highly problematical "; moreover, he considered it essential that the cruisers and destroyers should return to the convoy before dark. This view was confirmed by events.

Neither shadowers nor striking force from the *Ark Royal* found the enemy. The two shadowers left the *Ark Royal* at 1448, being informed that the enemy was 60 miles 078°, steering 190°. As mentioned above, two important signals then came in from a Royal Air Force reconnaissance aircraft. The first, made at 1445, reported that the Italians had altered course to 360°. This was received by the *Ark Royal* at 1510, but wireless congestion arising from the issue of the new orders detaching Admiral Curteis delayed its transmission to the shadowers. The other signal, timed 1503, reported the enemy's course as 060°, and amended the position in the original report (1340), making it 14 miles to the northward. This amended position was within 6 or 7 miles of the actual position, but the course 060° was merely a brief alteration to the eastward, to avoid a reported submarine. This was received by the *Ark Royal* at 1543, and the amended position and new course were passed to the striking force by wireless.[2] A few minutes before, at 1540, the striking force of twelve Swordfish had flown off, escorted by four Fulmars, with an estimated position of the enemy 54 miles 056°, steering 360°. Having reached the enemy's estimated position on the 060° course and seen nothing, they turned at 1700 and searched to the southward, then turned north again for 40 miles, but failed to locate the enemy, who had altered back to 360° at

---

[1] This signal was received by the *Nelson* at 1506 and by the *Ark Royal* at 1510.
[2] See Plan 6. A third signal, made by the R.A.F. shadower at 1515, reported that the enemy had altered course " to the north "; it was not received by Malta or by any ship. (Force " H " Report, paragraph 103)

1510 and by that time was some 50 miles to the westward of them at the extreme limit of radar range. Just before 1800 they reported their failure, and were ordered to return. Six landed on just after sunset and six after dark, all very short of petrol. The *Ark Royal's* shadowers were equally unsuccessful. Shadower A, proceeding to the eastward, met seven Italian fighters and was badly damaged and had to return. Shadower B had not received the 1445 report of the enemy's alteration of course to 360°, though he received the 1503 report of the amended position and of the enemy's being on course 060°. His A.S.V. set failed about 1700, and a visual search was unsuccessful. He returned after having been five hours and five minutes in the air.

The Italian Fleet, meanwhile, had continued to the northward till about 1700, when, on receipt of an encouraging signal from the Naval Staff,[1] Admiral Iachino altered course to south; but at sunset, just after 1800, he received orders to proceed to the east of Sardinia for the night and to await fresh instructions; he shaped course accordingly in an east-north-easterly direction.

23

Soon after Admiral Curteis had rejoined, at 1851, the fleet reached the mouth of the Narrows, where the convoy was to part company with Force " A " and continue its voyage under Admiral Burrough. When the news first came of the Italian fleet, Admiral Somerville had considered whether the convoy should steer southward along the coast of Tunisia instead of keeping east towards Sicily as arranged; but Admiral Burrough preferred the Sicilian route for the following reasons: "(a) The bolder course seemed more likely to deceive the enemy; (b) the convoy would be clearly silhouetted under the moon, while moving to the southward, and off the Tunisian coast could take no avoiding action; (c) convoy and escort in single line ahead from Cape Bon to south of Kelibia Light would extend to about seven miles, and would be very vulnerable to either aircraft or E-boat attack; (d) time of arrival at Malta would be delayed; (e) the enemy would be more likely to conduct a search to the south-west than to the north-east." Admiral Somerville agreed, " in view of the enemy's hurried withdrawal to the north-east," and at 1855 on the 27th they separated. The three battleships, the *Ark Royal* and the nine destroyers of Force " A " turned away westward. The five cruisers and nine destroyers of Force " X " took the convoy on, forming in Cruising Disposition No. 17 before dark (see Plan 8), and steaming at 14 to 15 knots.

Enemy aircraft were still about. Several Italian fighters had come within 20 miles or so of the fleet some little time before the convoy parted company, and for an hour the few Fulmars still available for patrol were engaged in keeping the enemy at a distance, lest they should observe the separation. Other Italian aircraft (probably fighters) approached the convoy between 1915 and 1930 as it passed through the Skerki Channel, but turned away when the cruisers opened fire. As soon as it grew dark, however, their torpedo bombers came, attacking the convoy repeatedly in ones, twos or threes between 2000 and 2040.

The sky was clear, with a half-moon shining on the starboard quarter, whereas the attacks were all on the port side: " an impossible night to see the birds, as any wildfowler will agree " said Commander Graham of the *Zulu*. And indeed, though the *Oribi* shot down one aircraft and the *Kenya* claims to have destroyed another with her 6-inch barrage, the ships had little chance of

---

[1] This signal stated that the British had only one battleship and one cruiser, and reported that Italian aircraft had sunk a cruiser and hit two more cruisers and possibly a battleship.

keeping the enemy at arm's length by their fire, hampered too as they were by the danger of hurting friends. Captain Hutton, of the *Laforey*, described the attack thus: " The appearance from the disengaged side of streams of shell of all calibres fired from H.M. ships and merchant ships was spectacular, but its effectiveness looked doubtful; some of it was quite indiscriminate, and revealed the convoy clearly to any other aircraft which may have been in the vicinity". There were luckily not much above a dozen aircraft there, or the convoy would probably have suffered heavily.

The *Cossack* (see Plan 8) sighted aircraft on the port side at 2027, and at 2029 a torpedo was dropped on the port bow of the *Sheffield*, which five minutes later had to turn with full helm to starboard to avoid another dropped on her port beam. At 2032, in 37° 31′ N., 10° 46′ E., the transport *Imperial Star* was struck by a torpedo on the port side aft. The *Oribi* was attacked at 2036, the torpedo being dropped 800 yards away just abaft the port beam, and avoided by the ship's turning stern on; her pom-poms and Oerlikon guns shot down the attacking aircraft.

The *Heythrop* went alongside the *Imperial Star*, took on board her 300 soldier passengers, and rejoined the convoy. The *Oribi* took her in tow and steered for Malta, distant 220 miles, Lieutenant-Commander McBeath deciding that she should go on rather than go back to Gibraltar. But the big transport's injuries made her unmanageable; with both screws and rudder gone and her stern deep in the water through the flooding of an engine-room (she was drawing 38 feet aft), she would only steer in circles. After two hours' towing they had to give it up; it was impracticable to tow her without tugs; and as she had valuable and secret stores on board, and there was risk of capture owing to her position, it was decided to sink her. The ship was scuttled with depth charges at 0340, the 28th; a huge fire broke out aft, and the *Oribi* shelled her to spread the blaze. When it seemed clear that she must soon be entirely gutted, the destroyer left her and went on to Malta alone. There was no trace of her the next day.

Towards the end of these moonlight actions, at 2030 on the 27th, the *Hermione* had parted company to shell the harbour and base at Pantellaria as a diversion. She reached her firing position north of the island about 0130, the 28th, and fired 122 high-explosive shells in five minutes at ranges of 12,000 to 13,500 yards by the light of starshell, causing columns of smoke to rise in the area fired at; she also dropped smoke floats a few minutes before opening fire " to give the impression that the convoy was passing." The bombardment was plainly visible to the convoy 50 miles away. The batteries on shore returned the *Hermione's* fire without effect, and she joined Admiral Burrough again at 0630.

After the torpedo attack at 2030 the convoy had a quiet night. Some aircraft were detected over 20 miles off an hour after the last attack, searching for the convoy farther south, others approached from the northward a little before midnight, others again crossed astern from the southward, but none came near enough to be dangerous. The moon set a few minutes after midnight, and thenceforward the night was uneventful. At 0615 on the 28th, Fulmars and Royal Air Force fighters from Malta arrived, " to give excellent protection," said Admiral Burrough, " for the remainder of the passage." About 0830, having heard by signal from Malta that no enemy ships were near his track, Admiral Burrough went on ahead with four cruisers to gain time for landing passengers and refuelling. He entered the Grand Harbour at 1130 with guards and bands paraded amidst the cheers of the whole city, assembled in crowds on the shore. Admiral Syfret, with the *Edinburgh* and the destroyers, brought the convoy into harbour a couple of hours later. They had several threats of attacks by Italian aircraft during the forenoon, but the Malta fighters drove off the enemy each time. The only ship lost was the *Imperial Star*.

24

Of the three transports that were to go from Malta empty to Gibraltar under cover of this operation, the *Melbourne Star* sailed on the 26th alone and reached Gibraltar without adventure on the 29th. The other two, *Port Chalmers* and *City of Pretoria*, left Malta together on the 27th, going through the Narrows westward along the coast of Tunisia the same night as the outgoing convoy passed through eastward farther north. Up to sunset that day a corvette had kept them company, but afterwards they sailed without escort. Soon after leaving Malta they had been seen and reported by enemy aircraft; and when passing Pantellaria at night they encountered a motor torpedo boat, with which the *Port Chalmers* exchanged fire. In the morning of the 28th the transports separated, the faster *Port Chalmers* going on at full speed and arriving at Gibraltar early on the 30th. Italian aircraft approached both ships several times during the 28th, but the transports, flying French colours, carefully refrained from firing at the aircraft. In the evening, however, three torpedo planes attacked the *City of Pretoria*; and she may have been attacked by a submarine at the same time. The transport hoisted her proper colours, fired at the aircraft, avoided their torpedoes, and made off under a smoke screen. Again in the night of 29th–30th September a submarine may have attacked her off the coast of Spain, but she reached Gibraltar unharmed a few hours after the *Port Chalmers*.

Admiral Somerville remarked on their conduct that " the able and resolute handling of both *Port Chalmers* and *City of Pretoria* in successfully driving off enemy attacks deserves high praise. Both masters showed excellent restraint in withholding fire at enemy aircraft, while there was a chance of their false colours being effective, and also in keeping wireless silence when attacked, except on the one occasion when *City of Pretoria* was attacked by torpedo bomber aircraft and her report might possibly have brought fighter assistance if *Ark Royal* had been in the vicinity."

The Admiral had not tried to give these ships direct protection. " In view of the low speed of *Nelson*," he wrote, " I did not consider that action to afford close support . . . was justified, since this would have involved an unacceptable reduction in the destroyer screen then available. I wished also to convey the impression that a general withdrawal of forces to the westward was in progress and would be continued." After leaving Admiral Burrough in the evening of the 27th, therefore, he took Force " A " westward at 14 knots, the flagship's best speed. In the morning of the 28th, the Royal Air Force reconnoitring aircraft reported the Italian fleet still cruising between Sardinia and Sicily, and there it remained all day, far from either part of the British fleet, finally withdrawing to the E.N.E. at 1518 that afternoon. Enemy aircraft shadowed Force " A " too, and at least once signalled a report; this was to some extent welcome to Admiral Somerville, who remarked, " By keeping the battleships concentrated until dark I hoped to have concealed damage to *Nelson*, and that consequently enemy surface vessels would keep clear while Force ' X ' made the passage westward from Malta." But as soon as it grew dark, having then arrived roughly in the longitude of Algiers, Admiral Somerville parted company. The speed of the *Nelson* had to be reduced to 12 knots at 2010 to lessen the strain on the bulkheads, the ship being down 8 feet by the bows with 3,500 tons of water in her. She arrived at Gibraltar with three destroyers on the 30th. Admiral Curteis had turned east with the *Prince of Wales, Rodney, Ark Royal* and six destroyers to meet Admiral Burrough.

25

Having landed passengers and stores and filled up with fuel at Malta, the ships of Force " X " sailed again in the evening of the 28th. Instead of keeping to the northward as he had come, Admiral Burrough went back along the African shore, and joined Admiral Curteis about 1030 on the 29th, when the combined force steered for Gibraltar, following a route different from that which Admiral Curteis had " already covered twice in thirty-six hours." The fleet divided into two groups at dusk that day, 29th September, Admirals Curteis and Burrough stretching ahead with some ships which entered harbour on the 30th, while Admiral Syfret arrived with the rest on 1st October.

The fleet's passage through the western basin was punctuated by a number of submarine attacks. There were six certain contacts or attacks between the evening of the 28th and the morning of 30th September, as well as other contacts not definitely submarine. The first took place at 1942 on the 28th, shortly before Admiral Somerville left the fleet, and the *Duncan* attacked with depth-charges, but without visible effect. Next morning, Admiral Curteis encountered two submarines on his way back to meet Admiral Burrough's force—the first about daybreak, the second two hours afterwards. In the first encounter, at 0612, two torpedoes passed under the *Gurkha*, which with the *Isaac Sweers* hunted the submarine unsuccessfully; in the attack at 0810 the *Gurkha* dropped a 14-charge pattern and may have damaged or destroyed the enemy. There was another attack in the afternoon, at 1645, by which time the fleet had arrived within some 40 miles of the *Duncan's* contact of the day before; the *Legion* and *Lively* hunted for an hour a submarine whose conning tower had broken surface and which had fired torpedoes at the fleet, but they could not claim any result. Lastly, there were two encounters on the 30th, perhaps with the same submarine. Between about 0330 and 0400, Admiral Curteis had indications of a submarine's presence on the surface, and heard what were probably torpedoes exploding at the end of their run, though the screening ships did not find the enemy. At 0930, when Admiral Syfret reached a position a little to the northward of this attack, the *Gurkha* and *Legion* hunted a submarine; and as Admiral Somerville recorded it, " there appears to be no reasonable cause to doubt " their full success.[1] It is now confirmed that the *Adua* was sunk on this occasion.

26

None of the nine Allied submarines on patrol had the luck to sight the Italian battleships. But Lieutenant-Commander Cayley in the *Utmost* attacked three cruisers in the afternoon of 26th September as they were steering northward towards Naples, having come through the Messina Strait, screened by eight destroyers and escorted by flying boats. Fortune, however, did not favour the *Utmost;* for one of the destroyers nearly rammed her, perhaps indeed passed over her, just as she was about to fire; and the high speed of the

---

[1] The following are the positions of the submarine attacks :—

Date	Position	
1942/28	37° 30′ N., 3° 45′ E.	(*Duncan*)
0612/29	37° 30′ N., 6° 25′ E.	(*Gurkha* and *Isaac Sweers*)
0810/29	37° 28′ N., 7° 14′ E.	(*Gurkha*)
1645/29	37° 26′ N., 4° 37′ E.	(*Legion* and *Lively*)
0930/30	37° 10′ N., 0° 56′ E.	(*Gurkha* and *Legion*)

enemy, estimated at 28 knots, spoilt the chance of catching up with the director angle and making a second attempt. Lieutenant-Commander Cayley then tried to report the enemy by wireless, but nobody seems to have received his signal. In the evening of the 27th the *Trusty* and *Upholder* had orders from Malta to shift their stations to the Bay of Naples, south-west of Ischia and Capri respectively, in the hope of intercepting the Italian battleships going back to port; they saw nothing, though they reached their new stations in good time: the enemy entered harbour early on the 29th, but may well have approached Naples by the route north of Ischia. On the 28th the *Urge* was moved away from the coast near Palermo to the probable track of cruisers returning to Messina, but again to no purpose. The Dutch *O.21* diving close off the south-east corner of Sardinia, cannot have been far from the enemy in the afternoon of the 28th, yet all she saw was a single destroyer, which passed inside her and went into Cagliari Bay.

Some submarines attacked merchantmen and torpedo craft; but Lieutenant Norman in the *Unbeaten*, south of the toe of Italy, refrained on the 27th for fear of " compromising *Unbeaten's* position for fleet operation." Admiral Cunningham thought this a mistake, " since the enemy must pass through " that area " whether he knows submarines are present or not." On the other hand, the Admiral of Submarines said that " an observed attack . . . might well have ruined any chances of H.M.S. *Unbeaten's* achieving her object of attacking or reporting Italian surface units," and that even a fleet tanker was not " a worthy target " in the circumstances.[1]

27

The most dangerous part of the convoy's voyage proved to be the moonlight passage through the Narrows, when the *Imperial Star* was torpedoed and lost. Admiral Somerville said of this danger that " it cannot be emphasized too strongly that, if operations of this character are carried out during moonlight, the hazards are increased to a very considerable extent. Had the enemy concentrated his torpedo aircraft in attacking from dusk onwards, he might well have succeeded in torpedoing a large proportion of the convoy." In comparison, the danger from the air during daylight was much less serious, the determined and successful attack on the *Nelson* notwithstanding; nor, in the Admiral's words, did the Italian fleet ever constitute a serious threat. Admiral Somerville noted " the excellent co-operation " by the Royal Air Force, whose fighters' services to the convoy Admirals Burrough and Syfret specially remarked on.[2] Apart from that, the bombing and machine-gun attacks on airfields in Sardinia and Sicily on 27th and 28th September " undoubtedly reduced to a considerable extent the scale of air attack which the enemy intended to launch."

These three operations—" Excess ", " Substance " and " Halberd "— brought 29 ships through the Narrows (apart from the 10 ships of the Malta-Egypt convoys in January) with a loss of one sunk and two damaged. The cost to the fleet was by no means small. It amounted to one battleship (*Nelson*) damaged; one aircraft carrier (*Illustrious*) severely damaged; one cruiser (*Southampton*) sunk and two damaged (*Gloucester, Manchester*); one destroyer (*Fearless*) sunk and two damaged (*Gallant, Firedrake*). These losses weighed little at the time against the joyous cheers that rose from the walls of Valetta as the ships entered the beleaguered harbour. England had not forgotten them. Her Navy still held the pathways of the sea.

---

[1] M.020005/41. H.M.S/M. *Unbeaten's* Report.
[2] See also Appendix F.

PART II. CONVOYS IN 1942

(Battle Summary No. 32)

CHAPTER IV

Operation "M.G.1", March 1942

28

IN MARCH 1942 the naval situation in the Mediterranean—and, indeed throughout the world—was more difficult than at any time hitherto during the war. The quarter ending that month saw a higher tonnage of merchant shipping sunk in the Atlantic than in any previous period, and this was on the increase; in the Arctic, the protection of the convoys to North Russia was throwing a very severe strain on the Home Fleet, due to the advent of daylight after the winter darkness and a redisposition of the German Fleet; and the tremendous events in the Far East following the Japanese entry into the war in December 1941, made themselves felt everywhere, and not least in the Mediterranean. In the eastern basin, neither capital ships nor carriers were available in the British Fleet, while Italy had four or five battleships fit for service and strong forces of shore-based aircraft at her disposal. In the western basin, Force H was preparing for the operation which resulted in the occupation of Diego Suarez (Madagascar) in May.

An attempt to send a convoy from Alexandria to Malta in February had failed, two ships being destroyed and the third disabled by air attack. But the Commander-in-Chief, Admiral Sir Andrew Cunningham, determined to try again, employing his whole strength of cruisers and destroyers under Rear-Admiral Philip Vian to fight the way through and with shore-based fighter aircraft patrolling overhead at times more than 300 miles from their base. This operation, known as M.G.1, was the last planned by Admiral Cunningham before he gave up the command of the station to Admiral Sir Henry Harwood in April; and it led to a brilliant action known as the Battle of Sirte[1] between surface ships in which Rear-Admiral Vian, using methods

---

[1] A Battle Honour—" Sirte "—was subsequently awarded for this action. The Italians refer to it as the *Second* Battle of Sirte, and to the action fought on 17th December 1941 (see *N.S.H., Mediterranean*, Vol. II) as the *First* Battle of Sirte.

like those proposed by Kempenfelt long ago, showed the power of a weak squadron to parry attempts by much stronger forces.[1] Unfortunately, only a small fraction of the cargoes " carried to Malta at such risk and price," said Admiral Harwood, was safely discharged. One ship was bombed and sunk by aircraft the day after the battle; another was towed disabled into Marsaxlokk and never reached the Grand Harbour, though a part of her cargo was recovered; continual air attacks after their arrival hindered unloading the other two, and they were sunk eventually with their holds still nearly full.

29

The ships available for the escort were three cruisers, an anti-aircraft ship, with ten " Fleet " and six (originally seven) Hunt-class destroyers from Alexandria, besides a cruiser and a destroyer from Malta that were to meet the convoy west of Crete.[2] The " Hunts " were to carry out an anti-submarine search between Alexandria and Tobruk in the night of 19th–20th March, the night before the convoy sailed, and during daylight on the 20th; they were then to oil at Tobruk, and to join the convoy in the morning of the 21st. The sweep was unfortunate, for the *Heythrop* was torpedoed by a submarine on the 20th, and sank whilst on her way to Tobruk in tow a few hours later. The convoy itself was to leave Alexandria with a small escort in the morning of 20th March, Rear-Admiral Vian following with the main body in the evening to catch up with the convoy next morning at the eastern end of the passage between Cyrenaica and Crete, whence earlier convoys had suffered heavy air attacks. Having met the two ships from Malta in the morning of the 22nd, the convoy was to proceed at full strength until dark that day, steering well to the southward of the natural course for Malta. At nightfall Rear-Admiral Vian was to turn back for Alexandria with his three cruisers and the " Fleet " destroyers (Force " B "), while the convoy finished its voyage with the ships from Malta, the anti-aircraft ship and the " Hunts," reaching its destination at dawn on the 23rd. Admiral Cunningham reckoned upon interference by surface ships during daylight on the 22nd or the night following. " Should this occur," ran his order on the subject, " it is my general intention that the enemy should, if possible, be evaded until darkness, after which the convoy should be sent on to Malta with the destroyer escort, being dispersed if considered advisable, and the enemy brought to action by Force " B." The convoy should only be turned back if it is evident that the enemy will otherwise intercept in daylight and east of longitude 18° E."

Four vessels of the Malta submarine flotilla and one from Alexandria—the *Proteus*—were also employed against surface attack, two on patrol south of the Strait of Messina, three off Taranto. The submarines off Taranto had each two stations: " A," " B " and " C " up to 22nd March; " R," " S " and " T " farther inshore, on the 23rd (see Plan 9). Only *P.36* saw anything of the Italian fleet on its sailing; she sighted some destroyers and had hydrophone effect of bigger ships standing out of the Gulf of Taranto in the night of 21st–22nd March, and thus was able to give timely warning to Rear-Admiral Vian. On the other hand, three submarines had opportunities for successful action before the operation began, while waiting to fulfil their

---

[1] *Vide* Kempenfelt to Middleton, July 1779: " Much, I may say almost all, depends upon this fleet; 'tis an inferior against a superior fleet; therefore the greatest skill and address is requisite to counteract the designs of the enemy, to watch and seize the favourable opportunity for action . . . to hover near the enemy, keep him at bay, and prevent his attempting to execute anything but at risk and hazard, to command their attention and oblige them to think of nothing but being on their guard against your attack." (*The Barham Papers*, I, p. 292.)

[2] See Appendix I.

part in protecting the convoy. On 14th March, *P.34* of the Messina patrol sank a submarine off Punto di Stilo, north-east of Cape Spartivento; and the *Unbeaten* sank another on the 17th on her regular station, Position " N." Lastly, the *Upholder*, being sent into the Adriatic to kill time, sank a submarine within 2 miles of the port of Brindisi on the 18th. She had also a long shot in a very rough sea on the 23rd at the Italian battleship *Littorio* returning to Taranto after the action of the previous day, but was unsuccessful, as will be told in its place.

Both the Army in Libya and the Royal Air Force helped to defend the convoy against attack from the air. The Army made feint advances on 20th and 21st March, to threaten enemy airfields, and thus to divert aircraft from attacking the convoy; these movements proved very successful, in particular the shelling of Martuba landing-ground on the second day of the advance. The Royal Air Force was to attack air stations in Cyrenaica and Crete to keep aircraft grounded.[1] Fighter patrols were to accompany the convoy " as far as possible "—a duty nobly performed until 0900[2] on the 22nd, when the aircraft were over 300 miles from their base. Air reconnaissance was to be flown both from Libya and Malta; but in the event heavy enemy attacks on the airfields prevented reconnaissance from Malta. Torpedo striking forces were also arranged for—Beauforts from Libya and a naval air squadron from Malta.

30

The convoy, known as M.W.10, consisting of the commissioned supply ship *Breconshire* and three merchant ships, sailed from Alexandria in the morning of 20th March with the anti-aircraft ship *Carlisle* and six destroyers, Rear-Admiral Vian following in the evening with the *Cleopatra* (flag), *Dido*, *Euryalus* and four destroyers. The two forces met some 70 miles northward of Tobruk in the forenoon of the 21st, by which time five of the six " Hunt " destroyers from Tobruk had also joined the convoy, and all proceeded westward together at 12 knots with relays of fighter aircraft overhead. The sixth destroyer from Tobruk, held up there by a fouled propeller, joined in the evening; and at 0800 next day, the 22nd, the *Penelope* and *Legion* joined from Malta in 34° 10' N., 19° 30' E. The force was thus complete and well on its way, having passed through the danger area between Crete and Cyrenaica without attack. By this time, however, Rear-Admiral Vian knew that he was unlikely to be left in peace much longer. Some German transport aircraft, crossing from Libya to Crete, had reported the convoy the previous evening,[3] and at 0518 that morning the following signal (timed· 0131/22) had come from Submarine *P.36*: " Three destroyers and hydrophone effect of heavier ships in 40° 08' N., 17° 07' E., course 150° at 23 knots."

This force was actually the battleship *Littorio*, wearing the flag of the Commander-in-Chief, Admiral Iachino, and four destroyers, which had sailed from Taranto shortly after midnight and was steaming to the southward with Convoy M.W.10 as its quarry, after being joined by two 8-inch cruisers (*Gorizia*, *Trento*), a 6-inch cruiser (*Bande Nere*) and four destroyers under Admiral Parona from Messina.

---

[1] No. 826 Naval Air Squadron, working with the Royal Air Force, bombed targets at Derna on the nights of the 20th–21st and 21st–22nd " to assist in creating a diversion while a convoy was on passage to Malta " (A.0991/42).

[2] Zone Time minus 2 is used throughout this chapter.

[3] The *Cleopatra*'s group had also been reported by submarines off Cyrenaica on the 21st.

P.36's signal indicated to Admiral Vian that air attacks must be expected at any moment, whilst an Italian fleet might appear in the afternoon. The air attacks began at about 0930, just half an hour after the last fighter patrol had to leave the convoy, and continued at intervals till dark. It was estimated that all told some 150 aircraft were employed, torpedo- and high-level-bombers, shadowers and spotting aircraft. The forenoon attempts were not dangerous, however, being only a few torpedo shots at long range by Italian S.79 aircraft—"futile attacks," as Captain Nicholl of the *Penelope* called them, on which " there are no particular remarks to make." The convoy was protected by a double screen, an inner air warning screen of cruisers and destroyers stationed close in with an anti-submarine screen of destroyers two miles ahead; and the half-dozen or so of torpedoes dropped were all released beyond the outer screen without effect. On the other hand, the attacks by German bombers later in the day were much more serious; most of the ships of war were away engaging the Italian fleet, and the merchantmen and their actual escort were hard put to it to avoid damage.

31

At 1230, Rear-Admiral Vian assumed his organization for a surface action and signalled his intention to form the striking force on a northerly course, should the enemy appear. He was determined that the convoy should go to Malta, " even if enemy surface forces made contact." In this organization, the ships were ordered in divisions as follows:—

    1st. *Jervis* (Captain Poland, D.14), *Kipling, Kelvin, Kingston*

    2nd. *Dido* (Captain McCall), *Penelope, Legion*

    3rd. *Zulu* (Commander Graham), *Hasty*

    4th. *Cleopatra* (flag), *Euryalus*

    5th. *Sikh* (Captain Micklethwait, D.22), *Lively, Hero, Havock*

    6th. *Carlisle* (Captain Neame), *Avon Vale* (smoke-laying)

On the enemy's approach, the ships of the first five divisions were to stand out from the convoy and concentrate by divisions as a striking force (see Fig. 1). Meanwhile, the 6th Division would prepare to lay smoke across the wake of the convoy; and the remaining destroyers—*Southwold* (Commander Jellicoe), *Beaufort, Dulverton, Hurworth* and *Eridge*—which already formed part of the inner screen, would be redisposed as a close escort. In case the Rear-Admiral decided against an immediate close engagement, he had a special signal to " carry out diversionary tactics using smoke to cover the escape of the convoy," when the convoy was to turn away, while the concentrated divisions laid smoke screens at right-angles to the bearing of the enemy, reversing course in time to attack with torpedoes as the enemy reached the smoke. A month previously, the cruiser squadron and some of the destroyers had practised the manœuvre required—" to move out from a cruising disposition designed to meet air attack into a disposition suitable for surface action with the least possible delay."

They were soon to carry it out in earnest.

32

The first sign of the enemy's approach came at 1332, when a shadowing aircraft dropped four red flares ahead of the convoy. Then at 1410 the *Euryalus* reported smoke to the northward, and at 1427 four ships bearing

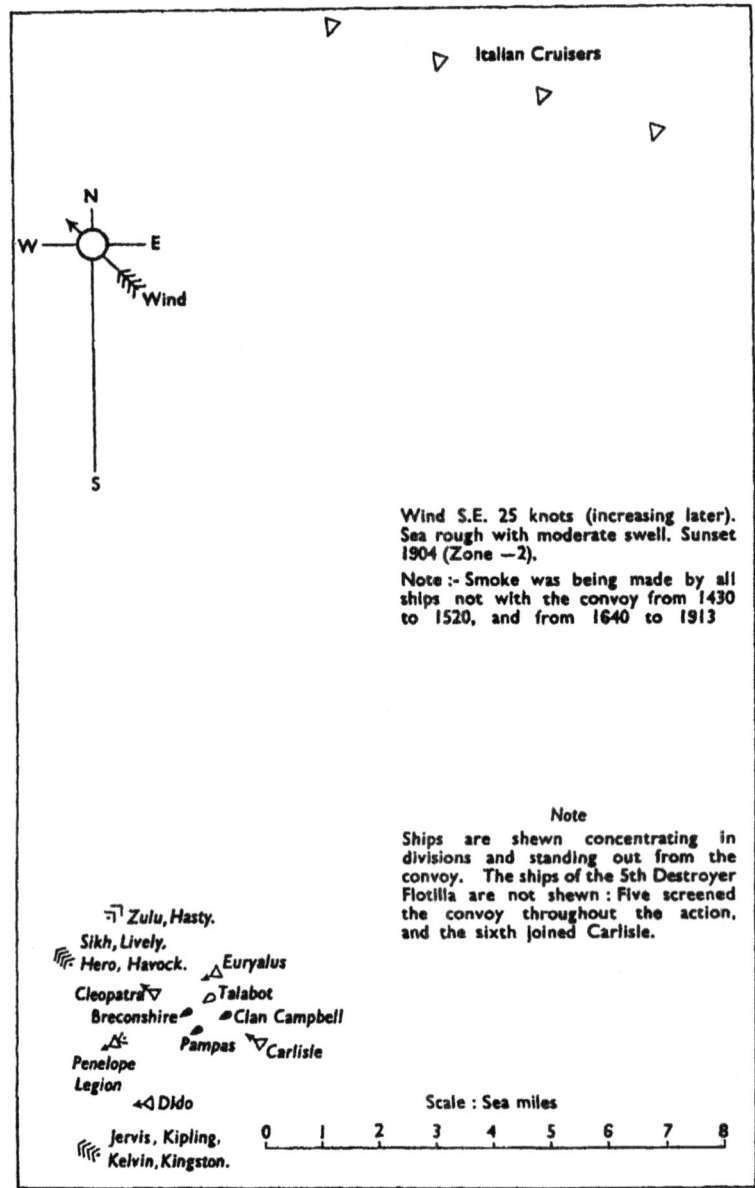

FIG. 1.   FIRST SIGHTING BY *Euryalus*, 1427

015°, while the *Legion* at the same time reported one ship bearing 010°, distant 12 miles. At first the enemy were thought to include three battleships, but they proved to be cruisers—it was thought one 8-inch and three 6-inch ships—and they had arrived a couple of hours sooner than was expected.[1] As we

---

[1] Actually, two 8-inch, one 6-inch and destroyers—Admiral Parona's force from Messina. The *Gorizia* sighted Admiral Vian's ships at 1425.

have seen, some Italian ships had sailed from Taranto about midnight, 21st–22nd, and *P.36* had detected them at 0131, but had been unable to make a definite report of their composition; nor did she report a second contact with heavy ships two hours later.[1] Whether the force that now appeared had come indeed from Taranto, at a higher speed than Rear-Admiral Vian allowed for, or was a separate force from Naples or Sicily, was not known. The Rear-Admiral must have learnt of its coming so soon with mixed feelings. On general grounds he would have liked to put off the meeting till the evening and as late in the convoy's passage as possible. Yet he wrote that " it was clear that the enemy must be driven off by dark "; for the ships of Force " B " could not oil at Malta, and so could not afford to be entangled in operations at night far to the westward; nor could the convoy afford to continue long off its proper course, when every hour's delay increased the danger from the air on the morrow.

As soon as he received the second report from the *Euryalus*, Rear-Admiral Vian made his special manœuvring signal and the ships of the striking force drew off to the north " exactly as detailed in the operation orders," forming divisions in line ahead, while the convoy and its close escort were sent away south-westward. A few minutes afterwards, at 1433, the divisions turned east to lay smoke, with a freshening south-easterly wind to blow the smoke across the wake of the merchantmen.[2] The four Italians, hitherto standing towards the convoy in a very loose line abreast, appeared to turn south-east beam on to open fire,[3] though still out of range, and at 1442 they altered right round to north-west. By that time they were recognized as cruisers only, so Rear-Admiral Vian made the signal to steer towards them, leading the way with the *Cleopatra* and *Euryalus*. At 1456 these two ships began a concentrated shoot on the 8-inch cruiser at a range of about 20,000 yards, but the Italians turned away north soon after fire was opened and at 1508 this engagement ceased. The Italian 6-inch ship then turned back for a few minutes,[4] and straddled the two British ships in a sharp exchange of fire at extreme range; at 1515, however, she hauled away again to join her consorts. Owing to the interference of their own smoke, few of the other British ships even saw the enemy during this brief action; the only other ship engaged was the *Lively*, which fired an occasional round from her 4-in. guns as she made out a target through the smoke. The enemy having gone off, Rear-Admiral Vian steered to rejoin the convoy. There was no apparent damage on either side, but the Rear-Admiral felt able to report to the Commander-in-Chief at 1535, " Enemy driven off."[5] An hour later he overtook the convoy.

33

The *Carlisle* and *Avon Vale*—the special smoke-laying division—had already joined the convoy. They had turned at about 1520, when they saw that the

---

[1] Lieutenant Edmonds remarks that " it was not feasible either in this case "—at 0330—" or at 0131 to fire by asdic, as the hydrophone effect was of more than one ship and was spread over a large area."

[2] " As soon as our ships were sighted by the enemy . . . he spread a smoke cloud which after only 40 seconds completely covered the convoy and blotted out a large area of the surrounding sea."—Admiral Iachino's report.

[3] According to the Italian account, the cruisers did not turn to the south-east, but stood on to S.S.W. and W.S.W. till 1429 (see Plan 10). Possibly the movements of his destroyers, at least one of which was taken for a cruiser, may have given rise to this impression.

[4] This movement of the *Bande Nere* is not shown in the Italian plan, and there is no mention of the incident in their report.

[5] Admiral Parona's instructions confined him to a reconnaissance role until after junction with the C-in-C., which he was then steering to effect.

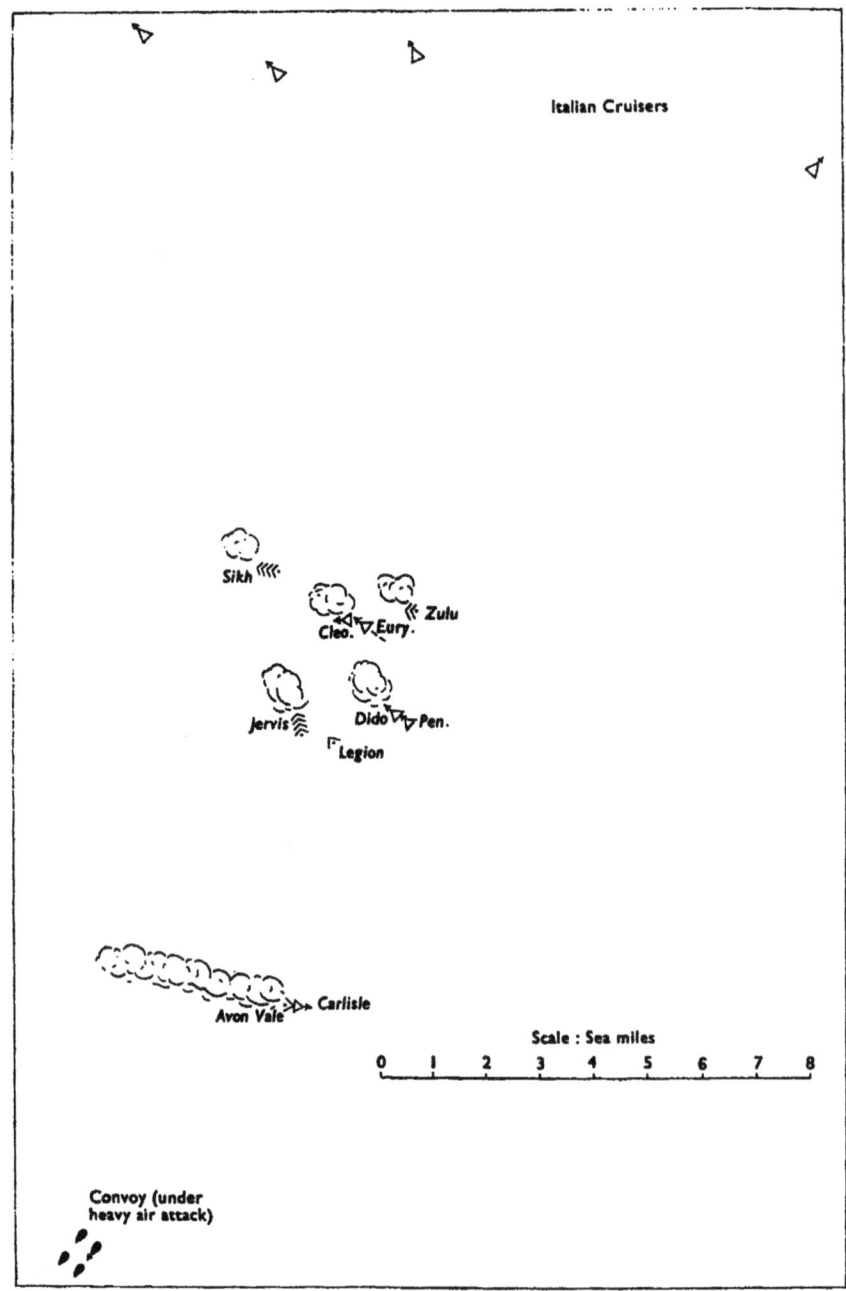

FIG. 2. ENEMY WITHDRAWS TO NORTHWARD, 1500

striking force was coming south again and that the convoy was being attacked from the air. Some single aircraft had dropped bombs harmlessly among the ships of the striking force during the engagement with the Italian squadron, and the *Carlisle* had a narrow escape from bombs while still laying smoke to the southward[1]; but "a heavy and sustained" assault upon the convoy had begun at 1445. The enemy were German Ju.88 bombers, varying in number from three to nine aircraft at a time, and they made both high-level and diving attacks from 9,000 ft. The steady shooting of the escort and the skilful handling of the convoy spoilt the attacks, which were entirely unsuccessful. Commander Jellicoe of the *Southwold* gave particular credit to the guns' crews on the forecastles of the destroyers, "who were fighting their guns under most difficult conditions" in the heavy sea then running "and were drenched from the start." Rear-Admiral Vian remarked that "whilst the striking force was rejoining, the sound of the 4-inch fire from the Hunts and *Carlisle* was most impressive, resembling continuous pom-pom fire, even though heard at a distance of 8 to 10 miles." But it was very expensive in ammunition; a little after 1600, as the striking force was coming up, the *Carlisle* reported having used one-third of her outfit, while the *Southwold* signalled, "Nine attacks so far; 40 per cent of 4-inch ammunition remaining." Accordingly, the Rear-Admiral ordered the five ships of the 1st Division to join the escort.[2]

34

Meanwhile Admiral Iachino's force, the *Littorio* and four destroyers, had been coming down from the northward on course 190° at 28 knots. The first enemy report he received came in from a shore-based aircraft at 0955 and placed a considerable naval force in 34° 10′ N., 19° 10′ E., steering 270° at 14 knots.

Admiral Iachino was determined to keep his forces to the westward of the enemy, in order to bar the passage to Malta, arguing that if (as actually occurred) the convoy turned to the southward, the delay would expose it to further air attack, and might give him another opportunity for surface attack next day. This decision governed his tactics throughout the day.

Accordingly, as enemy reports came in, he gradually hauled round to the south-westward, altering from 180° to 200° at 1353 and finally to 230° at 1618. At 1530 Admiral Parona's three cruisers joined him and were stationed in line abreast 5,500 yards to port of the *Littorio*. At the same time one of the *Littorio's* destroyers, the *Grecale*, had trouble with her steering gear and was ordered back to Taranto. An hour later (1631), in very bad and shortening visibility aggravated by "vast masses of smoke spread by the English vessels,"[3] the enemy came in sight. They were some 10 miles farther west than expected, and 12 minutes later the *Littorio* altered course to 270°.

35

To return to Admiral Vian: no sooner had the striking force overhauled the convoy than Italian ships came in sight again to the north-east. This time it was a truly formidable force, which eventually appeared to consist of one *Littorio*-class battleship, two 8-inch cruisers, and four smaller ships, all thought to be 6-inch cruisers. There followed sporadic fighting for some two and a half hours, from about 1640 to 1900, the British striking force laying smoke east and west to bar the way, while the Italians tried to work round the smoke to reach the convoy, which made off to the southward—still heavily

---

[1] As a result of her movements to avoid the bombs, the *Carlisle* came into collision with the *Avondale* in the thick smoke at 1505. Only superficial damage was sustained.
[2] The *Legion* had attached herself to this division during the surface engagement.
[3] Admiral Iachino's report.

attacked from the air.   Rear-Admiral Vian wrote of the " enormous area of
smoke, which lay well in the existing weather conditions of a 25-knot wind
from south-east.   The enemy tried to make touch with the convoy by passing
round the western end of the smoke, to leeward, and was therefore effectually
held away from the convoy, as he would not approach the smoke, which was

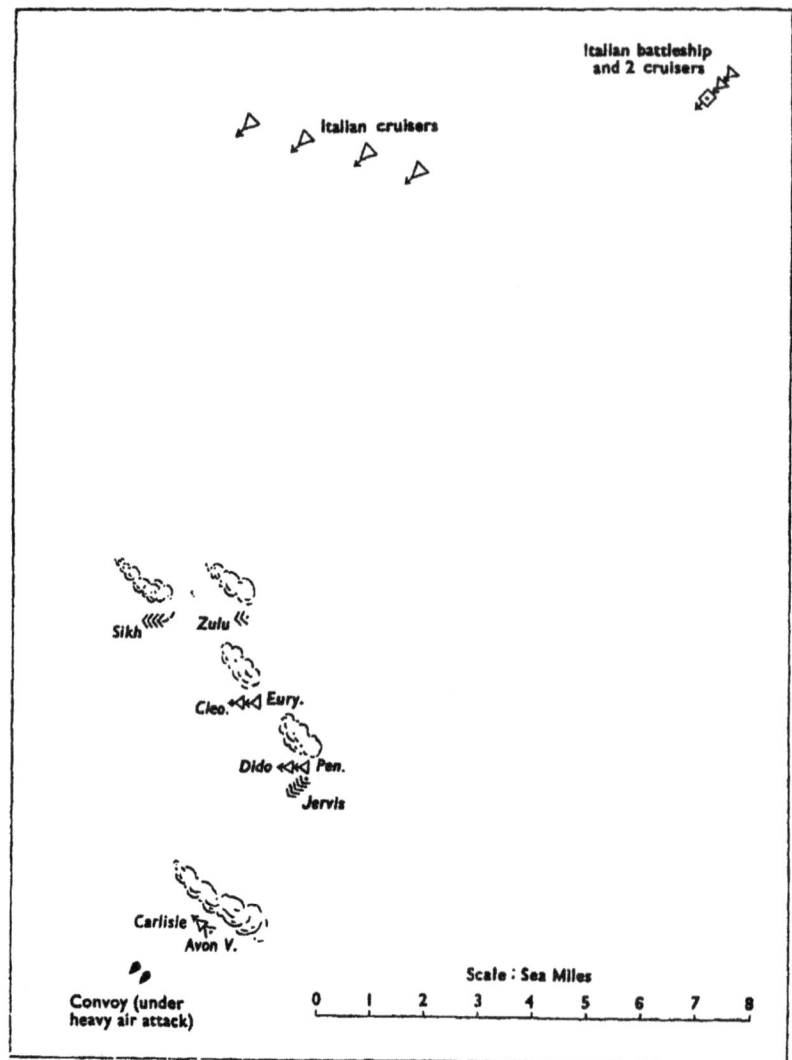

FIG. 3. SECOND CONTACT, 1640

drifting towards him."   He remarked, too, that " the enemy's most effective
course of action was to pass to windward of the smoke," that is to the eastward;
but they preferred what seemed the shortest way between the convoy and its
destination.   While the smoke screen thus fulfilled its main purpose of
protecting the convoy, besides to some extent shielding the British ships of

war from the fire of their stronger opponents, it naturally hampered the British ships' gunnery and restricted their view of the enemy's motions, and indeed of their consorts. The increasing sea had also its effect, the ships washing down fore and aft, and the bridges and director control towers of even the cruisers being drenched with spray, whenever they were steaming to windward. Meanwhile, the Italians had some assistance from spotting aircraft, which pointed out the positions of British ships in the smoke; on the other hand, they had the disadvantage of the lee gage, and one ship at least was seen to use only her upper—" B " and " X "—turrets in consequence. Certainly the British force had the better of the encounter and gained its object.

The first sighting report had come from the *Zulu* at 1637—four unknown ships bearing 042°, distant 9 miles; and this was followed at 1640 by a report from the *Euryalus* of three cruisers bearing 035°, distant 15 miles. As the situation developed, however, it appeared that the westward group of Italian ships were two 8-inch and two 6-inch cruisers,[1] some 10 miles away, with one battleship and two cruisers[2] farther east and about 15 miles from the British flagship, both groups steering a south-westerly course at high speed. As soon as the second report was received the divisions of the British striking force stood away to the northward to meet the enemy, as they had two hours before, only this time without a signal to proceed—except the 1st Division, which held on for a time towards the convoy according to Rear-Admiral Vian's previous orders. The *Cleopatra* and *Euryalus* led out on course 010° and started immediately to lay smoke. At 1643 they opened fire at a range of some 20,000 yards on the westernmost Italian, an 8-inch cruiser, the British ships firing individually instead of attempting a concentration as they had in the earlier engagement. The 8-inch ship and a 6-inch cruiser at once returned the fire, and the latter hit the bridge of the *Cleopatra* with her second salvo.[3] The Italian battleship, outside the British ships' range, opened fire also at this time, a splinter from a 15-inch shell hitting the *Euryalus*. At 1648 Rear-Admiral Vian turned westward into his smoke and ceased fire. Meanwhile, the *Dido* and *Penelope* had come into action against the Italian cruisers, as had the four destroyers of the 5th Division, but the *Zulu* and *Hasty* did not find a target within their reach.

The *Dido* and *Penelope* could not see their fall of shot, owing to the smoke and spray; neither they nor the *Cleopatra* and *Euryalus* could claim hits at this stage of the fight. When the Admiral turned away, they followed after him, losing sight of him as he entered the smoke. Captain McCall of the *Dido* thus described the situation: " The smoke was at that time extremely dense; 15-inch guns could be heard firing at no great distance, occasional large splashes were seen, and the positions of destroyers were obscure; so that a very exciting period ensued until we emerged from the smoke, steering an easterly course, at 1703, when three enemy cruisers were sighted in line ahead on a south-westerly course with the battleship close to them on an opposite course."[4] Captain Micklethwait, of the *Sikh*, believed that his division scored hits on " what was thought to be two destroyers," which soon turned north and disappeared. These were probably two of the *Littorio's* destroyers which Admiral Iachino had sent in to attack with torpedoes; seeing them quickly straddled, he ordered them to disengage. No hits were scored by either

---

[1] Actually two 8-in., one 6-in. cruisers.
[2] Actually 1 battleship. 2 destroyers.
[3] The shell hit the starboard side of the Air Defence position, putting it out of action, also W/T and radar. One officer and 14 ratings were killed; one officer and four ratings were seriously wounded. Splinters from near misses killed one rating and caused superficial damage.
[4] This alteration of course by the *Littorio* is not mentioned in the Italian account.

side. The four British destroyers were some way to the westward of the British cruisers; and at 1649, just after their first encounter, they sighted two cruisers and the battleship to the north-east 6 miles away, as it seemed to Captain Micklethwait, so he hastened westward to gain a favourable position for attacking with torpedoes. At 1659, three cruisers appeared on about the

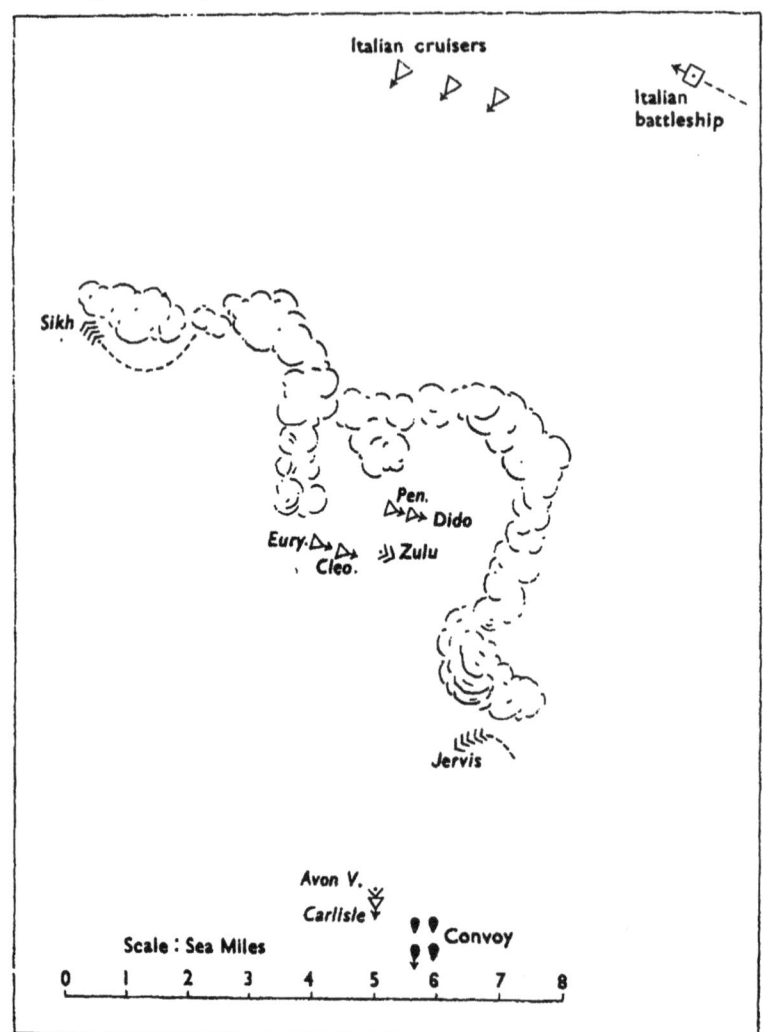

FIG. 4.   ENEMY ATTEMPTS TO GET TO LEEWARD OF SMOKE, 1705

same bearing only 5 miles off—possibly the western group of Italians again; and, turning up north-westward, Captain Micklethwait engaged these ships through the smoke till 1705, when the battleship came in sight once more farther east.   Then he altered away " to avoid punishment."[1]

[1] The three cruisers reported by the *Dido* as in line ahead at 1703 were probably in a loose line abreast about a mile apart.   The distances of the enemy reported by Captain Micklethwait at 1649 and 1659 are considerably less than those shown on the combined track chart in M.08720/42.

Rear-Admiral Vian hauled round gradually to the south-eastward at
about 1700. For the next ten minutes or so his two ships fired at the flashes
of the enemy's guns to the northward, or at ships dimly seen through the
smoke, at a range of some 14,000 yards, still without apparent effect. The
Dido and *Penelope*, having turned to the eastward about the same time as the
flagship, were now ahead of her, and when they cleared the smoke they
engaged the Italian cruisers, which were steering to the south-west 13,000 yards
away, with the battleship east of them, steering something north of west.
The *Dido*, opening at 1704, fired nine broadsides at an 8-inch ship and claimed

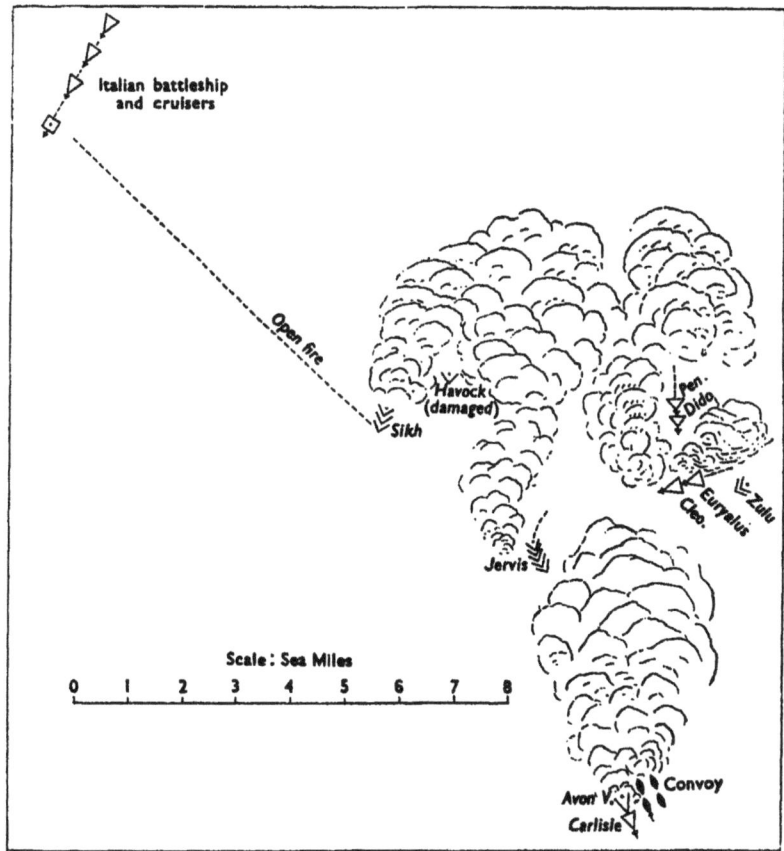

FIG. 5. 5TH DIVISION HOLDING OFF THE ENEMY, 1740

at least two hits; the *Penelope*, coming later out of the smoke, fired a few
rounds at a 6-inch ship, possibly hitting her with the first salvo.[1] But the
two British cruisers had come under fire from the battleship; " and as we were
getting rather far from the smoke screen," Captain McCall bore away south,
finding shelter in the smoke at 1712 and sighting the flagship soon afterwards.
The Rear-Admiral turned west at 1714 and south-eastward at 1720, continuing
so till 1730 and firing a few rounds at a ship seen through the smoke at 1727,
though he considered afterwards that the target was out of range. At 1730
he turned east for five minutes, with the other cruisers and the *Zulu* and

[1] According to the Italian account, no hits were scored at this time.

Hasty conforming generally to his movements, " in search of two enemy ships not accounted for, and which I thought might be working round in the rear" to reach the convoy from to windward.   The Italians in fact did not change from their plan of cutting off the convoy by steering the most direct course the smoke screen allowed.   And, as it turned out, Rear-Admiral Vian's stretch to the eastward at 1730, short as it was, nearly gave them their chance. Captain Micklethwait's division of destroyers kept them at bay.

These ships had been standing to the southward since 1705, watching the enemy at a distance of 10 miles or so.   They had not escaped punishment;

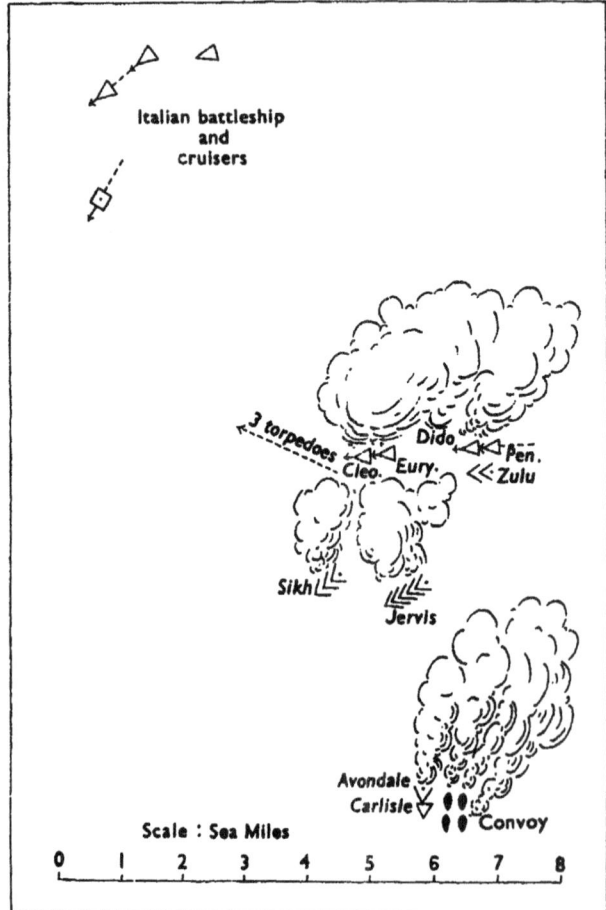

FIG. 6.   TORPEDO ATTACK ORDERED, 1805

for at 1720 a near miss from a 15-inch shell damaged a boiler in the *Havock*, reducing her speed to 16 knots,[1] and she had to be sent to join the convoy. None the less, the other three destroyers turned northward a few minutes after this with a view to attacking with torpedoes; but, deciding the conditions were not yet favourable, Captain Micklethwait turned away again and shaped course to the southward to keep between the Italians and the convoy, laying

---

[1] No. 3 boiler-room was flooded and the boiler damaged.   Structural strength members were cut.   Two officers and five ratings were killed; one officer and eight ratings were wounded.

smoke all the while. At 1740 they sighted the battleship again 16,000 yards off to the north-west, steering to the southward at high speed, and they opened fire on her with their 4·7-inch and 4-inch guns. Seas were sweeping over their forecastles, they were moving heavily in the swell, and smoke too interfered with shooting, while the range was far too great to observe the fall of shot of such light calibre guns. Indeed the *Lively* and *Hero*, astern of the *Sikh* and with her smoke between them and the enemy, could seldom see what was happening, though the *Lively* opened fire whenever she had a target to aim at.[1] According to the Italians, the *Littorio* was frequently straddled and turned to the south-west to open the range. She of course returned the fire, and at 1748 straddled the *Sikh*, which then fired two out of her four torpedoes, " in order to avoid sinking with all torpedoes on board and in the hope of making the enemy turn away," but to no effect. By 1800 the Italians were drawing ahead on the convoy; it looked as if they might gain their object after all. Captain Micklethwait made a signal to the convoy to steer south (its former course being south-westerly), while he endeavoured to extend the smoke screen westward, still continuing his " somewhat unequal contest " with the enemy.

In the meantime the British cruisers had come back. Rear-Admiral Vian had turned again at 1735, when some 6 miles south-eastward of the 5th Division and 14 miles from the Italians. At 1742 the *Cleopatra* fired a few salvoes at the battleship at extreme range: then for twenty minutes smoke covered all, and the ships with the Rear-Admiral tried in vain to cut their way through it to see the enemy. At 1759 he made the general signal, " Prepare to fire torpedoes under cover of smoke." At 1802 the *Cleopatra* cleared the smoke, sighted the battleship 13,000 yards off, and opened fire with all turrets; while the *Euryalus*, still in smoke astern of her, fired by radar. Then at 1806 the *Cleopatra* turned to port and fired her three starboard torpedoes as the battleship disappeared again behind the drifting smoke. No hits were seen, and no other ship fired. By the time they were out of the smoke, the opportunity had passed; the enemy had turned away and was hiding in a smoke screen of her own. But Rear-Admiral Vian believed it was his flagship's torpedoes that impelled the Italian to alter course, " further delaying the moment at which she might sight the convoy and slightly relieving the pressure on the 5th Division."[2] After the attack the Rear-Admiral went east again, not yet easy in his mind about the missing Italian cruisers, which might be still working to windward; at 1817, however, he could see there were none of the enemy in the north-east quarter, so he turned round once more to support the destroyers of the 5th Division. Their fight ended—for the time being—at 1819. Captain Micklethwait then hauled right round to the northward to lay a new screen of smoke.[3]

---

[1] Captain Micklethwait commended these two ships for " following astern of *Sikh* through salvoes of large and small shell fire " when not " even in a position to see what was going on."

[2] According to the Italian report, this alteration was made in an attempt to clear the smoke and not on account of the *Cleopatra's* torpedoes, which they had not seen fired.

[3] There is doubt as to the *Sikh's* position relative to the *Littorio* at this time. The plan accompanying the report of the action places her about 19,000 yards from the battleship (see Plan 10); but Captain (D) 22nd Flotilla's report, Gunnery Notes, states:—

" Towards the end of the battleship engagement when the range had closed to about 6,000 yards, nearly all salvoes, except overs, could be seen. This period was not of long duration, but the target was definitely found and a straddle observed at about 1820 at a range of 6,000 yards "—

a discrepancy of 13,000 yards. Errors in dead reckoning during an engagement of this nature in heavy weather and thick smoke are inevitable. It seems probable that in fighting the *Littorio* off, the *Sikh* was actually steering considerably farther to the westward and northward than shown in Plan 10 from about 1800 till her turn to the northward at 1820; but if this was the case she must have altered course to the south-westward earlier than shown for the *Lively* to have fired torpedoes at 7,000 yards range at 1851.

It was now the turn of the 1st Division under Captain Poland. At 1631, before the Italians came in sight, this division had been ordered to join the convoys to strengthen its anti-aircraft fire. The five destroyers set off accordingly; but when Captain Poland received the news of the enemy's approach, and two words of a mutilated signal from the flagship, he decided to follow the convoy at a distance, laying smoke between it and the enemy, instead of joining it. His first view of the battle came at 1745, gun flashes appearing to the north-west through the smoke laid by the 5th Division, which he could see was under heavy fire from 15-inch guns. At 1808 he received a signal timed 1758 from Captain Micklethwait that put the Italians

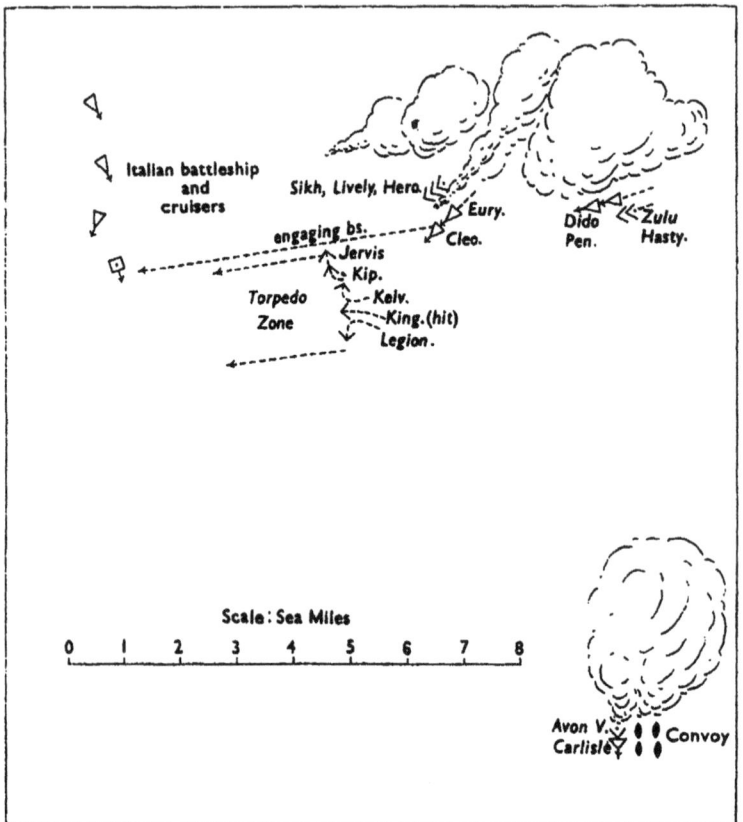

FIG. 7. TORPEDO ATTACK BY 1ST DIVISION, 1841

only 8 miles[1] from the convoy, and four minutes later he altered up from south-west to north-west to close the enemy. An attack by some torpedo aircraft deflected him from his course for some minutes, but at 1834, then steering north, he sighted the battleship west-north-west 12,000 yards away and determined to attack immediately with torpedoes. The division turned together to west, which brought the ships into line abreast, and increased speed to 28 knots, the 4·7-inch ships as they ran in carrying out a concentration

---

[1] This was an under-estimate; actually they were about 11 miles apart.

shoot, for which hits were claimed; the *Legion*, mounting 4-inch guns, withheld her fire till the range came down to 8,000 yards. The enemy were steering south, and three cruisers in line ahead were now in sight astern of the battleship; all returned the British destroyers' fire, but their shooting, said Captain Poland, "was very erratic." At 1840 the first cruiser, an 8-inch ship, turned away 90° to starboard, while the other two cruisers turned in a few points to port.[1]

At 1841, with the range down to 6,000 yards, the destroyers turned and fired torpedoes, the *Jervis*, *Kipling*, *Kelvin* and *Kingston* turning to starboard, the *Legion* to port. A 15-in. shell hit the *Kingston* as she was about to turn[2], yet she managed to fire three torpedoes. Altogether they fired twenty-five, all of which were avoided by the Italians, though at the time it was thought that one had hit the *Littorio*, which had turned away when she saw the destroyers firing, and withdrew to the north-westward, accompanied by the cruisers. The British ships retired to the eastward under smoke.[3]

During the attack the 1st Division was supported by the guns of the *Cleopatra* and *Euryalus* on the return of these ships from the eastward. This partly accounted for the erratic shooting of the Italians, whose one hit was that which crippled the *Kingston;* as Captain Grantham of the *Cleopatra* reported it, " The enemy battleship was firing in divided control, the forward turrets at the destroyers ahead and the after turret rather wildly in the rough direction of the *Cleopatra* and *Euryalus*." Having turned at 1817, Rear-Admiral Vian brought his division west with the *Dido* and *Penelope*, the *Zulu* and *Hasty* following at some distance astern. The *Cleopatra* sighted an enemy cruiser at 1830, and they exchanged a few salvoes at 20,000 yards, but were interrupted by smoke laid by the 5th Division on its northward stretch. Five minutes later all four Italians came in sight; thenceforward, for some twenty minutes, the *Cleopatra* engaged the battleship whenever smoke allowed, and the 8-inch cruiser at other times, and the *Euryalus* also engaged the battleship. At 1841, range 12,500 yards, the battleship was seen to be on fire from a hit abaft her after turret; and more hits were observed as she retired after the destroyers' attack. The last shots were fired at 1856; but about the same time the 5th Division attacked with torpedoes. After breaking off their gun action at

---

[1] This turn is not shown on the Italian plan.

[2] The shell passed through the ship and exploded beyond. Fires broke out in the engine-room and boiler-room, which were quickly extinguished: upper deck suffered serious damage, impairing structural strength, and pom-pom, Oerlikon and searchlight supports were extensively damaged. One officer and 12 ratings were killed, and 21 ratings were wounded.

[3] The details of torpedoes fired by the 1st Division are as follows:—

SHIP	No. OF TORPEDOES FIRED	REMARKS
Jervis	5 out of 9	" Owing to difficulty in controlling the swing in the prevailing bad weather, was able to fire only five torpedoes."
Kipling	All 5	—
Kelvin	4 out of 5	Fired two prematurely at 1835, having mistaken the signal to turn to run in for a signal to fire.
Kingston	3 out of 5	Two torpedo-tubes damaged by gunfire.
Legion	All 8	—

All ships aimed at the battleship except the *Jervis*, which chose the third ship in the enemy's line for her target.

Commander Jessel of the *Legion* steered a south-westerly course on the run-in, instead of west, because he thought the ships too much bunched together, and because he did not wish to lose bearing on the enemy. Owing to shell splashes he did not see the signal to turn to starboard to fire; but he had already trained his tubes to starboard, *i.e.* for a turn to port, for the reasons that led him to hold away south-westward on the run-in, so he turned to port.

1819, the three ships still in company had laid smoke on a northerly course till 1835, and then turned south-west again. Their stretch to the north, however, had given them a good start for an attack when the Italians retired north-west, and Captain Micklethwait seized upon the opportunity. Unluckily, as he turned to fire at 1855, smoke hid the target from all except the *Lively*, which fired all eight torpedoes, though without success. Once again the enemy scored one hit with their guns, a splinter of a 15-inch shell entering the *Lively* on her waterline as she was about to fire.[1]

The battle was over. Four weak cruisers and eleven destroyers had held at bay a capital ship, three cruisers and 7 destroyers for nearly two and a half hours in stormy weather, obliging them, in the words of Kempenfelt, " to think of nothing but being on their guard against your attack "—for that is

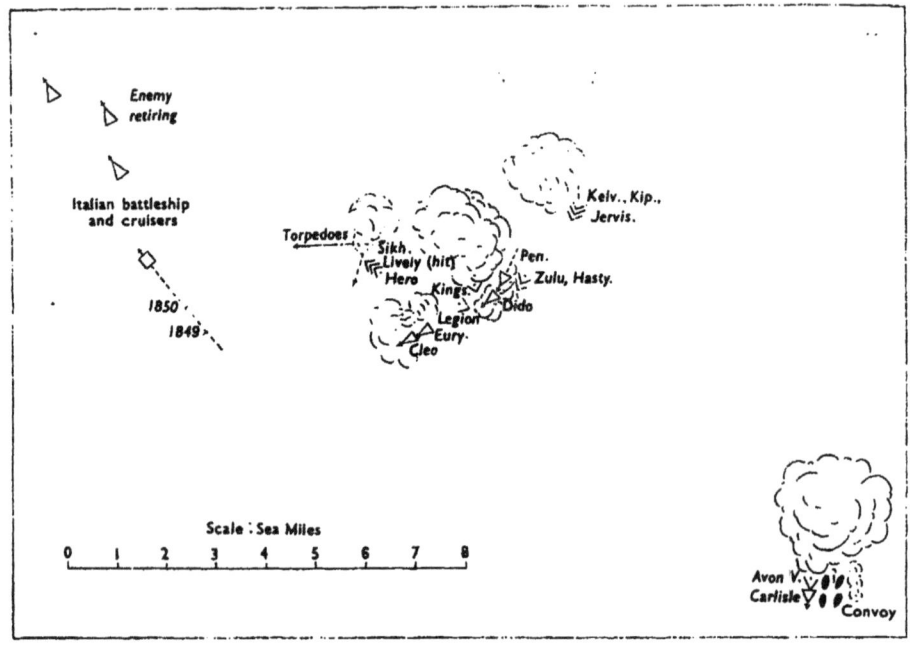

FIG. 8. ENEMY BREAKS OFF THE ACTION, 1855

what it amounted to. And at last, as the sun was setting that Sunday evening, 22nd March, the British force saw the enemy abandon their object and steer away homewards. Yet the Italians do not seem to have suffered much material damage. They received a few hits from guns of 4-inch up to 6-inch calibre, mostly on the battleship, but they seem to have been overawed by the constant readiness of Rear-Admiral Vian and his ships and by the threat of sudden torpedo attack coming out of the smoke; it was certainly the determined attack by the 1st Division that finally turned them back. In achieving this result the British ships fired 36 torpedoes and a great deal of gun ammunition; over 1,550 rounds were expended by the cruisers and about 1,300 by the destroyers. Much of the gunfire was inevitably ineffective,

---

[1] The base of the shell entered the fore lower mess deck, which flooded, and passed through the bulkhead to the after lower mess deck, which partially flooded later. There were no casualties.

for the range was often uncertain and the shell splashes invisible owing to smoke, the state of the weather and the long range at which the action was for the most part fought.[1] By taking advantage of every opportunity, however, the British ships proved their constant eagerness to fight, and deterred the Italian fleet from running risks with them.

36

All this time the convoy and its close escort had been under attack from the air. An occasional German bomber and one or two flights of Italian torpedo aircraft had attacked or threatened attack on ships of the striking force, sometimes requiring the attention of the cruisers' 5·25-inch guns to get quit of them; the *Euryalus* shot down one aircraft at 1733 and another at 1906. But instead of combining air attack with surface action to disable the striking force and so clear the way to the convoy, the enemy chose to spend the weight of their attack from the air directly upon the convoy. Up to about 1800, the aircraft were German Ju.88 bombers, after which some Italian S.79 and German He.111 torpedo aircraft attacked. The bombers generally came singly and down wind, on the port side of the convoy, approaching at about 8,000 ft. and releasing their bombs at 2,000 to 3,000 ft. They attacked with resolution and skill, considering the strength of the wind, but accomplished nothing beyond almost exhausting the ammunition of the escort, though that indeed helped towards success next day. These four hours of continual air attack in that heavy weather tested the British skill in gunnery and seamanship and the endurance of the ships' companies. Many aircraft were kept at arm's length or induced to drop bombs or torpedoes at a safe distance. Five were shot down, of which the *Breconshire* and *Pampas* each accounted for one, while the others fell to the *Carlisle* and the six destroyers.[2]

As soon as the Italian ships had disappeared, Rear-Admiral Vian collected his force and steered to close the convoy, 10 miles or so to the southward.

---

[1] The ammunition expended by individual ships varied greatly, depending on how often they were clear of the smoke. The expenditure by British and Italians was as follows:—

	BRITISH					ITALIAN					
	6 in.	5.25 in.	4.7 in.	4 in.		15 in.	8 in.	6 in.	4.7 in.	4 in.	3.5 in.
Cleopatra	—	868	—	—	Littorio ..	181	—	445	—	—	21
Dido	—	200	—	—	Gorizia ..	—	226	—	—	67	—
Euryalus	—	421	—	—	Trento ..	—	355	—	—	20	—
Penelope	64	—	—	—	Bande Nere ..	—	—	112	—	—	—
Jervis..	—	—	106	—	Aviere ..	—	—	—	84	—	—
Kipling	—	—	110	—	Ascari ..	—	—	—	0	—	—
Kelvin	—	—	73	—	Oriani ..	—	—	—	0	—	—
Kingston	—	—	56	—	Alpino ..	—	—	—	0	—	—
Sikh	—	—	450	—	Bersagliere ..	—	—	—	0	—	—
Lively	—	—	—	275	Fuciliere ..	—	—	—	0	—	—
Havock	—	—	92	—	Lanciere ..	—	—	—	0	—	—
Hero	—	—	88	—							
Zulu	—	—	0	—							
Hasty..	—	—	4	—							
Legion	—	—	—	?							
	64	1,489	979	275		181	581	557	84	87	21

[2] According to Commander Jellicoe of the *Southwold*, about 60 bombers and at least nine torpedo aircraft attacked during the afternoon and evening.

At 1940, in the growing darkness with the convoy not yet in sight, the Rear-Admiral decided to shape course for Alexandria with Force " B " and to send the convoy to Malta under the arrangements laid down in the operation orders. The two ships from Malta, the *Penelope* and *Legion*, parted company accordingly to overtake the convoy and return to their base; the *Havock* had joined the convoy already, and the *Kingston* was on her way to do so, both too badly damaged in the action to go back to Alexandria in the face of a rising gale. Rear-Admiral Vian proceeded eastward with the remaining three cruisers and eight destroyers. Captain Hutchison, of the *Breconshire*, the convoy commodore, had in fact complied with the operation orders on his own initiative at 1900, dispersing the ships on diverging courses with a destroyer or two apiece for escort, each ship to make her best speed so as to reach Malta as early as possible next morning; they had been intended to arrive at dawn, but the Italian fleet, by forcing the convoy south of its route, had given the German bombers a second chance, as Admiral Iachino had foreseen. Aircraft appeared as soon as it was light on 23rd March, in spite of the thick weather; and the ships had to run the gauntlet of attacks all the way to the entrance of the Grand Harbour, with their escorts, desperately short of ammunition, firing only when the danger became immediate.

The first ship of the convoy to arrive was the *Talabot*, at 0915, and she was closely followed by the *Penelope*, each ship accompanied by a destroyer. " We proceeded up harbour," reported the *Havock*, " to the cheers of the populace." Both merchantmen had had narrow escapes two hours earlier, two bombs actually hitting the *Pampas* without exploding, and their last assailants were driven off only a few minutes before they passed the breakwater. But that was the end of Fortune's favours. The *Breconshire*, with the *Carlisle* and three destroyers in company, arrived within 8 miles of the harbour at 0920, having survived a score of attacks only to be hit and disabled at last. The *Carlisle* prepared to take her in tow, circling round her meanwhile to keep off the enemy, for aircraft continued to attack. The *Penelope*, however, coming up later, decided herself to tow the *Breconshire*, as the *Carlisle* was almost out of ammunition; but the great draught of the damaged ship and the heavy swell running made towing impossible; so she was anchored, and three destroyers stayed to protect her. Finally, the *Clan Campbell* was hit at 1030, when some 20 miles short of her destination, by a bomb dropped from a height of only 50 ft.; she sank quickly, but her escort, the *Eridge*, saved most of her crew. For the time being, all the ships of war escaped injury except the *Legion*, which was damaged by a near miss and had to be beached in Marsaxlokk.

The three surviving ships of the convoy were lost within a few days of their arrival, as well as some of the men-of-war that brought the convoy in. Actually, the first loss was due to a mine, the *Southwold* being sunk by a mine on 24th March, while standing by the *Breconshire* outside Grand Harbour. The *Breconshire* herself reached Marsaxlokk in tow on the 25th, in spite of bad weather, but sank there on the 27th after further damage from bombs; she had suffered continual attack for four days. The *Legion* was sunk from the air on the 26th, soon after reaching the dockyard from Marsaxlokk. The *Talabot* and *Pampas* were hit that day too; and the former had to be scuttled, lest her cargo of ammunition should explode, while all the latter's holds but two were flooded. Last of all, Submarine *P.36* was bombed and sunk on 1st April, and the *Kingston* on the 11th. But the loss of cargoes was worse in the circumstances, perhaps, than the loss of ships. Only 5,000 tons out of nearly 26,000 tons carried in the convoy was safely landed, including some oil fuel saved from the *Breconshire*. And it was several months before supplies in large quantities again reached Malta.

37

Attempts on the homeward bound Italian Fleet were made without success. A torpedo striking force of Beaufort aircraft, sent from Libya in the evening of the 22nd, and No. 828 Naval Air Squadron from Malta were unable to make contact with the enemy before dark, so were recalled by order of Admiral Cunningham without having attacked. There were still the submarines, but the state of the weather gave them little chance of success. It was " visibility very poor in heavy rain and high seas," said one; and finding it impossible to patrol at periscope depth they generally had to keep listening watch down at 70 ft. The *Upholder*, however, in Position " S " off Taranto (see Plan 9), detected hydrophone effect of ships to the southward in the evening of the 23rd. After closing for a quarter of an hour, she sighted " dull shadows," of the bridge and funnels of a battleship. Two minutes later, at 1738, she fired her four torpedoes at 4,000 yards, though Lieutenant-Commander Wanklyn considered it " a forlorn hope " to fire under those conditions; all missed, the Italian apparently zig-zagging away during their run. In the night of the 24th–25th two cruisers were reported by aircraft about 120 miles east-north-east of Malta, steering for the Strait of Messina at 15 knots. The *Unbeaten*, then some 45 miles west of the reported position, on her way back to Malta from patrol, was ordered to intercept them. Her best speed in that weather was 7 knots, and she eventually had to abandon the chase, though for an hour she saw flares dropped by aircraft beyond the horizon.

The Italians did not get away scatheless, however. During the night of the 22nd–23rd March the weather got worse and worse; by midnight speed had to be reduced to 16 knots. The *Littorio* held on for Taranto, but the cruisers and most of the destroyers made for Messina. The *Bande Nere*[1] and all the destroyers suffered severe damage in the gale; two of the latter—the *Scirocco* and *Lanciere*—sank next day. Most of the damage was ascribed by Admiral Iachino to too-light hull construction, inefficient water-tight arrangements, scuttles, etc., and vulnerability of pumping arrangements. Even the *Littorio* shipped large quantities of water, which put the electric firing machinery of one of her 15-in. turrets out of action for some time.

38

The ships of Force " B " had an arduous passage back to Alexandria, though suffering rather from the dangers of the sea than from the violence of the enemy. Rear-Admiral Vian wished to go as far as possible through " Bomb Alley " between Cyrenaica and Crete before daylight, but the easterly gale forced him to reduce speed considerably, and at dawn on the 23rd he had only reached the longitude of Benghazi; moreover, all the destroyers except one had fallen astern, while most of them had suffered damage from the weather. On the other hand, though shadowing from the air began early, the force was spared attack until the afternoon, when the worst of the gale was past. No doubt the weather was the cause of this respite, though fighter aircraft of the Royal Air Force managed to give the ships protection all day at very long distances from their base. There were half a dozen attacks in all, usually by single aircraft, between 1610 and dusk. Two only were dangerous: at 1610, six Ju.87 aircraft bombed the *Lively*, which was a mile astern of the force, and she had to " act the part," as the Rear-Admiral put it, to avoid being hit; at 1900, three S.79 aircraft attacked the *Zulu* with torpedoes, but

---

[1] The *Bande Nere* reached Messina on 24th March, but was sunk on 1st April to the south-east of Stromboli by the *Urge* (Lieut.-Commander Tomkinson).

also without success. The damage suffered by the *Lively*, in the battle and in the gale, prevented her from keeping station when better weather after dark allowed Rear-Admiral Vian to increase speed, so he detached her to Tobruk. The rest of the ships arrived at Alexandria at midday on the 24th, " honoured to receive the great demonstration " they were given for their victory.

Commenting on this operation, the Commander-in-Chief, Admiral Sir Henry Harwood, remarked on the good handling of the merchant ships and the excellent work done by the Naval liaison officers embarked in them. " There can be no doubt," he wrote, " that the defeat of the heavy air attacks on the convoy on 22nd March was due in no small measure to the excellent seamanship and discipline displayed by the merchant ships."

" During the action on 22nd March, the determination and team-work of all ships more than fulfilled the high standard that had been expected. This, combined with the resolute leadership and masterly handling of the force by Rear-Admiral Philip L. Vian, K.B.E., D.S.O., produced a heartening and thoroughly deserved victory from a situation in which, had the roles been reversed, it is unthinkable that the convoy or much of its escort could have survived."

CHAPTER V

Operation "Harpoon", June 1942

39

AFTER THE CONVOY in March 1942 a few special cargoes reached Malta in submarines and in the fast minelayer *Welshman*, but the fortress had to wait till the middle of June for the next attempt to supply it on a large scale. This was chiefly due to the unceasing assaults on Malta from the air; as Admiral Sir Henry Harwood, the new Commander-in-Chief, Mediterranean, wrote in his report of the operation in March, " It is evident that before another Malta convoy is run, air superiority in the island must be assured." Accordingly, strong reinforcements of fighter aircraft were sent to Malta, flown off from the *Eagle* and U.S.S. *Wasp*. By the middle of May the bombing attacks had slackened, largely as a result of great air battles on the 9th and 10th, when the enemy lost heavily both in bombers and in their fighter escorts; more British fighters arrived early in June.[1]   In these improved circumstances it was decided to make another attempt to supply the island, and a double operation was planned: a convoy of six ships from the United Kingdom through the Strait of Gibraltar—Operation " Harpoon "—and another of eleven ships (Convoy M.W.11) from Egypt—Operation " Vigorous "—the two convoys being timed to reach Malta on consecutive days.   This, it was hoped, would divide the attention of the enemy between the two convoys while they were on passage.   Mining of the harbour approaches had greatly increased since March[2] (when the *Southwold* was lost), and as Malta was almost entirely without resources to deal with this danger, it was arranged that minesweepers should accompany the convoys to sweep them into harbour, and subsequently to strengthen those stationed at Malta.

The result of these operations was disappointing. In the end two ships of the western convoy only arrived, while the eastern convoy had to give up the attempt and turn back to Alexandria. Although the actual losses in merchant ships were all due to air attack, the principal cause of ill success was probably the lack of surface force, which submarines and aircraft were unable to replace.

---

[1] On 9th May, 60 Spitfires reached Malta from U.S.S. *Wasp* and H.M.S. *Eagle*. They destroyed or damaged 30 enemy aircraft the same day and 60 the following day. " Daylight raiding was brought to an abrupt end."—Malta War Diary.

[2] Actually, the mining was even more serious than was known at the time.

The main strength of the Italian fleet—battleships and cruisers based on Taranto—was employed against the eastern convoy. Though they did not meet, the threat of attack by a battle fleet diverted the convoy from its course for so long that, under repeated attacks from the air, the ships of the close escort ran so far short of ammunition as to preclude the convoy's going on. In the same way two cruisers and five destroyers from Sardinia, meeting the western convoy south of Pantellaria with only an anti-aircraft ship and nine destroyers, held it up for three hours. Air attacks during the action and soon afterwards, beyond the reach of effective protection by fighter aircraft from Malta, sank one merchantman and disabled two, which had to be sunk but might have been saved except for the presence of Italian ships.

Though complementary to each other, these operations were entirely separate. For the sake of clearness, therefore, Operation " Harpoon " only will be described in this chapter and Operation " Vigorous " in the next; but it should be borne in mind that they were actually taking place at the same time.

40

The plan for Operation " Harpoon " was similar to that adopted in the latter part of 1941. The convoy sailed from the United Kingdom with an escort of Home Fleet ships under Vice-Admiral Curteis, who conducted the operation, ships of the North Atlantic Station from Gibraltar strengthening the escort as the convoy entered the Strait.[1] As before, the heavy ships (Force " W ") turned back on reaching the Skerki Channel at the entrance of the Sicily-Tunis Narrows, while the convoy went on with a smaller escort (Force " X "), and an oiler with her own escort (Force " Y ") cruised on a rendezvous to fuel ships of the convoy escort during the passage. The escort, however, was much weaker than those it had been possible to provide in the previous summer and autumn. There was only one capital ship, the *Malaya;* and the aircraft carriers *Eagle* and *Argus*, both old ships, had between them hardly the capacity of the *Ark Royal* which had been lost in November, 1941. Furthermore, instead of a respectable squadron of cruisers for the last stage of the passage, there was only the anti-aircraft ship *Cairo*, besides smaller ships. The full strength as follows:—[2]

FORCE " W "

Capital ship, 1 (*Malaya*)
Aircraft carriers, 2 (*Eagle, Argus*)
Cruisers, 3 (*Kenya*—flag, Vice-Admiral Curteis—*Liverpool, Charybdis*)
Destroyers, 8.

FORCE " X "

A.A. ship, 1 (*Cairo*, Captain C. C. Hardy, S.O.)
Destroyers, 9
Minesweepers, 4.

Force " X " had instructions to " bear in mind the conflicting requirements of the safe arrival of the convoy and the need for economy of fuel, and to a lesser extent of ammunition, so that no extra ship need enter Malta." The *Cairo* and destroyers, in fact, were to return without entering harbour, unless they had to replenish fuel and ammunition.

Six minesweeping motor launches, as well as the four fleet sweepers, accompanied the convoy and were to join the Malta command on arrival The *Welshman*, with a special cargo, also accompanied the convoy as far as

---

[1] Some ships from other commands were attached for the occasion.
[2] See Appendix J.

the Narrows, but then went on alone at 28 knots. Four submarines were stationed on a line between Sardinia and Sicily.

The Royal Air Force at Gibraltar provided anti-submarine patrols for the first part of the passage inside the Strait. Malta provided air reconnaissance, long- and short-range fighter protection, and torpedo striking forces by Royal Air Force and naval aircraft so far as resources allowed; but " Malta's major effort " was required for Operation " Vigorous " to the eastward.

41

Operation " Harpoon " commenced with the departure of the convoy (WS19Z) from the Clyde on 5th June. It soon became apparent that several of the merchant ships were not capable of maintaining the scheduled speed of 14 knots,[1] but by " cutting corners " the Mediterranean was entered up to time during the night of the 11th–12th, the ships of the Home Fleet escort oiling at Gibraltar in reliefs during the passage through the Strait. Nearly 2,000 miles to the east the preliminary movements of operation " Vigorous " were taking place at the same time. The North Atlantic ships of the escort joined that night and next morning, as did one of the convoy—the tanker *Kentucky*—which was already at Gibraltar.

By 0800,[2] 12th June, the force was at full strength and proceeding to the eastward at 12 to 13 knots. That day passed without incident, except the sighting of a Spanish merchant ship in the evening. On the 13th, however, the convoy was shadowed continuously by German and Italian aircraft, and reported by a submarine, despite the efforts of the fighter and anti-submarine patrols from the *Eagle* and *Argus*, which destroyed one Italian Cant.Z1007. This was the day appointed for meeting Force " Y " and refuelling the escort, but delay occurred through the oiler being some 25 miles off her rendezvous,[3] and oiling was not finished till late at night, the *Cairo* and eleven destroyers completing from the *Brown Ranger* and three destroyers from the *Liverpool* to save time.[4]

At 2245 on the 13th, intelligence of cruisers and destroyers leaving Cagliari was received, and the convoy was believed to have been reported by a submarine[5] at 0242, 14th; otherwise the night passed without incident. At dawn shadowing aircraft appeared once more. The convoy was then approaching the danger area for attack from the air stations in Sardinia, where it was believed the enemy had some 40 bombers and 35 torpedo aircraft.

42

At this stage it will be convenient to take note of the situation as it appeared to the Italians, and how they proposed to deal with it. Information of the

---

[1] The Admiralty subsequently took up with D. of S.T. the question of checking actual speeds of merchant ships during the planning stage.

[2] Zone Time minus 3 is used throughout this chapter.

[3] Admiral Curteis recommended that in future the refuelling force should if possible accompany the remainder.

[4] Force " Y " remained cruising ready to oil ships of Force " X " on their return passage. On this Captain Russell, of the *Kenya*, remarked—" That the oiler *Brown Ranger* was allowed to cruise for some six days or more unmolested across the enemy submarine areas appears to be the fault of the enemy."

[5] According to the Italian report, the submarine *Uarsciek* attacked the formation at 0245. 14th June, and claimed to have hit one vessel, and the *Giada*, attacking a few hours later, claimed to have scored two torpedo hits on the *Eagle* (or another unit near her) at 0605, after which she was subjected to prolonged hunting. There is no mention of these attacks in the British reports.

departure of the "Harpoon" forces from Gibraltar had reached the Italian Naval Staff in the morning of the 12th June, and early next day air reconnaissance in the eastern Mediterranean reported the departure of a large convoy from Alexandria. Appreciating that these movements were both directed towards the supply of Malta, they at once set in train measures to deal with the situation. The bulk of the Italian Fleet was then at Taranto, a detachment of two 6-in. cruisers—the *Eugenio di Savoia* and *Montecuccoli*— and five destroyers being at Cagliari. It was decided that the Taranto forces should be used in the eastern Mediterranean against the convoy from Egypt, which from the number of ships reported was deemed to be the more important of the two. These operations will be described in the following chapter.

To deal with the "Harpoon" Convoy, a large number of submarines was disposed in the western basin and off Malta (by the morning of the 15th June 20 submarines were so deployed). Concentrated air attacks south of Sardinia and also after passing Cape Bon were planned; and the Cagliari cruiser force was to attack the convoy at dawn on the 15th June. In addition, torpedo boats and coastal motor boats were to attack in the Sicilian Channel; but, as things turned out, the weather and the darkness of the night precluded these latter attacks.

43

To return to the "Harpoon" Convoy: at 1000, 14th June, the first radar warning came, and at about the same time fighters from the *Eagle* shot down an Italian torpedo aircraft, one of a number gathering for an attack some 20 miles away. It was a bright clear morning, with hardly a cloud in the sky. There was little wind, but such as there was came from nearly astern, west to north-west; and this made it difficult for the British fighter crews, especially those working from the twenty-five-year-old *Argus*, with her small margin of speed, unless she were to haul right round to the wind and so leave the shelter of the destroyer screen. The convoy was steering east in two columns in line ahead, the flagship *Kenya* leading the port column and the *Liverpool* the starboard with the *Malaya* and *Welshman* in line ahead astern of the convoy. The motor launches also followed the convoy, adding to the volume of close-range fire and available for rescue work. The carriers were to port of the convoy, manœuvring independently, each with her A.A. escort and a destroyer, viz., *Eagle, Cairo, Wishart,* and *Argus, Charybdis, Vidette.* The remaining fifteen destroyers and four fleet sweepers formed an all-round screen spread from 3 to 3¼ miles from the convoy—an unusual extension that " proved satisfactory," said Vice-Admiral Curteis, " and all ships fired both outwards and inwards with a freedom which would have been impossible with a closer screen."[1]

The attacks began at 1030. The first was a shallow dive-bombing attack by two groups, each of four or five Italian fighter-bombers (CR.42), one approaching from astern at 12,000 ft. and diving to 6,000 ft., the other coming out of the sun ahead at 6,000 ft. and dropping bombs at 3,000–4,000 ft. Their target was the *Argus* and her consorts on the port beam of the *Malaya*, and one bomb fell close to the *Charybdis*. Two of the enemy were shot down after their attack by a section of the *Eagle's* Fulmars, which were controlled by the *Argus* and afterwards landed on board her, the policy being to employ the

---

[1] Under the daytime cruising disposition the carriers and their attendant ships formed one group stationed on the weather quarter of the convoy; but they seem to have worked in two separate groups on 14th June, though generally on the same side of the convoy.

Hurricanes from the *Eagle* as a high fighter force and the Fulmars from the *Argus* as a low force.[1]

A much more serious attempt followed half an hour later, when some 28 Savoia torpedo aircraft escorted by 20 Macchi fighters carried out a combined attack with 10 Cant. high-level bombers. The Savoias approached from the northward in two waves of equal strength, the first at 1110 and the second soon afterwards. The first wave passed through the screen on the port beam 500 ft. or so above the water, rounded the rear of the convoy, and attacked from the starboard side, splitting into groups before firing. They dropped torpedoes at a height of 100 ft. and a range of 2,000 yards; and they hit the *Liverpool*, leading the starboard column, as she turned to meet the attack, and also the Dutch ship *Tanimbar* in the rear, the latter sinking within a few minutes. The second wave, attacking the port column, dropped their torpedoes first and at longer range, perhaps deterred by the heavy gunfire; their aim being further upset by an emergency turn towards them ordered by Vice-Admiral Curteis, they did not secure a hit. The Cant. bombers came also in two formations, flying in out of the sun ahead some 10,000 ft. up. They seem to have aimed their attacks at the *Eagle* on the port bow and at the *Argus* on the quarter of the convoy, but none of their bombs fell dangerously near.

A little before noon, several torpedo aircraft made harmless attacks at long range. They were probably stragglers turned back from the earlier attacks by gunfire and anxious only to be rid of their torpedoes.

On the whole the Italians seem to have attacked gallantly. Captain Russell of the *Kenya*, for instance, remarked on their outstanding bravery, and Captain Armstrong of the *Onslow* called the attacks unexpectedly impressive, though other officers were not so kind. On the other hand, had their timing been more exact and the two torpedo attacks delivered together instead of one after the other, they would probably have proved more successful. The British fighters shot down three Italian fighters and three torpedo aircraft, which was a notable achievement in view of what Captain Rushbrooke of the *Eagle* called "the most inadequate measure" of protection that was all his ship and the *Argus* could provide; for they had at most six Hurricanes and four Fulmars in the air at a time, whereas the enemy had a score of shore-based fighters attending on the striking force. Three British aircraft were lost, one being shot down by a ship in the screen. The convoy and escort destroyed seven of the enemy, all Savoia 79, both long- and close-range fire taking their toll. Captain Waller of the *Malaya* remarked on the efficiency of the 6-inch barrage in inducing the Italians to drop torpedoes prematurely. He also lamented the idleness of his 15-inch guns for want of suitable ammunition against aircraft. Captain Philip of the *Argus* made the same point, and indeed went further: "A modern edition of the old carronade for use at short range," he said, "might well provide a successful solution; in short, all that is needed for these insolent aircraft is a big blast from something."[2]

44

The *Liverpool* had been hit in the engine room and she could only steam at the rate of 3 or 4 knots on one shaft. She was ordered back to Gibraltar,

---

[1] See Appendix J for the original equipment of the two ships. The *Argus* carried Swordfish aircraft as a torpedo striking force and for anti-submarine work.

[2] The number of aircraft shot down by ships' fire, seven in all, is the assessment by the Gunnery and Anti-aircraft Warfare Division, Naval Staff. Individual claims amounted to 28, not including those made by merchantmen (the *Troilus* claimed two); it is impossible, therefore, to identify the successful ships.

towed by the *Antelope* and screened by the *Westcott*, a long voyage that for the
first twenty-four hours or so was punctuated by air attacks. At 1640, some
three and a half hours after proceeding, five C.R.42 fighter-bombers attacked
from astern out of the sun, luckily without hitting, though one or two bombs
fell near enough to increase the ship's list. At 1800, the tow having parted,
there was a harmless attempt by eleven high-level bombers followed by an
equally harmless attempt by seven torpedo aircraft, the latter heavily escorted
by fighters; the *Liverpool* and *Westcott* each destroyed a torpedo plane. At
2015, when once more in tow, she was attacked by five high-level bombers,
their bombs again falling wide. At 2230, six torpedo aircraft made a twilight
attack at very long range, only to lose one of their number to the cruiser's
barrage. Then at 1420 next day, the 15th, three torpedo aircraft made a
final unsuccessful attempt, after which the ships were not again molested.
Two tugs arrived from Gibraltar the same afternoon; and at sunset one of
them took over the tow, releasing the *Antelope* to join the *Westcott* as an anti-
submarine screen, which had become the more urgent service. On the 16th
some corvettes arrived. Apart from a shadowing submarine that night, which
was thrown off after dark, the rest of the voyage passed without incident. The
Liverpool reached Gibraltar in the evening of 17th June.

45

The fruitless attacks on the damaged *Liverpool* in the afternoon and evening
of 14th June evidently occupied the remaining aircraft available in Sardinia;
for after its hard service in the forenoon that day the convoy went freely on,
except for shadowers, until it came within the reach of Sicilian air stations
in the evening. Then at 1820, German bombers first appeared, about
10 Junkers 88 aircraft approaching the convoy from astern at 10,000 ft. and
diving to 6,000 ft. to make the attack. " As is usual in the Mediterranean,"
remarked Vice-Admiral Curteis, " it was very difficult to see these till they
had reached the bombing position, and gunfire was ineffective." Both the
carriers had narrow escapes, the *Argus* in particular; a bomb pitched fine on
her port bow, dived under the ship, and burst under the starboard bow. No
ship was damaged, however, nor were any bombers brought down, though the
six British fighters on patrol harassed the enemy and forced several to jettison
their bombs. One Fulmar was lost.

As in the morning, the shallow dive-bombing attack preceded a heavy
combined torpedo and bombing attack; but in the evening the lapse of time
was greater, and dive-bombers as well as high-level bombers took part in the
massed attack. It was a combination of Italians and Germans: 16 Savoia
79 torpedo planes, strongly escorted by Macchi fighters, with 10 Junkers 88
and 15 Junkers 87 bombers. The first to appear were the Savoias, which
approached from the north-east—to port—at about 2000, flying well above the
water; they worked round the stern of the convoy outside gun range to glide
down and attack on the starboard side. In the meantime, a few minutes
after the S.79s had been sighted, two groups of Ju. 88s came in from ahead
at 12,000 ft. and dropped their bombs without effect as they flew across the
screen and along the columns of the convoy. Next, the Ju. 87 dive-bombers
arrived on the port bow and attacked the port wing of the screen, diving
from 7,000 ft. to 1,000 ft., and narrowly missing the *Icarus* and *Wrestler*, though
they had probably hoped to reach the *Eagle*, which was to port of the convoy;
the coming of the dive-bombers, said Captain Armstrong of the *Onslow*,
" entirely took the screen's attention away " from the torpedo aircraft. These
last closed to attack at about 2020. The Vice-Admiral had ordered three
emergency turns to port to keep the sterns of the convoy towards the aircraft,

thus giving them but poor targets.   Most of them concentrated on the *Malaya*, *Argus*, *Charybdis* and *Vidette*, then together some two miles out on the starboard quarter, and they managed to drop three torpedoes within 300 yards of the carrier, though her handiness enabled her to avoid them.[1]

The *Malaya's* distance from the convoy was due to an encounter with an enemy submarine.   The *Middleton* in the screen ahead had sighted a periscope during the dive-bombing attack.   She dropped a depth-charge, and was followed by two other destroyers which hauled out of the screen to drop charges over the position of sighting, but without making asdic contact " owing to the numerous wakes in the vicinity."   The submarine evidently went deep under the advancing merchantmen, for her periscope next appeared broad on the starboard bow of the *Malaya* astern.   The battleship was turning to starboard to meet the air torpedo attack then developing, and she continued her turn towards the submarine until the periscope disappeared close ahead of her;   then she reversed her helm to rejoin the convoy, making a warning signal to the *Speedy*, which was in the screen on the starboard quarter.   The *Speedy* had seen the destroyer dropping charges, and she gained a good asdic contact and attacked, firing continuously at aircraft all the time;   Lieutenant-Commander Doran claimed that he destroyed the submarine.[2]

This was the last encounter before the force divided at the Narrows. Compared with the big air attacks from Sardinia in the morning, the attempts between 2000 and 2020 were timed in better combination, and some officers considered the torpedo attack more vigorously carried out.   Yet the evening attacks were fruitless, which must be chiefly ascribed to the convoy's emergency turns away, for neither gunfire nor fighter aircraft were nearly as successful as in the morning.   Radar warning of the enemy's approach gave time to increase the British air patrol from four to eight fighters;   but they were busily engaged with the far more numerous Italian fighters, and could do little to spoil the attacks.   They shot down two torpedo aircraft, however, and the ships' fire destroyed a third.   Three British fighters were lost—one in action, one unfortunately shot down by the fleet, and one which crashed when landing down wind.   Altogether, on 14th June, the 16 Hurricanes and 6 Fulmars carried shot down 11 enemy aircraft, and damaged and drove away others, at a cost of 7 British aircraft.   The *Eagle* and *Argus* lacked adequate equipment for fighter-direction;   and they could only maintain 10 aircraft at the most in the air.   As the Director of the Naval Air Division subsequently remarked, " The results achieved by the small force of naval fighters are most outstanding."[3]

As the force reached the entrance to the Narrows at 2100, four Beaufighters from Malta arrived to relieve the hard-worked naval airmen: and at 2130 Vice-Admiral Curteis hauled round to the westward with Force " W," while the convoy stood on with Force " X " under Captain Hardy of the *Cairo*. The five remaining merchant ships formed single line ahead for the passage along the Tunisian coast with the men of war screening them: the *Cairo*, nine destroyers, four fleet sweepers and six motor launches.   At 2205, as it was growing dark, eight Ju. 88s made a shallow dive-bombing attack, dropping down from 6,000 ft. to 3,000 ft. to release their bombs.   They approached out of the dusk ahead and had the convoy clear against the western sky, but they were unsuccessful;   they lost two aircraft, one shot down by a Beaufighter,

---

[1] The *Welshman* had replaced the *Liverpool* as guide of the starboard column in the convoy; but the *Welshman* parted company at 2000 and went to Malta alone, the Polish destroyer *Kujawiak* taking her station in the convoy.
[2] This is not confirmed by Italian sources.
[3] Staff Minute on M.08465/42 (Record Office, Case 8285).

the other by the ships' fire. This was the end of the day's fighting. Severe as had been the massed air attacks west of the Narrows, a greater trial and heavier losses awaited the convoy on the morrow.

Though up to time at noon, 14th June, the convoy was one and a half hours late on scheduled time for passing Cape Bon. This was due partly to delay caused by avoiding action and partly to the convoy's speed not being up to expectation[1] and was to have serious consequences, as it resulted in the convoy being one and a half hours further from Malta Spitfire protection at dawn on the 15th.

46

It will be remembered that the Italian plan provided for an attack on the convoy at dawn on 15th June by the cruisers and destroyers based on Cagliari. This force had accordingly sailed to the eastward in the evening of 13th June and put in to Palermo on the 14th, there to await news of the approach of the convoy.

The movement had not passed unnoticed by the British. The westernmost British submarine on patrol, *P.43*, attacked them at 1931, 13th, some 60 miles from Cagliari; she claimed to have hit a cruiser, but was mistaken. Two hours later the next submarine on the patrol line, *P.211*, sighted them also, but was too far off to attack.[2] On receiving the submarines' reports, Vice-Admiral Leatham at Malta arranged for a striking force of Wellington aircraft to intercept the enemy. These aircraft, or a reconnaissance aircraft, sighted the Italians north-west of Cape San Vito in Sicily at 0255 on the 14th, but lack of flares to light up the targets foiled attack. Two and a half hours later air reconnaissance showed the enemy to be off Palermo; at 1800 the two cruisers were reported in harbour there; and at 2125 (just when Admiral Curteis was parting company from the convoy) the two cruisers and four destroyers were sighted putting to sea, but the reconnoitring aircraft could not determine their subsequent course. Vice-Admiral Leatham judged that the enemy were bound eastward to join the Italian main fleet, which had sailed from Taranto the same evening, doubtless intending to intercept the convoy then on its way to Malta from Egypt (Operation " Vigorous "). Accordingly, he stationed a naval air patrol over the Strait of Messina, while a naval air striking force at Malta stood by to attack should the reconnaissance aircraft gain touch. The requirements of air support for the other operation— " Vigorous "—precluded further action.

Vice-Admiral Curteis, who was taking Force " W " westward, also received the report of the enemy's leaving Palermo, and had to decide whether to strengthen Force " X " with either or both of his cruisers, the *Kenya* and *Charybdis*. He was then, at 2315 on the 14th, in about 37° 30′ N., 9° 30′ E., over 50 miles from the convoy, which would be nearly 100 miles further on by dawn on the 15th.[3] He too judged that the Italians were unlikely to be a danger to the convoy, and that the escort was strong enough " to deter them from doing any harm "—especially as they would expect to be attacked by air from Malta. Apart from this, he was anxious for the safety of his aircraft carriers, which would need the cruisers' support while within striking distance of the air bases in Sardinia; furthermore, there was barely time to overtake the convoy by the morning. " With the force available," he said, " a decision

---

[1] See Section 40 *ante*.
[2] See Plan 11.
[3] Dawn was about 0630, Zone Time minus 3.

either way was a gamble; if the *Liverpool* had been present, there would have been no doubt in my mind." He decided against sending either ship.[1]

Actually, the two cruisers with five destroyers, after rounding Cape San Vito, had steered for the area south of Pantellaria, with the intention of attacking the convoy at first light next day. Thus in the early morning of the 15th the convoy and its escort faced an enemy considerably superior in the range of its guns, if in nothing else.

47

At daybreak on the 15th June the convoy was through the Narrows and some 40 miles off the African coast, steering away to the east-south-eastward for its destination, when the Italian surface forces appeared on the scene.

Captain Hardy first knew of the enemy's presence through a Beaufighter which was on its way to patrol above the convoy, and which at 0620 reported two cruisers and four destroyers 15 miles on the port beam of the British force. The convoy was then steering south-east at 12 knots; and the merchantmen were formed in two columns again, with the *Cairo* ahead, five "Fleet" destroyers in the screen to starboard, four "Hunts" to port, and the mine-sweepers and motor launches astern. A few minutes later the Italians could be seen from on board ship, outlined hull down against the brightening sky to the eastward. They were broad on the port bow, steering a slightly converging course at high speed, and drawing ahead of the convoy; before long it was clear that they were two 6-inch cruisers with five destroyers (3 ahead and 2 astern), not four as was first reported.[2] Commander Scurfield in the *Bedouin* led out the "Fleets" to attack, while the *Cairo* and the rest of the escort started making smoke to cover the merchant ships, which were ordered to turn away to starboard and to seek shelter in Tunisian waters; for Captain Hardy's "immediate intention was to gain time and to fight a delaying action in the hope that an air striking force could be sent from Malta."

At 0640 the Italian cruisers opened fire at a range of over 20,000 yards; their second salvo straddled the *Cairo*, and others fell near the convoy before the smoke screen took effect. The British ships could not yet reply, the range being too great for their 4·7-inch and 4-inch guns; indeed, some never reached effective range, though "for moral effect" they fired a few rounds. As the 11th Division—"Fleets"—gathered way, they became strung out in a loose line of bearing, nearly line ahead, in the order, *Bedouin*, *Partridge*, *Ithuriel*, *Marne*, *Matchless*, though the last ship worked up to 32 knots in the endeavour to keep up. The first two ships opened fired on the cruisers at about 0645, with their guns at the maximum elevation; but in a quarter of an hour both ships, the *Bedouin* and the *Partridge*, were badly hit and stopped, and the fight passed them by. The *Ithuriel* held her fire till she got within 15,000 yards; then she engaged a cruiser, which she eventually hit at a range of 8,000 yards. The *Marne* also engaged a cruiser ahead, starting at over 18,000 yards. In the meantime, however, the Italian destroyers had fallen astern of the cruisers; three of them, in fact, soon left the line and disappeared to the northward, having apparently taken no part in the action.[3] The last two[4] opened fire on the *Marne* from her port beam at about 0700, and she and

---

[1] This difficult decision was subsequently approved by the Admiralty.
[2] See Plan 12 for ensuing action.
[3] This is how it appeared to the British. The Italian account states that these destroyers "brilliantly withstood the encounter with the cruisers and the many similar enemy units" till at 0809 they were detached to the assistance of the damaged *Vivaldi*.
[4] According to the Italian report these two destroyers, *Vivaldi* and *Malocello*, had been detached to attack the merchant ships.

the *Matchless* astern of her replied. The British ships quickly found the range, hit one of the enemy (the *Ugolino Vivaldi*), and drove them off. Then they pressed on to engage the cruisers, which were all the time keeping at a respectful distance, and zigzagging and making smoke to upset the aim of the British ships.[1]

As soon as the convoy was well behind its smoke screen and on its way to the westward, the *Cairo* and the 12th Division of destroyers—" Hunts "—steered south after the enemy as well, the destroyers firing on the two Italian destroyers engaged by the *Marne* and *Matchless* as they passed at extreme range. At about 0700, the *Cairo* again came under fire from the cruisers, which were each using two turrets against her and two against the ships of the 11th Division to port of her, and she received a hit from a 6-inch gun; she herself fired her 4-inch occasionally, though without much hope of harming the enemy. At 0715 Captain Hardy decided to concentrate his three remaining large destroyers on the *Cairo*, and he ordered the *Ithuriel* to join him.

According to her report, that ship was only 8,000 yards from the enemy when the signal reached her, and under heavy and accurate fire, though it was then that she scored her hit on the cruiser. The *Marne* and *Matchless* continued in action half an hour longer, and for a time the former was less than 10,000 yards from the enemy; the shooting on both sides was accurate, though neither succeeded in hitting. At 0745 the Italians turned away to port, on which Captain Hardy hauled round to the northward and ordered all the destroyers to rejoin.

The convoy 15 miles away in the north-west and hitherto steering westward turned south-east again at this time. At 0705, deprived of the support of the *Cairo* and destroyers and without air protection, the convoy had been attacked by eight Ju. 87 dive-bombers, which sank the *Chant* and disabled the *Kentucky* at a cost of one German aircraft shot down. The *Hebe* took the *Kentucky* in tow, and the convoy went on till 0745. Then, however, as the enemy had not sent ships to deal with the merchantmen, and the British force appeared to be holding its own, Commander Pilditch, commodore of the convoy, decided to return to his course for Malta in the hope of meeting fighter aircraft.[2] This course brought him back towards the main escort, and he could not continue on it long; for the Italians had turned northward soon after Captain Hardy, and were following the British ships—warily indeed, but keeping them under fire. At 0834, therefore, as he closed the convoy, Captain Hardy ordered it to reverse its course, while the *Cairo* and the destroyers laid a smoke screen across its track. This seems to have baffled the Italians, which first turned south-west and then at 0840 hauled round to the north-eastward and stood away. Sending the " Hunts " to the convoy, Captain Hardy led the " Fleets " after the enemy, the *Cairo* receiving a second hit at this time. For the time being, however, the Italians had given up the game; by 0930 they were out of sight, and the British ships turned back to meet the convoy.

An hour later the merchant ships were on their proper course, with the escort at full strength (except the *Bedouin* and *Partridge*, whose fortunes will be described later), and with long-range Spitfire aircraft from Malta overhead. But the convoy had not reached the end of its trials. At 1040 a few German bombers approached, but they were driven off before they could drop their bombs and the fighters shot one down. Unluckily, this exhausted the fuel

---

[1] The track marked " 11th Division " on Plan 12 is that of the *Marne*. The courses and times for the *Ithuriel* ahead and the *Matchless* astern were slightly different.

[2] The Beaufighter that originally sighted the Italian ships seems to have gone back to Malta at once to report in full. No other aircraft made contact with the convoy till 0930.

and ammunition of the Spitfires, which were working at the limit of their range; and when another attack started, at 1120, the relief flight had not yet come. It was a combination of high-level and dive bombing by Ju. 88 and Ju. 87 aircraft, ten all told. Gunfire destroyed one of the Germans, and one or two were shot down afterwards by the relieving Spitfires, which arrived during the attack; but the *Burdwan* was disabled. There was still 150 miles to go, with the likelihood of further attacks from the air and with Italian ships not far away, so Captain Hardy resolved to sacrifice the damaged *Kentucky* and *Burdwan* as the best way to save the rest of the convoy, whose speed would be otherwise reduced to about 6 knots; he ordered the *Hebe* and *Badsworth* to sink the cripples, which enabled the two good ships remaining to go on at their best speed.[1] Dive-bombers attacked again at 1315, and again there happened to be no fighter aircraft in company; this time, however, the Germans were unsuccessful, and one bomber out of 12 attacking was shot down by the ships, while the relief flight of Spitfires came in time to destroy two more as they retired. That was the last attack from the air before the convoy arrived under the protection of short-range Spitfires in large numbers. The next threat of attack came from the Italian surface force, which appeared once more.

After the engagement in the morning the Italian cruisers had gone back to join the destroyers,[2] one of which (*Vivaldi*), as it turned out, had been badly damaged by the *Matchless* and *Marne*. While preparing to take her in tow, the Italians were disturbed by British aircraft; for, as Captain Hardy had hoped, Malta had been able to send a small torpedo striking force to attack them. Four naval Albacores under Lieutenant-Commander Roe, followed by two Beauforts, attacked about 12 miles south of Pantellaria at 1030, unluckily without success. The two cruisers and two destroyers afterwards went south again, doubtless learning from their allies in the air that there were stragglers from the convoy to pick up. They found the *Hebe*, which was on her way back to the convoy, having left the *Kentucky* sinking astern. The *Hebe* sighted the enemy a long way to the northward at 1255; in half an hour they had closed enough to open fire, and they eventually hit her. Receiving her report at 1341, Captain Hardy left the convoy and stood towards the Italians with the *Cairo* and his three large destroyers; besides the *Hebe* to protect, there were other ships coming back from the scuttled merchantmen, and the *Bedouin* and *Partridge*, which Captain Hardy believed to be following the convoy. At 1355 the Italians gave up the chase, presumably on sighting the *Cairo*, and turned to engage a target to the westward This could only be the *Bedouin* and *Partridge;* but Captain Hardy felt bound to return to the convoy, then nearly 15 miles off, though it meant leaving the two damaged destroyers to their fate.

48

The *Bedouin* and *Partridge* meanwhile had been making strenuous efforts to overcome the damage they had received. The former had received at least a dozen 6-in. hits, and was completely disabled, though Commander Scurfield, hoping continually to be able to steam shortly, made a sanguine report to Captain Hardy as late as midday. The *Partridge* was ready to steam at 12 knots again by 0745, three quarters of an hour after being put out of action. She prepared to take the *Bedouin* in tow, but the preparations were

---

[1] This decision was subsequently approved by the Admiralty.
[2] The decision of the Italian admiral to withdraw his whole force on account of one damaged destroyer seems rather to have lost sight of his object. The *Vivaldi*, towed by the *Premula*, reached Pantellaria at 1530.

interrupted by two Italian destroyers, which had to be driven away. By 1000, however, Lieutenant-Commander Hawkins had his consort in tow, and the two ships were proceeding slowly towards the convoy, which they had orders to join. They met it at 1145, still hoping to get one engine to work in the *Bedouin;* but later on this hope had to be abandoned, and Commander Scurfield then thought it best to make for Gibraltar. At 1320 the Italian squadron came in sight again, and two destroyers were apparently closing the British ships, while there were also dive-bombers about. The *Partridge* accordingly slipped the tow by order of Commander Scurfield and laid smoke round the *Bedouin.* As the cruisers approached, after their chase of the *Hebe,* the *Partridge* stood away to draw their fire, and in this she succeeded, being straddled at long range at 1400. But she was disappointed of her further intention of returning to her consort. At 1425 an Italian aircraft torpedoed the *Bedouin,* which sank within a few minutes, after managing first to shoot down her assailant.[1] Italian torpedo aircraft also sank the derelict *Kentucky* and *Burdwan* at about the same time.

The *Partridge* remained under fire from the Italian ships, which had an aircraft spotting for them, and whose shots fell close in spite of her smoke screen. After a while the enemy turned away, apparently under an air attack, which must have been made by their friends. Four German bombers, however, attacked the *Partridge* at 1530, and near misses jammed her rudder hard over. It took more than an hour to get it amidships, and during that time she had to lie stopped. She saw Italian ships approach the position where the *Bedouin* had sunk, some seven miles to the eastward, and thought they were picking up survivors. " It is deeply regretted," wrote Lieutenant-Commander Hawkins, " that, even if the ship could not be saved, the *Bedouin*'s commanding officer and her ship's company could not be rescued by a British warship."[2] When able to proceed, the *Partridge* went to the westward, intending to make good defects under shelter of the land; but a signal from Vice-Admiral Leatham at Malta ordered her back to Gibraltar, where she arrived without further incident on the 17th. The Italian ships made no effort to destroy the *Partridge,* but steered away to the northward,[3] and at 1700 on the 15th again encountered British naval aircraft near Pantellaria. These were three Albacores that Vice-Admiral Leatham had sent to attack with torpedoes in aid of the *Bedouin* and *Partridge.* The aircraft, not finding the enemy on the way out from Malta, sighted them by chance on the way back; but the attack did not succeed, and one Albacore was shot down by the swarm of fighter aircraft the enemy had then in company. The last news of the Italian ships came from Submarine *P.42* the same evening. At 2045, the 15th, she sighted two cruisers and two destroyers steering north at high speed close to Marittimo and beyond her reach.

49

Captain Hardy rejoined the convoy at 1530, the 15th after the last encounter with the Italian squadron. At 1730 the *Welshman* joined south of Linosa, having reached Malta that morning and been sent out again by Vice-Admiral Leatham as soon as she had landed her cargo. Then, at 1910, there was another air attack. Up to that time radar warnings and fighter direction by

---

[1] Approximate position: 36° 12′ N., 11° 37′ E.

[2] Actually, the Italians made no attempt at rescue work at this time, and it was not till 2000 that an Italian rescue plane picked up a few. An hour later an Italian hospital ship arrived and picked up the remainder (208 out of a total crew of 241), being bombed by her own aircraft during the rescue.

[3] They received orders from the Naval High Command at 1520 to return to harbour.

the *Cairo* had enabled the strong escort of Spitfires to keep enemy aircraft at a safe distance and to frustrate two attempted attacks during the afternoon. At 1910, however, 12 German bombers managed to attack, and without doing actual harm they nearly hit the *Matchless, Troilus* and *Welshman.* A last attempt, at 2040, was foiled by the fighters and the ships' guns.

There remained one danger to overcome—the mines that the enemy had laid so industriously off Malta in the past few months; and they took their toll as the two merchant ships and their escort entered harbour that night. In the original plan it was hoped that the *Cairo* and the destroyers would not need to go into harbour; but the heavy fighting on the 14th and 15th required them to replenish with ammunition from the slender store at Malta. Owing to mistakes, the convoy and the main escort arrived at the entrance before the sweepers, which ought to have been sweeping ahead of them. The *Badsworth* and *Kujawiak* struck mines off Zonkor Point, a few miles short of Grand Harbour, and the *Orari, Matchless* and *Hebe* were mined just outside the breakwater. All except the *Kujawiak* reached harbour only slightly damaged, but the Polish destroyer was lost.[1]

Having arrived at Malta in the early morning of the 16th, the *Cairo* and the four undamaged destroyers sailed again for Gibraltar in the evening. On the 17th, as they skirted along the African coast, they were shadowed from sunrise onward, but not attacked until midday, when they were past the Galita Bank. From then until 2030 that evening German bombers pestered them continuously. The Germans came sometimes in flights of six, though generally in twos and threes, concentrating specially upon the *Ithuriel*, which reported the afternoon's progress as a " struggle for existence "; but apart from a few leaks caused by near misses no harm was done and the *Cairo* shot down a bomber. At 2017 they joined Vice-Admiral Curteis with the *Kenya* and *Charybdis* in 37° 30' N., 4° 30' E.

After leaving the convoy in the evening of the 14th the Vice-Admiral had taken Force " W " some 400 miles to the westward of Sardinia, in order to avoid observation and attack while awaiting the return of Force " X." His ships had been shadowed as a matter of course on the 15th, and two small groups of torpedo aircraft attacked that afternoon; but Hurricanes from the *Eagle* forced them to drop their torpedoes at long range and shot down one aircraft. From the morning of the 16th to noon on the 17th, he cruised with the *Kenya* and *Charybdis* on his rendezvous, sending his battleship, the two aircraft carriers and the destroyers to Gibraltar. Then he went east again to meet Captain Hardy, and after the junction had been made they returned to Gibraltar together.

This was the end of Operation " Harpoon." Out of six ships in the convoy, two reached their destination, the other four all being destroyed by air attack. But these two ships landed two months' supplies, enough to tide over the sorely-tried fortress till August. About 200 aircraft attacked the convoy and escort during the operation, losing 13 to the carrier-borne fighters and 16 to the ships' guns, besides several shot down by Royal Air Force fighters from Malta.[2] Of the escorting ships, two destroyers were lost, and a cruiser, three destroyers and a minesweeper damaged.

---

[1] The report of the Board of Inquiry held upon this matter is in M.010042/42. Subsequent sweeping by the newly-arrived flotilla showed that the minefield was even more extensive and more thickly sown than was appreciated before the convoy arrived. The *Matchless* and *Badsworth* escorted the *Troilus* and *Orari* to Gibraltar in August during Operation " Pedestal ".

[2] From the time the convoy came within range of Malta-based aircraft until the surviving ships reached harbour, the R.A.F. flew 414 sorties in support of the convoy—292 by short-range Spitfires, 97 by long-range Spitfires and 25 by Beaufighters.

CHAPTER VI

Operation "Vigorous", June 1942

50

WHILE THE "HARPOON" forces were battling their way through to Malta from the west, operation "Vigorous" in the east was encountering even more formidable opposition, which eventually compelled the abandonment of the attempt.

The convoy from Egypt in March (or part of it) had succeeded in reaching Malta owing chiefly to the exertions of the slender force of cruisers and destroyers under Rear-Admiral Philip Vian. The same officer led the surface escort in the attempt in June that was complementary to Operation "Harpoon" from Gibraltar. For this occasion the strength of the Mediterranean Fleet was augmented by borrowing from the Eastern Fleet, so that Rear-Admiral Vian had seven cruisers, one anti-aircraft ship, and twenty-six destroyers as the main escort for eleven merchant ships.[1] There were also four motor torpedo boats, which were to be towed by merchantmen, ready to slip and attack should opportunity arise; four corvettes; two minesweepers, which were to sweep ahead of the convoy when approaching Malta; two unarmed rescue ships; and the former battleship *Centurion*, unarmed except against air attack, but masquerading as a capital ship.[2] In default of real battleships, however, the convoy was to depend for protection against the Italian main fleet rather on submarines and air striking forces than on its surface escort; for in midsummer an inferior force could not hope to gain as much by evasion and delay as it did in March. In these circumstances the general conduct of the operation rested directly with the Commander-in-Chief himself, and with the Air Officer Commanding-in-Chief, Air Marshal Sir Arthur Tedder, the two officers working together in "a special combined operations room" at the headquarters of the Naval Co-operation Group, Royal Air Force.

"In previous operations, available submarines had been disposed in the close approaches to Messina and Taranto. Apart from valuable early sighting reports and an occasional attack on returning enemy forces, these dispositions had produced little result."[3] This time, therefore, the submarines were to

---

[1] See Appendix J.
[2] The Italians were not seriously perturbed by this ruse, having assessed her as "probably another unit camouflaged" as early as 13th June.
[3] Commander-in-Chief, Mediterranean, report in M. 013471/42.

be used differently. From the point of view of surface attack, the critical day of the operation would be that on which the convoy passed through the " central basin " between Crete and Malta. Up to that morning nine submarines were to carry out normal diving patrols on lines north of the route, so placed as " to cover the enemy's most probable movements," but from which the submarines could reach the positions required on the critical day—the next stage of their task. On that day, they were to proceed on the surface formed as a screen, parallel to the convoy and between it and the enemy's line of approach from Taranto; and they were to have " complete freedom of action to intercept any enemy force which may be reported." The next day, when the convoy should have arrived in Malta, the submarines were to dive again, some on a line of stations from which they should help to cover the return of the surface escort to Alexandria, and the others in the Messina approaches, where they might have an opportunity of intercepting Italian ships returning through those waters.[1] As things turned out the plan was not fully carried out. The Italian fleet sailed earlier than the scheme allowed for, and the convoy was turned back by order of the Commander-in-Chief so as to avoid meeting the enemy. The moving screen of submarines thus became impracticable, and instead the patrol lines were adjusted according to the information received of the enemy's movements. Four submarines sighted the Italian fleet as it came south in the morning of 15th June, though one only was able to attack; and one sighted part of the fleet as it went north again that night, unfortunately outside her reach.

The air striking forces came from both Malta and Egypt. Some forty aircraft were employed: Wellingtons and Beauforts armed with torpedoes from Malta, torpedo Beauforts from a landing-ground in Egypt near the Libyan border, and United States Liberator bombers from as far away as the Suez Canal. It was intended to synchronize the bombing with the two main torpedo attacks by Beauforts, despite the long distances to be flown and the widely separated bases. But the plan proved too ambitious, though the Beauforts from Egypt managed to attack within a few minutes of the Liberators in the forenoon of the 15th. The Malta Beauforts had attacked three hours earlier, as the Italian fleet was crossing the submarine patrol line; and they disabled the cruiser *Trento*, which was sunk later by Submarine *P.35*. One bomb from the Liberators hit the battleship *Littorio*, which was hit again by a torpedo from a Wellington late that night when going back to Taranto. But that was the sum of the airmen's success. The damage inflicted during their passage south did not deter the Italians. They continued on their course towards the convoy for six hours after the attack by the Liberators, and although they were never nearer than 100 miles they succeeded so far as to stop the convoy from finishing its voyage. For the convoy itself was heavily attacked by German aircraft that day and the day before; it lost time and distance by the diversion that the threatening approach of the Italian fleet imposed upon it; and when it might have retraced its course, in the evening of the 15th, it had not ammunition enough remaining for the air attacks it must still expect before reaching Malta.

---

[1] The positions marked on Plan 13 are those on the first patrol lines, the only lines actually occupied. The choice of further positions to which submarines could be moved was limited by the speed of submarines; and this presumably accounts for the Messina approaches patrol, to which the slow U-class vessels were to go. The scheme may be compared with that adopted for the Russian convoys in July and September the same year. Instead of forming a moving screen, the submarines in the northern theatre occupied successive patrol lines according to the progress of the convoy. (See Naval Staff History, Battle Summary No. 22, *Arctic Convoys, 1942–45*.)

51

In order to mislead the enemy and to deny them knowledge of the convoy for as long as possible, the ships were loaded at various ports between Beirut and Alexandria.   Part of the convoy—M.W.11C—was to sail with a special escort from Port Said on 11th June, some thirty-six hours before the main body; it was to go as far west as 24° 50′ E., nearly to Tobruk, arriving there at dusk on the 12th, and then to turn back to meet the rest of the convoy. Admiral Harwood hoped by this means to draw the Italian fleet to sea prematurely, " exposing them to attack and running them short of fuel "— but this ruse did not succeed.   The rest of the convoy was to assemble at Haifa and Port Said in two parts, M.W.11A and M.W.11B, which were to join at sea and go to a rendezvous off Alexandria, where Convoy M.W.11C and part of the permanent escort were to join on 13th June.   The remainder of the ships of war were to sail from Alexandria later with Rear-Admiral Vian and to overtake the convoy a little east of Tobruk in the morning of the 14th.   For the first part of the passage, the route lay within the range of protection by shore-based aircraft against enemy submarines and air attack. Fighter protection was difficult to give, because the land battle in Libya demanded a share of the few aircraft available and because the enemy's advance had deprived the Royal Air Force of its airfields there; yet protection was given, by Hurricanes at first and then by longer-ranged Beaufighters and Kittihawks, to the limit of endurance.[1]   As the course of the operation was governed largely by the movements of the Italian fleet, good air reconnaissance was essential, alike for the Allied submarines and air striking forces to fulfil their tasks and for enabling the convoy itself to evade attack; extensive searches were carried out accordingly from Malta and Egypt by day and by night, but the aircraft available for the purpose were too few to keep the enemy under continuous observation.

The four ships of Convoy M.W.11C, sailing on 11th June as arranged, escorted by the *Coventry* and eight destroyers, were found by German bombers in the evening of the 12th, when about to turn east again to rendezvous with the main body.   A dozen Ju. 88 aircraft attacked, and one merchant ship was damaged by a near miss and had to be sent to Tobruk with two destroyers for escort.   The rest of the force turned back at the appointed time and met the main convoy off Alexandria in the afternoon of the 13th.   As another of the convoy had to return to harbour, being unable to maintain the speed of the convoy, 13 knots, only nine out of the original eleven ships left the rendezvous.   They proceeded with the *Coventry*, ten destroyers and four corvettes, the *Centurion* and the two rescue ships, and the four motor torpedo boats; but the torpedo boats had to go back the same night, the weather being too rough for towing.   In the morning of the 14th the force was completed by the junction of the two minesweepers and of Rear-Admiral Vian in the *Cleopatra*, with the cruisers *Dido*, *Hermione*, *Euryalus*, *Arethusa*, *Newcastle* (flag, Rear-Admiral Tennant) and *Birmingham* and fourteen more destroyers, and by the return of the two destroyers detached to Tobruk on the 12th—these last two ships had hunted an enemy submarine, till she was no longer a menace to the convoy, whilst rejoining.   On the other hand, the corvettes *Erica* and *Primula* had to part company owing to defects; yet another merchant ship, the *Aagtekirk*, was found to be too slow, so was sent to Tobruk; and the destroyer *Tetcott* went with her.   The *Aagtekirk* did not reach harbour.

---

[1] To lessen the weight of enemy air attack from Crete, parties were landed there before and during the operation to raid air stations.   For instance, Captain Lord Jellicoe with some French soldiers landed from the Greek submarine *Triton* in the night of 13th–14th June, and did some damage at Maleme, though not so much as was believed at the time.

About 40 German dive-bombers, Ju. 87 and Ju. 88, attacked at 1220[1] that day, when the merchantman and her escort were within a dozen miles of Tobruk, and the *Primula* was following them a few miles astern. The *Aagtekirk* was hit and sunk and the *Primula* was damaged by near misses. The two ships of war shot down three of the attacking aircraft between them.

52

The main convoy had been threatened from the air the previous night. From sunset on the 13th to 0430 on the 14th, enemy aircraft had dropped flares almost continuously to guide attacks, while a few bombs were dropped near the screen. After 0430 the enemy had turned their attention to Rear-Admiral Vian as he overhauled the convoy. One or two small bombs fell close to the flagship *Cleopatra* at that time, and the enemy went on dropping flares round the cruisers till daylight. Then, however, owing largely to the exertions of the fighter aircraft, there was no further sign of the enemy till the afternoon, though the convoy was well inside " Bomb Alley " between Crete and Cyrenaica; at least one strong formation of German bombers, escorted by fighters, was intercepted and dispersed by two squadrons of British fighters, which the Western Desert Command detached at a moment's notice from the land battle.[2] Even the afternoon attacks were individually less formidable than that which overwhelmed the *Aagtekirk*, though the enemy succeeded in sinking one merchant ship and damaging another at a cost of six bombers shot down by the escort and convoy out of 60 or 70 that attacked between 1630 and 2115. There were seven attacks, generally by 10 or 12 aircraft at a time, Ju. 87 and Ju. 88; they approached from astern or the quarter at a height of 10,000 ft., and dived in ones or twos to 3,000 or 4,000 ft. to release their bombs. The one attack that brought success to the enemy took place between 1730 and 1800. This time as many as 20 aircraft approached together on the beam and split into groups of three to attack. They hit and sank the *Bhutan*, sternmost ship of a wing column, and damaged the *Potaro* by near misses, but she was able to stay with the convoy. The rescue ships *Antwerp* and *Malines*, having picked up the survivors from the *Bhutan*, were detached to Tobruk.[3]

Towards the end of the air attacks, at 2000 on the 14th, a submarine appeared on the starboard bow of the force and nearly torpedoed the *Pakenham* in the outer screen; she was attacked with depth charges, but without success. A few minutes later, at sunset, the fighter patrol reported a flotilla of six motor torpedo craft—E-boats[4]—to the north-westward, and shortly afterwards the enemy were seen hull down from the *Euryalus* on the starboard bow of the convoy. The fighters were directed to attack; but the E-boats had an escort of German fighters, which held off the one British aircraft that complied, the others being engaged with enemy bombers. Accordingly, the E-boats remained undisturbed.

At 2115, by which time it was dark, Rear-Admiral Vian assumed his night

---

[1] Zone Time minus 3 is used throughout this chapter.

[2] " R.A.F., Middle East " (H.M. Stationery Office, 1945), p. 57. See also the report of No. 201 (Naval Co-operation) Group, R.A.F., in M.013471/42.

[3] The eight merchant ships and the *Centurion* were formed in four columns, with the two rescue ships between the inner columns. The seven cruisers and the *Coventry* were disposed as a screen round the convoy 1,200 yards out. There was an all-round air-warning screen of Hunt class destroyers and smaller vessels, 1,600 yards outside the cruisers; and an anti-submarine screen of Fleet destroyers, from ahead to either quarter, 2,500 yards beyond the air-warning screen.

[4] These were German E-boats, based on Crete.

disposition, in which he had a regular anti-submarine screen ahead and on the bows, a special " night screen " of two cruisers and four destroyers on each quarter, and single destroyers 5 miles out on either bow and quarter of the convoy. Enemy aircraft were dropping flares, evidently to assist submarines and E-boats as well as bombers, which still attacked sporadically; and Rear-Admiral Vian claimed that his force, thus disposed, " proved an unattractive proposition " to the E-boats, especially with the whole area lit up as it was by the flares. Certainly the *Airedale* and *Aldenham*, stationed out on either quarter, found little difficulty in driving off five boats that approached from astern at midnight. But Rear-Admiral Tennant, leading one of the night screens, remarked that " flares gave one a very naked feeling, when dropped overhead, and it is surprising that the E-boats did not achieve a great deal more success." For two successes they did achieve a few hours later.

This arose out of the convoy's reversing its course, which was an awkward manœuvre at night in that formation and with ships out of position through turning to avoid bombs. At 2315, having learnt that an Italian force of two battleships and four cruisers had sailed from Taranto and would probably meet him on his present course at 0700 in the morning, Rear-Admiral Vian signalled to the Commander-in-Chief, " Do you wish me to retire? " For, with fine weather and a light north-westerly breeze, he could not hope " to hold off such a force from early morning to dusk." Admiral Harwood intended the convoy to make as much westing as possible, whilst leaving sea-room for the submarines and aircraft to attack the Italian fleet, and therefore ordered the Rear-Admiral to continue till 0200 and then to " turn back along the same track." The convoy turned accordingly at 0145, the 15th. In carrying out the manœuvre, Rear-Admiral Tennant's ships dropped several miles astern; and at 0350, while coming up to regain station, his flagship, the *Newcastle*, was torpedoed by an E-boat from 500 yards on the bow. The enemy was sighted in time for the *Newcastle* to avoid one torpedo and to receive the other well forward, and after shoring up the damaged compartments the ship was still capable of 24 knots' speed; in the meantime, Rear-Admiral Tennant sent his other cruiser and one destroyer to join the convoy, keeping three destroyers with the *Newcastle*. Before the *Newcastle* and her escort overtook the convoy they were attacked again and the *Hasty* was hit by one torpedo at 0528. She was so badly damaged that she had to be sunk by a consort.[1]

53

Meanwhile an Italian squadron consisting of the battleships *Littorio* and *Vittorio Veneto*, the cruisers *Gorizia*, *Trento*, *Garibaldi* and *Duca d'Aosta*, and 12 destroyers had left Taranto at 1430, 14th June, with the intention of intercepting the convoy at dawn, 15th. When the convoy altered course to the east (0145, 15th) the Italian fleet was rather more than 230 miles away in the north-west, pressing south towards the line of passage to Malta.

The first news of them to reach the British came from a Malta aircraft, which sighted them clearing the Gulf of Taranto at 1845 on the 14th, and reported two battleships with four destroyers in company and four cruisers with four destroyers a few miles farther on. Photographic reconnaissance of Taranto by a Malta aircraft at 2000 showed that three " Cavour "-class battleships still lay " in their nets " there, but that the two " Littorio "-class ships, two 8-inch and two 6-inch cruisers and eleven destroyers had sailed. This information,

---

[1] On this occasion the E-boat was not seen, and it was thought that the torpedo came from a submarine. It has since been confirmed by German sources that it was E-boat *S55*.

however, did not reach Admiral Harwood until 0300 on the 15th, and at midnight he had only the first sighting at 1845—signal received at 2230, the 14th—on which to base his reply to Rear-Admiral Vian's question whether to retire.[1] The next report of the Italians' progress came at 0224, the 15th, but gave only a part of their force: one battleship, two cruisers and two destroyers in 37° 30′ N., 19° 35′ E., course 190°, speed 20 knots, at 0200. No further news arrived until 0630, except that the little torpedo striking force of Wellington aircraft had left Malta at midnight to attack; but at 0525 Admiral Harwood ordered the convoy to steer north-west again, for he considered its return into " Bomb Alley " more dangerous than an advance towards the Italian fleet. In compliance with this order Rear-Admiral Vian turned back towards Malta at 0655. The Italians had just crossed the submarine line, leaving behind them an 8-inch cruiser disabled by air attack, though neither the Commander-in-Chief nor Rear-Admiral Vian was to know of it for some time to come.

There had been two attempts upon the Italian fleet by aircraft from Malta. The Wellingtons were dispatched at midnight on the strength of the first sighting report and the photographic reconnaissance of Taranto. The aircraft found their target at 0340; but the Italian smoke screen was so effective that one only of the four was able to attack, and both its torpedoes missed. The nine Beauforts attacked at dawn, as the enemy were passing over the submarines. The Italians were steering south in two groups, disposed apparently as follows: two battleships and two cruisers, screened by five or six destroyers, with two cruisers and five or six destroyers several miles to the westward. According to the Italian report, the aircraft first attacked the cruiser group to the westward, approaching at 0610 and disabling the sternmost cruiser, *Trento*, which turned away and steamed slowly westward with two destroyers. Then the Beauforts attacked the battleships, but without success, though on their first return to Malta they claimed hits on both. The Italians avoided attack by making large alterations of course. Lieutenant Maydon, of Submarine *P.35*, who missed a chance of his own through their turning away, thus described what he saw. " *P.35* was in the unenviable position of being in the centre of a fantastic circus of wildly careering capital ships, cruisers, and destroyers . . . of tracer-shell streaks and anti-aircraft bursts. At one period there was not a quadrant of the compass unoccupied by enemy vessels weaving continuously to and fro. It was only possible to count the big ships: destroyers seemed to be everywhere. It was essential to remain at periscope depth, for an opportunity to fire might come at any moment; one was in fact tempted to stand with periscope up and gaze in utter amazement."

The submarines, in accordance with the original plan of the operation, had left their stations on patrol during the night of 14th–15th June to go south-west to their starting positions on the moving screen, parallel to the convoy, which they were to have formed on the 15th; but after the enemy's sailing was known (2230, 14th), they were ordered back to the previous patrol lines. The route of the Italian fleet crossed the western line of four U-class submarines of the Tenth Flotilla, three of which sighted the enemy. *P.35*, warned by the signal giving the enemy's position at 0200 and sighting aircraft flares to the northward soon after 0400, steered westward to intercept the Italians, which she expected to sight at dawn. She saw two battleships and two cruisers at 0545, and started to attack them. But a few seconds before she was due to fire (in the circumstances described in the last paragraph), the enemy turned away 90° under air attack, and the submarine lost her chance. The battleships circled round the damaged *Trento* to the westward (for they appeared beyond her),

---

[1] The reported positions of the Italian fleet are marked on Plan 13.

worked to the eastward again, and coming south gave Lieutenant Maydon another opportunity. At 0646, he fired his four torpedoes at the second battleship at a range of 5,000 to 6,000 yards, but without success. *P.34*, in her station at the patrol line, first sighted the fleet to the north-westward at 0615 during the Beauforts' attack. Lieutenant Harrison saw the battleships steering east after closing the *Trento*, while the three remaining cruisers screened by four destroyers came south towards *P.34*. He started an attack at 0622, arrived inside the screen and was about to fire, when the enemy turned 90° towards, passed over him and altered course to the southward again out of range. At 0700 the two battleships appeared once more, standing south with five destroyers, but *P.34* could not reach them. *P.31*, on the other side of the Italians' track, sighted them against the dawn sky at 0604, when she was already on their beam at extreme range.

Three submarines of the faster First Flotilla to the eastward also tried to intercept the Italian fleet. Receiving the 0200 sighting report, whilst going back north-eastward to their old positions under the new orders, they turned to head off the enemy, going at full speed on the surface. The *Thrasher* and *Taku* both gave up the attempt after some three hours, the latter misled by a second sighting report, timed 0420, which made the enemy's course south-westerly instead of southerly; otherwise, as her captain calculated, she would have met them about 0800. The *Thorn*, having started her westward stretch near the enemy, was able to dive in good time a little east of their line of advance. At 0700 she sighted a column of smoke in the north-west, which was evidently the *Trento* on fire, and at 0725 saw the masts of what proved to be the Italian battleships. She could not, however, approach nearer than 12.000 yards. There remained the disabled *Trento* for the three ships of the Tenth Flotilla, all of which closed her as soon as the main body of the fleet had passed. *P.31*, the farthest away, had begun to close at 0620; and according to Lieutenant Kershaw she was still " burning gloriously " three hours later, with her crew gathered on the quarterdeck and with two destroyers laying a smoke screen round her; but he had still an hour's diving before she would be within range. Lieutenant Harrison, of *P.34*, seeing her " definitely out of action and incapable of movement ", decided that his first duty was to withdraw out of sight of the destroyers to signal the situation to the Commander-in-Chief " and to return later and sink the cruiser if still necessary ". *P.35* forestalled both her consorts. Lieutenant Maydon hit the *Trento* with two torpedoes at 1006; her fore magazine blew up and she sank immediately.

Before this the main body of the Italian fleet, continuing southward towards the convoy, had been attacked by the torpedo and bombing air forces from Egypt. The eight Liberators arrived first, beginning their attack at 0905 after a flight of five and a half hours from their base.[1] The Italians were still steaming in two groups, battleships with a destroyer screen to the eastward, cruisers and destroyers 4 or 5 miles west of them. The American aircraft approached out of the sun on the bow of the battleships, and dropped their bombs from an average height of 14,000 ft. They claimed half a dozen hits on each battleship; but the Italians admit only one hit on the *Littorio*, though many bombs fell around them. Four German fighters had joined the Italians at 0800, but they do not seem to have been in company during this attack, for the Liberators report " erratic " gunfire from the ships to be the only opposition they met with until they were many miles on their way home. The Beauforts were not so fortunate. Twelve aircraft set out at 0625, but five Messerschmitt 109 fighters intercepted them half-way to the target; two Beauforts were shot down, while five more had to turn back owing to damage

---

[1] A ninth Liberator had to abandon the attack and return, owing to defective engines.

received in the encounter or to excessive fuel consumption, and one of them never arrived. The remaining Beauforts reached the enemy at about 0940 under the eyes of the Americans, who saw the torpedo aircraft flying close to the water below them as they finished their own attack. The Italians met the British attack with a heavy fire at long range, damaging two Beauforts. On the other hand, by altering course 90° when they were bows on to the aircraft, they helped the attack. The British airmen believed that at least one of their torpedoes hit a battleship, while the watching Americans reported hits on a cruiser and a destroyer, but in fact not a ship was touched. And all the gallantry of the airmen, all the skilful leading that enabled the little striking forces to find their targets on each occasion, had not availed: the Italian fleet stood on.

54

Admiral Harwood had already decided to turn the convoy east once more until he should learn the results of the air attacks. Finding from an air reconnaissance report, timed 0828, that both battleships, three cruisers and nine destroyers were within 150 miles of the convoy and steering south-east, he ordered Rear-Admiral Vian to steer 105°; and the convoy altered round at 0940. Then came the claim of the Malta Beauforts to have hit both Italian battleships. On this, at 1151, Admiral Harwood ordered the convoy to resume its course for Malta; and giving the Rear-Admiral the supposed result of the Beauforts' attack, he told him that an 8-inch cruiser was believed to be also damaged and retiring, and that a further attack by British aircraft was intended in the afternoon. Lastly, he repeated an order he had given early in the morning (0705/15): " Avoid contact until aircraft have attacked, which should be by 1030. If air attack fails, every effort must be made to get convoy through to Malta by adopting offensive attitude. Should this fail, and convoy be cornered, it is to be sacrificed and you are to extricate your forces, proceeding to the eastward or westward." Meanwhile, however, the air reconnaissance had stopped, the latest report being timed 0944. The Commander-in-Chief began to suspect that the cruiser might be the only Italian ship seriously damaged; he did not know whether the convoy had suffered attack and damage, nor how it stood for fuel and ammunition. At 1245, therefore, he signalled to the Rear-Admiral, " I must leave decision to you whether to comply with my 0705/15, or whether to again retire with hope of carrying out a night destroyer attack, if enemy stand on."[1]

55

Rear-Admiral Vian received the signal to turn again for Malta at 1345. By that time a fresh reconnaissance aircraft was shadowing the Italian fleet. He soon had its first report, which showed that the enemy were standing on, whereas his two best ships, the *Newcastle* and *Birmingham*, were damaged.

---

[1] Air Vice-Marshal Sir Leonard Slatter, commanding No. 201 (Naval Co-operation) Group, who wrote the Air report of the operation, commented on Admiral Harwood's difficulties " on account of the very meagre information provided by air reports " both in the night of 14th–15th and in the forenoon of 15th June. " Striking forces and shadowers," he said, " should report at once any results observed from attacks. This is of the greatest value to the Commander-in-Chief, and was not done in this operation." Again, " During the whole of the morning the Commander-in-Chief, Mediterranean, was greatly hampered in making a decision as to whether to turn the convoy towards Malta, as no results of our air attacks on the enemy had been received, and it was not known whether Malta had attacked or not." (M.013471/42).
    Admiral Harwood said he received the results of the Malta Beauforts' attack at 1115. His belief that a cruiser was retiring damaged was presumably founded on an air reconnaissance report timed 0810 and received about 0830.

" My heavy striking force, the Fourth Cruiser Squadron, being somewhat under the weather, I held on to the eastward awaiting the Commander-in-Chief's reactions to Aircraft T's report." At 1420 he received Admiral Harwood's discretionary signal, timed 1245, which confirmed his decision to continue eastward.

The *Newcastle*, it will be remembered, had been hit by an E-boat's torpedo early that morning and had her speed reduced. The *Birmingham's* injuries (she had two 6-inch guns out of action) were the result of an air attack at midday—for the convoy was back in " Bomb Alley ". About 20 German dive-bombers (Ju. 87) had attacked from the quarters at 1150, and six of them concentrated upon the *Birmingham*, which was stationed on the port side ahead of the merchant ships, scoring a near miss; the convoy suffered no other damage, and one of the attackers was brought down by the ships' fire. A further attack took place at 1525, when between 30 and 40 dive-bombers, escorted by Messerschmitts, approached from astern. A dozen aircraft attacked the *Airedale*, stationed in the air-warning screen on the starboard quarter; she was smothered with hits and near misses and completely disabled, and another destroyer had to sink her. The other aircraft, generally in groups of three, attacked the convoy itself, but without success, except that nine aircraft concentrating upon the *Centurion* inflicted slight damage from near misses. Four of the enemy were shot down, one falling to the guns of the *Centurion*, and others may have been destroyed by British fighters after the attack.

Meanwhile, the general situation had changed; for the Italians had given up the chase. At 1515, when rather more than 100 miles astern of the convoy, they hauled round to the north-westward, and at 1605 the shadowing aircraft reported them well away on the course for Taranto. The moment Admiral Harwood was waiting for had come, and as soon as the position was clear he made the following signal to Rear-Admiral Vian (1625/15): " Now is golden opportunity to get convoy to Malta. Have Hunts, *Coventry*, minesweepers and corvettes enough fuel and ammunition for one-way trip? If so, I would like to turn convoy now, cruisers and destroyers parting company after dark and returning to Alexandria." Two hours later, having had no reply from the Rear-Admiral, he modified the plan, intending to send to Malta only the four fastest merchant ships of the seven remaining in the convoy, and adding the *Arethusa* and two large destroyers to their escort. But the first signal reached Rear-Admiral Vian during the most trying air attack of the day, under conditions that precluded his reversing the course of forty ships. Moreover, it was an hour before he could ascertain the quantity of high-angle ammunition still on board the destroyers; and upon that the decision rested.

The attack lasted two hours, beginning at 1720. " All known forms of attack were employed," said Rear-Admiral Vian, " the fire of the fleet being fully extended." The Germans and Italians evidently tried to synchronize high-level and shallow dive-bombing with torpedo attack—on a scale somewhat larger than that which the British and Americans had achieved against the Italian fleet in the morning. Nearly 30 bombers took part, while 10 Italian torpedo aircraft arrived towards the end of the attack. The high-level bombers came first, approaching from the western sun, unseen until they were nearly overhead; " without blind radar-controlled fire, many unopposed attacks would have been made." The bombing was accurate, from a height of 16,000 ft., and three ships had narrow escapes. Shallow-diving Ju. 88 aircraft followed at about 1800, as the high-level bombers were finishing. They attacked both screen and convoy from several directions, diving to 5,000 ft. The *Arethusa* and the *Centurion* suffered slightly, and the Australian destroyer *Nestor* was badly holed, all from near misses. Lastly, the Savoia 79s came in on both quarters at about 1900, attacking independently and dropping their torpedoes at long range to no purpose. The two Beaufighters on patrol with the convoy had intercepted four Savoias half an hour earlier and destroyed one. The ships' guns accounted for three Savoias and two bombers.

56

Rear-Admiral Vian answered Admiral Harwood's signal at 1842, during the dive-bombing attack. Exact figures were still impossible to get from the hard-pressed destroyers, but he estimated from their reports that they had under 30 per cent of ammunition left; it was being used fast, and he considered it insufficient for the passage to Malta. This crossed Admiral Harwood's second signal, ordering the four best ships to turn back for Malta with a strengthened escort. When it reached him the Commander-in-Chief decided that he must abandon the attempt; he signalled to the Rear-Admiral at 2053, " Return to Alexandria with your whole force."

The unhappy ending of the enterprise was made worse by the loss of two more ships of the escort. A last attempt from the air at dusk on the 15th did no harm, though bombs fell all round the convoy; but the *Hermione* was torpedoed and sunk in the night, and next morning the damaged *Nestor* had to be scuttled. The *Hermione* was on the starboard quarter of the convoy, which was zigzagging at 13 knots, when at 0127 on the 16th one or perhaps two torpedoes hit her and she sank in twenty minutes; there was no sign of the enemy, which was probably a submarine.[1] The *Nestor*, having been disabled in the dive-bombing attack at about 1800 on the 15th, was taken in tow by the *Javelin* and escorted by three more destroyers. That evening they were twice attacked unsuccessfully by small numbers of aircraft, and on each occasion they shot down one of the enemy. But the *Nestor* yawed badly through being down by the bow, and towing was difficult; at 0430 on the 16th the tow parted for the second time, soon after which a flotilla of E-boats was sighted. The British ships were still more than 200 miles from port, with their position known to the enemy, and they could only crawl through a long summer's day exposed to submarine and air attack, so Commander Rosenthal decided that to go on was to invite the loss of the *Javelin* as well as of his own ship, the *Nestor*, and at 0700 he scuttled her. The other four destroyers overtook the convoy late in the afternoon. Rear-Admiral Vian had had several submarine contacts in the early afternoon (position about 31° 30′ N., 28° E.), but had avoided attack. He arrived at Alexandria in the evening, sending on part of the convoy to Port Said.

57

The Italian fleet arrived at Taranto the same day, having narrowly escaped attack by submarines the previous evening and having suffered one torpedo hit from an aircraft in the night. Captain Ruck-Keene, commander of the First Flotilla, who was directing the submarines under the Commander-in-Chief, gave various orders on the 15th with a view to placing the submarines in the path of the fleet when it should go north again, so far as his scanty information allowed. But signals took so long to get through on that day (sometimes above four hours) that as Lieutenant Mackenzie of the *Thrasher* said, " The only possible course was to remain on the surface, and by the use of reports of the enemy from aircraft and other sources keep on the direct line between him and Taranto." Unfortunately, reports ceased at 1625, the

---

[1] It is now known that it was the German submarine *U.205*.

aircraft then shadowing the Italians being apparently shot down after making one signal, while its relief was chased and engaged by German aircraft on the way out from Egypt, and it did not find the Italian fleet. The small and slow submarines of the Tenth Flotilla were far to the westward of the Italians' return route—they had had their chance in the morning. So was the *Thorn*, which had then tried to intercept the enemy; but she did her best by going north at full speed in the hope of reaching ahead of the fleet next morning. The other four large ships of the First Flotilla, " all bristling with torpedoes ", as Lieutenant Bennington, the captain of the *Porpoise*, put it, made their way towards the enemy; and with a little more information they should have been able to attack. The *Thrasher* actually sighted the three Italian cruisers at sunset. The *Porpoise*, farther south, very likely missed seeing them only through being forced to dive by their escorting aircraft.

The *Porpoise* was well placed originally, for her position on the patrol line was the easternmost of all, and she had stayed near her station all the morning. Lieutenant Bennington shared Lieutenant Mackenzie's opinion that to stay on the surface was essential in order to ensure receiving all reports made and to be made ready to act on them at once.[1] " The all-important factor was to avoid being left in a position through which the enemy would pass in dark hours." At 1535, receiving the air report of the Italians' turn-back north-westward, he steered away at full speed to the southward to meet them. At 1935 he had to dive and go deep on sighting an aircraft which bombed him; it is most probable that the enemy passed him unseen at that time. The *Thrasher* had tried to intercept the Italian fleet on its way south in the morning. Working eastward again, she crossed ahead of its track on return at 2000, as Lieutenant Mackenzie thought, and he stood on some miles, hoping to put the enemy against the lighter sky to the westward. Then he too had to dive to avoid being seen by a patrolling aircraft. At 2038 he sighted through the periscope the masts and funnel-tops of three large ships nine or ten miles south-eastward, and closed to attack; but the enemy passed seven miles off about twenty minutes later.

There was still a chance of striking at the enemy from the air, and Malta sent out a reconnaissance aircraft and five torpedo Wellingtons that night. The reconnaissance aircraft found the Italian fleet at 2255—six and a half hours since the last air sighting report. The Wellingtons sighted the battleship division an hour later, but were baffled by the enemy's smoke screen. One aircraft persisted, however, and at 0040 on the 16th hit the *Littorio* forward with one torpedo. Thus the Italians lost a cruiser in the operation and had a battleship twice hit and put out of action for several months. Had the Allied submarines and aircraft really disabled the Italian fleet, it would have made all the difference to future operations for supplying Malta that summer. Later convoys would have been spared the diversion of course to avoid the surface threat, which added so much to the difficulty of fighting the way past Cyrenaica under air attack. As it was, no further convoy from Egypt sailed for Malta till November, and by then the German and Italian forces were in full retreat out of Libya.

In this unsuccessful Operation " Vigorous " a cruiser, three destroyers and two merchant ships were lost, and three cruisers, the special service ship *Centurion*, a corvette and two merchantmen were damaged. The Royal Air Force suffered considerable losses of fighter aircraft, though the fighters prevented several attempts upon the convoy and destroyed a number of

---

[1] A signal from Captain Ruck-Keene, timed 1315, ordered all submarines to remain on the surface, but it did not reach any of them till after 1700.

enemy aircraft. The ships shot down 21 out of some 220 aircraft that attacked them during the operation.

" Events proved with painful clarity," wrote Admiral Harwood, " that our air striking force had nothing like the weight required to stop a fast and powerful enemy force, and in no way compensated for our lack of heavy ships." [1]

---

[1] Commander-in-Chief, Mediterranean, report in M.013471/42.

CHAPTER VII

Operation "Pedestal", August 1942

58

OPERATION " PEDESTAL " was the culmination of the series of convoys to Malta. On its success or failure the fate of Malta may well have hinged. Both sides fully appreciated its importance, and both sides put all their previous experience into their offensive or defensive efforts. Probably no convoy in history has ever been subjected to such a scale and diversity of attack. In the event, though sorely mauled, sufficient ships got through to Malta to tide the island over until the great events of the autumn finally brought relief. But it was a near thing, and had the Italians used their surface forces as they had originally intended, they might well have prevented a single merchant ship from getting through.

For these reasons, this operation will be dealt with in greater detail than those previously described.

Strategically, the position in the Mediterranean was more difficult than at any other time. It was indeed the darkest hour before the dawn—though at the time few would have predicted how soon the dawn would come. In North Africa Field-Marshal Rommel's May offensive had brought the German and Italian forces as far as El Alamein—only 90 miles from Alexandria—by the beginning of July. There he was held. Fierce fighting throughout July, with local gains and losses on both sides, was followed by siege warfare which continued for some weeks in August. With all the Libyan airfields in the hands of the enemy and the powerful Italian fleet based on Taranto, the eastern Mediterranean route to Malta was practically closed to the Allies.

Meanwhile, Malta's situation as regards supplies was critical. After the " Harpoon "–" Vigorous " operations the Commander-in-Chief, Mediterranean, though fully appreciating the gravity of the situation, was doubtful whether it was worth even attempting to run in another convoy.[1] The question really was whether the island could hold out on the supplies brought by the two survivors of " Harpoon " until another convoy could be run from the west during the next moonless period. At home, owing to the partial failure of the last three convoys, there was general depression. The Governor of Malta, Field-Marshal Lord Gort, v.c., however, took a more cheerful view.[2] He reported on 20th June that the unloading of the two " Harpoon " ships was almost completed, and that he was actively examining how best to eke out Malta's supplies till late in September.

<h3 style="text-align:center">59</h3>

Under these difficult conditions the decision was taken to make another attempt from the west in August. No time was lost in commencing preparations. Acting Vice-Admiral Syfret, then on his way home after his successful occupation of Diego Suarez (in May), was chosen to command the operation and was ordered to disembark at Takoradi and fly to the United Kingdom. Accompanied by his S.O.O., he arrived home on 13th July and meetings between himself, the two flag officers who were to take part in the operation— Rear-Admirals Lyster, R.A.(A), Home Fleet, and Burrough, R.A. 10th C.S.— and the Naval Staff were at once started at the Admiralty, at which the details were carefully planned.[3]

Operation " Pedestal " was " Harpoon " over again on a larger scale, but without the corresponding operation from Egypt. The principal feature of the operation was the increased strength of carrier-borne air protection for the convoy. There were three " Fleet " carriers—the *Victorious* (flag, Rear-Admiral Lyster), *Indomitable* and *Eagle*—each with her attendant cruiser for anti-aircraft defence, and altogether 72 fighter aircraft—Hurricanes, Martlets and Fulmars—and 28 Albacores.

The full escort consisted of Force " Z ", comprising two battleships, the *Nelson* (flag, Vice-Admiral Syfret) and *Rodney*, the three carriers, three cruisers, *Sirius*, *Phoebe* and *Charybdis*, and twelve destroyers; and Force " X ", comprising three cruisers, *Nigeria* (flag, Rear-Admiral Burrough), *Kenya* and *Manchester*, the A.A. ship *Cairo* and twelve destroyers.[4]

On arrival at Skerki Bank at dusk on D3, the main force was as usual to withdraw to the westward, while Rear-Admiral Burrough with three cruisers, the *Cairo* and twelve destroyers (Force " X ") proceeded through the Sicilian Narrows as far as the approaches to Malta, where he would meet the Malta minesweeping flotilla, which would sweep the convoy into harbour. An ocean tug was to have accompanied the convoy (an innovation due to the experiences of operation " Harpoon "); but, as things turned out, she was diverted early in the operation to assist a damaged ship (the *Eagle*) and had not sufficient speed to catch up again. There was the usual provision for fuelling the escort during the passage: two fleet oilers and a tug with their own escort of

---

[1] Commander-in-Chief, Mediterranean, to Prime Minister, 18th June 1942 (P.M.'s files).
[2] Colonel Hollis to General Ismay, 20th June 1942 (P.M.'s files).
[3] The planning of this operation was considered far better than that of any of its predecessors, because it was started earlier and was done more thoroughly, and because the resources and facilities at the Admiralty were placed at the disposal of the Flag Officer concerned. After the operation was over a small Committee was set up at the Admiralty to consider whether any improvements in the planning arrangements for future operations of this sort could be made. Extracts from the report of this Committee which are considered of permanent value will be found in Appendix L. The whole report is contained in Record Office Case War History 8268.
[4] See Appendix K.

corvettes, known as Force " R ". There were also eight spare destroyers, additional to the main escort; they were used to strengthen force " R " whilst it cruised alone on its rendezvous, for other incidental duties, and to screen the *Furious*, which had to be included in the operation at a late stage in the planning, on her return to Gibraltar after carrying out a special service. This (Operation " Bellows ") consisted of flying off 36 spitfires to Malta, as it was realized that those already in the island would be quite inadequate to cover the convoy for the last stage of its voyage.

Another subsidiary operation (Operation " Ascendant ") was planned to take place under cover of the main operation—the passage of the two surviving ships of " Harpoon " which had reached Malta in June back to Gibraltar. Escorted by two destroyers, they sailed on 10th August and arrived safely on the 14th, undisturbed by the enemy.

Eight submarines took part in the operation. Two carried out normal diving patrols north of Sicily, one off Palermo, the other off Milazzo, farther east. The other six were given alternative patrol lines south of Pantellaria, one of which they were to take up at dawn on 13th August, according to the movements of enemy surface ships that might threaten the convoy from the westward. When the convoy had passed the patrol line, which it should have done by that time, the submarines were to proceed on the surface parallel to the convoy as a screen, as had been intended in Operation " Vigorous," and to dive away clear of the convoy at noon. It was expressly intended that they should be seen on the surface and reported by enemy aircraft in order to deter enemy ships from attacking the convoy. " Therefore," ran the order, " the line is to be maintained so far as air activity allows; but submarines have complete freedom of action on sighting any enemy ships, and should endeavour to attack cruisers or battleships." Actually, though Italian cruisers and destroyers put to sea from Cagliari and other ports, they did not come south of Sicily; and as soon as it was evident that the enemy could not reach the convoy the submarines were ordered to dive and retire, " thus concluding," said one of them, " two hours very intense hide-and-seek " with enemy aircraft. These submarines had no other contact with the enemy; but one off the north coast of Sicily torpedoed and severely damaged two Italian cruisers near Stromboli in the morning of 13th August.[1]

The Royal Air Force at Malta under Air Vice-Marshal Sir Keith Park was cast for an important part.[2] The strong torpedo striking force was kept in readiness to deal with a possible attack by the heavy ships from Taranto after the convoy had passed the Narrows. Attack by cruisers stationed at Cagliari, Naples and Messina had also to be considered; and it was anticipated—as turned out to be the case—that the enemy would strengthen his air forces in Sardinia, Pantellaria and Sicily. It was decided to use all the air striking forces of the island (except torpedo aircraft) to minimise this latter threat, and the plan eventually worked out defined the role of the air forces as:—

(*a*) to locate, report and shadow all enemy surface forces, in order to warn the convoy and escort;

(*b*) to protect " Pedestal " from air-borne attack;

(*c*) to destroy enemy surface forces which might jeopardise the safe passage of " Pedestal ";

[1] See Plan 14 for the positions of the submarines on patrol.
[2] The air forces at Malta were strongly reinforced from the United Kingdom and Egypt. The maximum numbers of aircraft serviceable at any one time during the operation were 100 Spitfires, 36 Beaufighters, 30 Beauforts, 3 Wellingtons, 2 Liberators, 2 Baltimores, 3 F.A.A. Albacores and Swordfish. In addition reconnaissance aircraft consisted of 5 Baltimores, 6 P.R.U. Spitfires, and 5 Wellington VIIIs.

(*d*) to dislocate the enemy's air forces on the ground, by means of low-flying attacks by Beaufighters, night bombing attacks on Sardinia by R.A.F. Liberators based on Malta, and by large scale night bombing attacks by U.S. Liberators based on the Middle East.

How these arrangements worked out will emerge in the course of the narrative, but it may be mentioned here that an attack on two stations near Cagliari in the night of the 11th/12th August proved particularly useful; according to the Italian report, six aircraft were destroyed on the ground and others put out of action—whilst the wakeful night (" notte de veglia ") passed by the aircrews handicapped them in their action against the convoy next day.[1]

In the eastern Mediterranean, the fleet carried out a diversion as another aid to the safe passage of the convoy from the westward. Though it was not possible to send supplies to Malta from Egypt at this time, Admiral Harwood sent a dummy convoy—M.W.12—to sea " with the object of preventing the enemy's directing the full weight of surface and air forces against the convoy being run from Gibraltar." Three cruisers and ten destroyers with three merchant ships sailed from Port Said in the evening of 10th August, and Rear-Admiral Vian with two cruisers, five destroyers, and one merchant ship sailed from Haifa next morning. The two forces joined that day, proceeded in company as far west as the longitude of Alexandria, where they arrived at dusk, the 11th, and then turned back, dispersing during the night. At the same time, to profit by possible movements of the Italian fleet, one submarine was stationed off Navarino, where the Italians had three cruisers, and two more were ordered to a position 100 miles west-south-west of Crete, where the dummy convoy should have arrived in the afternoon of the 13th, had it gone on. But the Italians stayed in harbour. "The only point of interest in this little operation," remarked Admiral Harwood, " was that considerable disappointment was expressed by the merchant ships taking part, when they found they were not going through to Malta."

Actually, this operation had an important effect on the fortunes of the convoy, since according to the Italian official history it was partly anxiety about this diversion which caused the enemy to call off a projected attack by a strong cruiser force, which would have found " Pedestal " in a state of considerable disorganisation after serious losses by air and E-boat attack the night before.

60

Operation " Pedestal " may be said to have started with the arrival of Vice-Admiral Syfret at Scapa Flow, where he joined the *Nelson* on 27th July. Most of the ships taking part were assembled there, and on the 29th he held a conference with the Flag and Commanding Officers concerned, at which the orders for the operation were gone through in detail.

On 31st July Rear-Admiral Lyster in the *Victorious*, with the *Argus*,[2] *Sirius* and four destroyers sailed to rendezvous with the *Eagle* and *Charybdis* from Gibraltar and the *Indomitable* and *Phoebe* from Freetown for exercises in the Atlantic (Operation " Berserk ") before joining Admiral Syfret's force west of

---

[1] N.I.D. 06680/44. In addition to the air attacks on Italian airfields, a party was landed from the submarine *Una* to raid Catania airfield in the night of 11–12th August; but the attempt was unsuccessful. (Mediterranean War Diary and M.052185/42).

[2] The *Argus* took part in Operation " Berserk," but then went to Gibraltar and had no share in the main operation.

the Strait of Gibraltar. Of this operation Admiral Syfret subsequently wrote that it was " of the utmost benefit in exercising fighter direction and co-operation between the three carriers."

Admiral Syfret himself left Scapa in the *Nelson* with the *Rodney* and six destroyers in the afternoon of 2nd August, and was joined next morning by the convoy—fourteen merchant ships, known as W.S. 21.S—escorted by the *Nigeria* (flag, Rear-Admiral Burrough), *Kenya* and destroyers which had sailed from the Clyde during the night. Just prior to sailing, but after the " normal " convoy conference, Admiral Burrough had held a meeting in his flagship with the masters of the merchant ships, at which the whole plan was explained to them in detail. A meeting with their radio operators was also held and all details regarding fleet communications and procedure were fully explained. " These two meetings were invaluable."[1]

The passage of the convoy from the United Kingdom to the rendezvous with the carriers west of the Strait of Gibraltar passed without incident, apart from many U-boat alarms. The convoy was repeatedly exercised in emergency turns and in changing from one cruising disposition to another, using both flags and short range wireless. The risk to security in breaking W/T silence was accepted and " as a result of these exercises the convoy attained an efficiency in manœuvring comparable to a fleet unit."[2]

On 7th August the *Manchester* with the *Furious*, which owing to technical difficulties in connection with her aircraft had been delayed in sailing from the Clyde, joined Admiral Syfret's flag; and the next day Admiral Lyster's carrier force also joined, except the *Indomitable* and screen, which had been detached to Gibraltar for fuel. She joined on the 9th, and that afternoon dummy air attacks were carried out on the force, which proved to be of the utmost benefit for exercising the radar reporting and fighter-direction organisation. The " attacks " were followed by a fly-past for identification purposes, which was of great value in giving everyone an opportunity for studying the characteristics and marking of the F.A.A. aircraft.[3] It is believed that this was the first occasion on which as many as five of H.M. aircraft carriers operated in company at sea simultaneously.

61

Convoy W.S.21.S. entered the Strait of Gibraltar in dense fog in the early hours of 10th August. The fog cleared at 0500[4] and by 0800 the convoy was clear of the Strait and making to the eastward at 13½ knots. This was the time appointed for the master of each merchant ship to open an envelope which had been handed to him before leaving the Clyde and which contained a personal message of good cheer signed by the First Lord of the Admiralty. Admiral Syfret subsequently remarked that this act of courtesy and encouragement was very highly appreciated.

Since 5th August various ships of the escort had been sent into Gibraltar to fuel during the nights, the last of them going there while passing through the Strait.[5] These ships rejoined the convoy at intervals during 10th August,

[1] Vice-Admiral Syfret's report (in R.O. Case W.H.S. 8268).
[2] Idem.
[3] These exercises, of course, entailed "a great volume of W/T and R/T traffic, which must have been very apparent to enemy or enemy-controlled listening stations. This risk to security was considered acceptable when balanced against the benefit to be derived from the practices."— Vice-Admiral Syfret's report.
[4] Zone Time minus 2 is used throughout this chapter.
[5] This inevitably gave warning to the enemy, but owing to the fog the first definite report reached the Italians from a passenger aircraft which sighted the British force in the afternoon of 10th August.

the last two destroyers arriving at 1600.[1]

At 0645, 11th August, there commenced an elaborate fuelling programme from Force " R ", which was finished by 2030 that evening, when " thanks very largely to the extreme efficiency "[2] shown by R.F.A.s *Dingledale* and *Brown Ranger*, three cruisers and 26 destroyers had completed with fuel. This evolution was helped by the weather, which was calm with a light easterly breeze.

German reconnaissance aircraft started shadowing soon after daylight, and thereafter they or Italian aircraft kept the convoy under continuous observation, despite the efforts of the fighters from the carriers. But the speed and the height of the Ju. 88s made the fighters' task a hopeless one. " It will be a happy day," wrote Admiral Syfret, " when the Fleet is equipped with modern fighter aircraft." There were also a large number of sightings and reports of torpedoes and U-boats in the course of the day, " a proportion of which may well have been actualities."[3] At noon, 11th August, the convoy was about 75 miles south of Majorca, zigzagging on a mean course 090°, and shortly afterwards the *Furious* (Captain Bulteel) hauled out on the port quarter and at 1229 started flying off her Spitfires to Malta from a position 584 miles from the island. After two flights of eight Spitfires had been flown off, the programme was rudely interrupted.

The convoy was in four columns at the time, on the starboard leg of the zigzag, with the heavy ships stationed close round it and a destroyer screen ahead; there were only 13 ships in the screen, however, the rest being engaged in screening the *Furious* or with Force " R " several miles away. Suddenly, without warning, at 1315 the *Eagle* (Captain Mackintosh)—on the starboard quarter of the convoy—was hit by four torpedoes from the German submarine *U.73*, which had dived through the screen and convoy columns undetected. All four torpedoes hit her port side within about 10 seconds; she heeled over sharply to port and sank in eight minutes.[4] The *Laforey* and *Lookout*, which were screening the *Furious*, were at once ordered to her assistance and with the tug *Jaunty* picked up 927 of her ship's company, including Captain Mackintosh.

This was a severe blow. Not only was the Royal Navy deprived of a well-tried and valuable carrier, but Admiral Syfret's force was bereft of 25 per cent of its fighter strength. Four of her aircraft then on patrol were subsequently landed on the other carriers.

After this unfortunate occurrence, the *Furious* completed operation " Bellows, " flying off the remainder of the Spitfires by 1450. In all 38 were flown off; one developed a defect and landed on the *Indomitable*, and the remaining 37 arrived safely at Malta.[5] In the evening the *Furious* was detached to Gibraltar, escorted by a division of spare destroyers which had joined the force during the

---

[1] Except the *Wrestler*, which was detained by defects. Her place was later filled by the *Amazon*, by direction of the Flag Officer, North Atlantic, at Gibraltar.

[2] Vice-Admiral Syfret's report. The Vice-Admiral remarked, " In previous operations it has not been necessary to provide for so large an oiling programme since ships going to Malta have been able to fuel there. In this case Malta had no oil to spare. The problem of oiling 3 cruisers and 26 destroyers at sea, under enemy observation and in U-boat-infested waters was an anxious one, failure of which could have seriously upset the whole plan."

[3] Vice-Admiral Syfret's report.

[4] Lat. 38° 05' N., Long. 3° 02' E.

[5] Admiral Syfret in his report stated that he was informed later in the day by Vice-Admiral, Malta, that 36 only had arrived, but the Vice-Admiral, Malta, writing on 26th August, gave 37 as the number.

afternoon. The passage was fortunate, for at 0100, 12th August, the *Wolverine* (Lieut.-Commander Gretton) rammed and sank the Italian submarine *Dagabur* in 37° 18′ N., 1° 55′ E.

Late in the afternoon of the 11th Admiral Syfret received warning from the Flag Officer, North Atlantic, that aircraft might attack the convoy at dusk, so he extended the destroyers to form an all-round screen. All this time the force was being shadowed by three or more aircraft and our fighters were kept extremely busy. At 2030 radar indicated that the attack was imminent, and not many minutes later reports of enemy aircraft were received from the screen. The last destroyers to oil opportunely rejoined at this time, thus bringing the force to full strength.

The attack began at 2056, a quarter of an hour after sunset. The enemy were 36 German bombers and torpedo aircraft, Junkers 88 and Heinkel 110, most of which attacked the convoy, while a few went on to attack Force " R " to the southward. The Junkers arrived first, diving down from 8,000 ft. to 2,000–3,000 ft. to drop their bombs, and subsequently claiming hits on an aircraft carrier and a merchantman; the Heinkels also claimed to have torpedoed a cruiser, but in fact no ship was touched. On the other hand, the ships shot down three bombers, one of which fell to the tug *Jaunty* (Lieut.-Commander Osburn, R.N.R.), then on her way to Force " R." Admiral Syfret described the barrage put up as " most spectacular." The attack lasted till about 2130; just before the end the *Quentin* confirmed an asdic contact and carried out three depth charge attacks. The British fighters which were up were unable to find the enemy in the failing light. They had to land on after dark, and in doing so some were fired on by our own ships.

No further incidents occurred during the night and the force continued its voyage unmolested. But dawn would find it within 150 miles of Cagliari; the whole day would be spent well within fighter-escorted range of the Sardinian airfields, and air attack on a very heavy scale was certain. There we will leave it for the present, and see how the enemy proposed to deal with the situation.

62

The first news of the " Pedestal " forces to reach the Italian Naval Staff had come from Ceuta early in the morning of 9th August. Definite confirmation of their having entered the Mediterranean, however, did not reach them till the afternoon of the 10th. The presence of the three carriers together with the battleships indicated a determination to fight the convoy through in the teeth of the heavy air attacks to be expected from Sardinia, and surface attack by their own main naval forces, should they be employed in the Western Mediterranean.

Previous experience enabled them to forecast the plan with considerable accuracy. They expected the heavy ships and carriers to turn to the westward on reaching the Sicilian Narrows, leaving a strong force of cruisers and destroyers to see the convoy through the remainder of the passage. They estimated that Cape Bon would be passed late in the afternoon of 12th August and Pantellaria during hours of darkness. There was no indication as yet that a complementary convoy from the eastern Mediterranean was contemplated, as in June.

Their plan followed much the same lines as that employed against "Halberd." Special air reconnaissance in the Western Mediterranean was arranged in collaboration with the German Air Force for 11th and 12th August. Submarines, of which there were available 18 Italian and two German, were disposed in five areas at intervals along the estimated convoy track from south of the Balearics to just west of Malta.[1] Twenty-three motor torpedo boats (five of them German) were stationed off Cape Bon, Pantellaria and south of Marittimo; and a destroyer was detailed to augment the minefields in the Narrows during the night of the 12th.

As regards surface forces, an acute oil fuel shortage prohibited the use of their battleships. On the assumption that the convoy would be accompanied through the Sicilian narrows by stronger forces than in June, but without battleships, it was arranged that the 3rd division—the 8-inch cruisers *Gorizia*, *Bolzano* and *Trieste*—and the 7th division—the 6-inch cruisers *Savoia*, *Montecuccoli* and *Attendolo*—with 11 destroyers should rendezvous about 100 miles north of Marittimo in the evening of 12th August, and intercept the convoy in the region of Pantellaria in the morning of the 13th; but this was subject to effective fighter protection being available in view of the increased number of aircraft in Malta. Any convoy from Egypt was to be dealt with by the 8th division (three 6-inch cruisers), based at Navarino. Some modifications were made to these plans during 12th August, especially as a result of a report which came in that morning of Admiral Harwood's dummy convoy.

So much for the naval part of the Axis plan. But their great effort was to come from the air. For this purpose they had concentrated about six hundred aircraft, bombers and fighters, on the Sardinian and Sicilian airfields of which about 200[2] were German, specially reinforced for the occasion from Crete and North Africa. The main attacks, which were carefully co-ordinated, were naturally planned for 12th August, when the convoy would be passing to the southward of Sardinia and fighter protection could be given to the bombers all day.

63

To return to the British forces: at first light[3], 12th August, radar reports of enemy shadowing aircraft began to come in and all ships went to the first degree of readiness for H.A. and L.A. guns. Twelve fighters were flown off at 0610, and this number was maintained in the air throughout the day, being reinforced when necessary. From then onwards " there were few moments " —to quote Admiral Syfret—" when neither aircraft, submarines, torpedoes nor asdic contacts were being reported."

The first air attack of the day took place at about 0915. Some twenty or more Ju. 88s, approaching out of the sun ahead, were intercepted by fighters 25 miles off. Only a dozen got through to the convoy, making high-level or shallow dive-bombing attacks individually without result. Eight Germans were believed to be shot down by fighters, who had also shot down three shadowers before the attack, and two by the ships' guns. All this time, too, there were submarine alarms. Destroyers dropped depth charges on obtaining asdic contacts and probably foiled attempts during the air attack and again at about 1130.

But the enemy's great effort from the Sardinian airfields came at midday, the 12th. It was to be a combined attack by some 70 aircraft, heavily escorted

---

[1] See Plan 14.

[2] Discrepancies as to these numbers occur in the German and Italian accounts, ranging from 480 as given by the German Admiral Weichold to 784 as given in the Italian Official Naval History. After examining various sources the British Air Ministry Historical Branch came to the conclusion that the probable numbers were:—*Bombers*, 334 (148 German, 186 Italian): *Fighters*, 273 (72 German, 201 Italian)—a total of 607 aircraft. Of these 90 were torpedo-bombers. These figures take no account of a force earmarked to bomb Malta, reconnaissance, escort and transport aircraft, rescue planes, etc.

[3] Sunrise 0653, Zone minus 2: beginning of Civil Twilight (sun 6° below horizon), 0615.

by fighters, carried out in stages and employing new methods. First, ten Italian torpedo-bombers were each to drop a " motobomba FF " (apparently a circling torpedo or mine, used for the first time in this attack) a few hundred yards ahead of the British force, while eight fighter-bombers made dive-bombing and machine-gun attacks; and the object at this stage was to dislocate the formation of the force and to draw anti-aircraft fire, making the ships more vulnerable to a torpedo attack, which was to follow in five minutes, though the Italians hoped also that the " motobomba " would do underwater damage—indeed, they claimed mistakenly to have sunk a merchant ship. The torpedo aircraft, 42 all told, were to attack in two groups, one on either bow of the convoy. The next stage was a shallow dive-bombing attack by German aircraft, after which two Reggiane 2001 fighters, each with a single heavy armour-piercing bomb, were to dive-bomb one of the aircraft carriers, whilst yet another new form of attack was to be employed against the other carrier, but defects in the weapon prevented this last attack from taking place.[1]

The enemy's plan was carried out in the main, though the normal torpedo attack was made half an hour instead of five minutes after the special mines had been dropped. British fighters met the minelaying aircraft, and shot down one of them as they approached; the other nine dropped their mines at 1215 in the path of the force, which turned at right-angles to avoid the danger, and heard the mines exploding harmlessly some minutes later. Only three of the fighter-bombers at this stage of the attack appear to have reached as far as the screen, but the *Lightning* (Commander Walters) had a narrow escape from their bombs. The torpedo aircraft arrived at 1245, likewise reduced from their original strength to 25 or 30, some being destroyed and others driven off by the British fighters. They attacked the convoy from the port bow, port beam, and starboard quarter, but dropped their torpedoes well outside the screen, 8,000 yards from the merchant ships they had been ordered to make their targets; the force turned 45° to port and back to starboard to avoid the attack, and the *Rodney* (Captain Rivett-Carnac), on the port quarter of the convoy, joined her 16-inch guns to the barrage fire with which the enemy were received. In the next stage, the German bombing attack, the enemy scored their one success. These aircraft, too, were intercepted on their way in; but about 12 out of perhaps 20 persevered, and, crossing the convoy from starboard to port, they dived to 3,000 ft. and damaged the *Deucalion*, leading the port wing column, while bombs fell close to several other ships. This was at 1318. Finally, at 1345, the two Reggiane fighters approached the *Victorious* (Captain Bovell), flagship of Rear-Admiral Lyster, " as if to land on." They looked like Hurricanes, and the ship was engaged in landing on fighters of her own; they dropped their bombs, one of which hit the flight deck amidships, fortunately breaking up without exploding; they then made off out of range before the *Victorious* could open fire. Altogether, nine enemy aircraft were credited to fighters in these attacks, and two to ships' fire.

The *Deucalion*, unable to keep up with the convoy was ordered to follow the inshore route along the Tunisian coast accompanied by the *Bramham* (Lieutenant Baines). Two bombers found these ships late in the afternoon, but their bombs missed. At 1940, however, near the Cani Rocks, two torpedo aircraft attacked; and a torpedo hitting the *Deucalion*, she caught fire and eventually blew up.

The convoy, passing some 20 miles north of Galita Island, spent the afternoon avoiding submarines, which were known to be concentrated in these waters. There were " innumerable reports " of sightings and asdic contacts, said

---

[1] This account of the Italian plan comes from N.I.D.06680/44; but the Italian report does not mention the attack by German bombers that followed the torpedo attack.

Vice-Admiral Syfret, and at least two submarines proved dangerous. At 1616 the *Pathfinder* (Commander Gibbs) and *Zetland* (Lieutenant Wilkinson) attacked one on the port bow, and hunted her till the convoy was out of her reach. The *Ithuriel* (Lieut.-Commander Maitland-Makgill-Crichton) stationed on the quarter, then attacked, brought the enemy to the surface, and finally rammed her; she proved to be the Italian submarine *Cobalto*. Meanwhile the *Tartar*, on the starboard quarter, saw six torpedoes[1] fired at close range at 1640, and the next ship in the screen, the *Lookout* (Commander Brown), sighted a periscope; together they attacked the submarine, continuing until she was no longer dangerous, but without gaining definite evidence of success. The Vice-Admiral commended " the constant anti-submarine vigilance " shown by the destroyers throughout the operation. " It is true," he wrote, " that the submarine which sank H.M.S. *Eagle* was undetected, but I am very sure that their watchfulness foiled many another attack." And as an illustration of the value of their work he remarked that the convoy made forty-eight emergency turns during the 10–12th August in consequence of warnings of submarines given by the screen.

At 1750, on her way to rejoin after sinking the *Cobalto*, the *Ithuriel* was unsuccessfully attacked by a few dive-bombers when a dozen miles astern of the convoy. This attack may have been made as a last attempt by the air forces in Sardinia or by part of the force from Sicily, which was then gathering to attack the convoy and with which the British fighters were already in touch. This force numbered nearly 100 aircraft—Ju. 87 and Ju. 88 bombers and S.79 torpedo aircraft, with a strong escort of fighters.[2] The enemy arrived at 1835, the bombers attacking both from ahead and astern (the direction of the sun), while the torpedo aircraft came from ahead to attack on the starboard bow and beam of the convoy. Vice-Admiral Syfret called their timing excellent, the result of careful position-taking as they approached the convoy; many aircraft must have waited some 25 miles away for nearly an hour before the moment came to fly in. As at midday, the Savoias dropped their torpedoes about 3,000 yards outside the screen, and once again the convoy was turned away to avoid them; but this time the destroyer *Foresight* (Lieut.-Commander Fell) was hit and disabled. The bombers made their chief effort against the *Indomitable* (Captain Troubridge), which was astern of the *Rodney* on the port quarter of the convoy. Four Ju. 88s and eight Ju. 87s, " appearing suddenly from up sun out of the smoky blue sky," said Captain Troubridge, dived steeply on the *Indomitable* from astern, some of the Ju. 87s coming down to 1,000 ft.; the carrier received three hits, her flight deck was put out of action, and her fighters had to return to the *Victorious*. Captain Frend of the *Phoebe*, astern of the *Indomitable*, said that his attention was mainly directed to the Savoias on the starboard bow, which appeared to be working aft, when the Junkers came down from 9,000 ft. almost overhead out of the shell-bursts to attack the carrier he was attending. The *Rodney* also had a narrow escape from a bomber that attacked her from ahead a few minutes before the attack on the *Indomitable*. The ships shot down one enemy aircraft; and the twenty or so Hurricanes, Martlets and Fulmars in the air destroyed seven more, though the enemy's fighters were probably twice as numerous as the British.

Altogether, the 60 British fighters available since the loss of the *Eagle* claimed 39 enemy aircraft of all sorts, at a cost of 13 British aircraft, whilst on 11th and 12th August the ships shot down nine of the enemy.[3]

---

[1] According to the Italian report, the submarine *Emo* fired *four* torpedoes at this time. The *Emo* survived the counter-attack.

[2] Vice-Admiral Syfret reported the strength as 12 Ju. 87s, 30 Ju. 88s, and 40 S.79 and other torpedo aircraft, besides fighters. The Italian account in N.I.D.06680/44 mentions only 8 Ju. 87s, 14 S.79s, and 28 fighters.

[3] According to Italian sources only 17 aircraft were lost on 12th August. Total of aircraft lost throughout the operation is given as 42 (21 German, 21 Italian).

The *Tartar* (Commander St. J. Tyrwhitt) took the damaged *Foresight* in tow and proceeded westward for Gibraltar; but next day, as they were persistently shadowed by enemy aircraft and submarines were about, it was decided to sink the cripple, lest both ships should be lost, and the *Tartar* torpedoed her a few miles from Galita Island.

This last air attack took place about 20 miles west of the Skerki Channel; and at 1900, when it was clearly over, Admiral Syfret turned away with Force " Z " and proceeded to the westward, leaving Rear-Admiral Burrough with Force " X " to take the convoy on.

64

So far, apart from the loss of the *Eagle*, things had gone well. The massed air attacks south of Sardinia had succeeded in damaging only the *Indomitable* and *Foresight*, and the 14 merchant ships, save for the *Deucalion*, were still intact. But an hour after parting from Force " Z " its previous good fortune deserted the convoy. Thrown into disorder by submarine and air attacks, which inflicted serious damage and losses on both convoy and escorts, the straggling ships offered an easy prey later in the night for the motor torpedo boats awaiting them south of Cape Bon. The trouble started with a remarkably effective submarine attack. The convoy was just changing its formation from four into two columns at the entrance to Skerki Channel when at 1956 the *Nigeria* (Captain Paton) and *Cairo* (Captain Hardy)—leading the columns— and the tanker *Ohio* were all damaged by under-water explosions practically simultaneously—whether from mines or torpedoes was not known. Actually, the Italian submarine *Axum* fired four torpedoes, which were responsible for the damage. The *Nigeria* turned back for Gibraltar, escorted by two destroyers (afterwards joined by a third), and Rear-Admiral Burrough shifted his flag to the *Ashanti* (Captain Onslow). The *Cairo*, with her stern blown off, had to be sunk. The *Ohio* struggled on. As all three ships had been damaged on the port side, the convoy, then led by the *Kenya* (Captain Russell) and *Manchester* (Captain Drew), altered course to the southward to avoid the danger, and in the process became " scrummed up " or " a heterogeneous mass "—as naval liaison officers in the merchant ships afterwards described it. Most of the ten destroyers[1] were standing by the damaged ships, and two of the cruisers had gone; most unfortunate of all, these two cruisers were the only ships fitted for fighter direction. The convoy was, moreover, deprived of the leadership of Admiral Burrough, while he was shifting his flag.

In these conditions, while trying to form the two columns previously ordered, the convoy was attacked from the air at 2030, half an hour after its earlier misfortune. Six Beaufighters from Malta were patrolling overhead, but— bereft of fighter direction and, incidentally, frequently fired on by our own ships—they were unable to see much in the growing dusk[2] and soon withdrew to Malta.[3] The enemy had an easy task. About 20 German aircraft, Ju. 88s, made dive-bombing and torpedo attacks, hitting the *Empire Hope* with a bomb and the *Clan Ferguson* and *Brisbane Star* with torpedoes. The first of these ships had to be sunk (by the *Penn*, which rescued her survivors); the second blew up—it was thought with the loss of all hands, but some reached the Tunisian

---

[1] Of the original twelve destroyers the *Bramham* had parted company in the afternoon to escort the *Deucalion*, and the *Foresight* had been disabled.

[2] Sunset was 2016, Zone minus 2: end of Civil Twilight, 2044.

[3] Air Vice-Marshal Park, referring to this incident in his report, remarked, " it is considered essential that as many as possible (up to 100 per cent) of warships should be capable of giving V.H.F. fighter direction." With this opinion Vice-Admiral Leatham, V.A., Malta, concurred. —V.A. Malta's report and enclosure in R.O. Case W.H.S.8269.

coast; the last eventually arrived at Malta. The *Ashanti*, which with the *Penn* had been laying a smoke-screen between the convoy and the light western horizon to prevent the ships being silhouetted, was very narrowly missed by a torpedo. Soon after this attack, at 2111, the *Kenya* was torpedoed by the Italian submarine *Alagi*, which fired four torpedoes at her. She fortunately saw the enemy in time to avoid all of them but one, which hit her on the forefoot; her speed was reduced to 25 knots, but she was able to stay with the convoy.

The situation was then as follows. The *Kenya* and *Manchester*, with two merchant ships and with the minesweeping destroyers *Intrepid*, *Icarus* and *Fury* sweeping ahead, had passed the Skerki Channel and were steering to pass inshore of Zembra Island on the way to Cape Bon. The *Ashanti*, with Admiral Burrough on board, was fast overhauling this main body. The destroyers *Pathfinder*, *Penn* and *Ledbury* were rounding up the remaining nine merchant ships, which, having separated during the air attack, were following along the route spread out over several miles to the north-westward. The *Deucalion* having sunk, the *Bramham* was returning from the vicinity of the Cani Rocks, and the *Nigeria* with the other three destroyers was well to the westward on her way to Gibraltar.

On learning of the fate of the *Nigeria* and *Cairo*, Admiral Syfret had detached the *Charybdis*, *Eskimo* and *Somali* to reinforce Admiral Burrough, but it would take them several hours to catch up with the convoy. " By this time," wrote Admiral Burrough, " the situation was becoming rather critical, as there was still a possibility of the Italian surface forces coming south to attack the convoy at dawn." Four cruisers and six destroyers steering to the southward had in fact been reported by Malta reconnaissance aircraft at 1922, in a position some 90 miles north of Marittimo.

65

The main body of the convoy, led by Admiral Burrough in the *Ashanti*, passed Cape Bon at midnight, 12th/13th August. Forty minutes later E-boats were detected to port, and soon afterwards to starboard, by Type 285 radar. " They used smoke cover and were extremely difficult to engage ";[1] and they took a heavy toll in a series of attacks that lasted until the convoy was well past Kelibia and on the course for Malta. Their first victim was the *Manchester*, torpedoed by two Italian E-boats at 0120, on the 13th, a few miles short of Kelibia. The *Pathfinder* (Commander Gibbs), detached to stand by her, went alongside twenty minutes later and took off about 150 of her ship's company, then rejoined Admiral Burrough in accordance with his orders. Subsequently, Captain Drew decided that the *Manchester* must be abandoned and scuttled.[2] This was done and she sank at 0500; most of the crew, including the captain, reached the shore and were interned by the French; but some were picked up later by destroyers sent to her assistance.

The other ships hit were all stragglers—the *Glenorchy*,[3] *Wairangi*, *Almeria Lykes*, *Rochester Castle* and *Santa Elisa;* they were attacked between 0215 and 0500 to the south-eastward of Kelibia, whilst taking a short cut to overhaul

---

[1] Rear-Admiral Burrough's report, in R.O. Case W.H.S. 8269.
[2] The sinking of the *Manchester* was subsequently the subject of a Court Martial and is dealt with in Naval Staff History, Mediterranean, Vol. II.
[3] The fate of the *Glenorchy* was unknown at the time, but from Italian sources it seems she was torpedoed off Kelibia at 0215, about an hour after the *Manchester*. As in the case of the *Clan Ferguson*, it was feared for some time that there were no survivors, but a telegram from the U.S. Consul at Tunis on 17th August reported that 130 survivors from these two ships were safe in Tunis.

the main body. The *Wairangi* and *Almeria Lykes* were abandoned in a sinking condition, but the *Rochester Castle* survived and, " merrily doing 13 knots ", she caught up the main body about 0530, two hours after being torpedoed. The *Santa Elisa*, the last to be torpedoed (about 0500), was also abandoned, her crew being rescued by the *Penn* and *Bramham*, who arrived on the scene with the *Port Chalmers;* at early dawn she was bombed by a lone Ju. 88 and sank in five minutes. All this damage was the work of about a dozen E-boats, and was inflicted without loss to themselves.

Meanwhile, the *Charybdis* (Captain Voelcker), *Somali* (Commander Currey) and *Eskimo* (Commander le Geyt) had joined Admiral Burrough's flag at 0330, just in time to take part in another running fight with several E-boats. It was in the course of this attack that the *Rochester Castle* was hit; the *Ashanti* was again narrowly missed.

At dawn[1], 13th August, the situation was as follows. In company with Admiral Burrough in the *Ashanti* were H.M. ships *Charybdis, Kenya, Intrepid, Icarus, Fury, Pathfinder, Somali* and *Eskimo* and M.T. ships *Rochester Castle, Waimarama* and *Melbourne Star.* As it became lighter the *Ledbury*, with the *Ohio* in company, was seen about five miles astern, overtaking the convoy rapidly. Some ten miles away to the north-west the *Port Chalmers* with the *Penn* and *Bramham* was in sight; and the *Santa Elisa* could be seen stopped and on fire. The *Dorset* was following alone. Lastly, the *Brisbane Star*, torpedoed the evening before, was hugging the Tunisian coast independently, intending to steer for Malta at nightfall. From signals received during the night the danger of attack by heavy Italian surface forces appeared to have abated. This must have been a relief to Admiral Burrough, for with his reduced escort and scattered charges a resolute attack ought to have had very serious consequences. It will therefore be of interest at this stage to see what the enemy cruisers had been about.

66

The first move of the Italian cruisers to carry out their part in the plan had been the departure of the 7th Division from Cagliari in the evening of the 11th August. As it chanced they were sighted leaving harbour by Beaufighters returning from attacks on neighbouring airfields, and subsequently shadowed while steering easterly in the Tyrrhenian Sea by a Wellington till 0130, 12th, when, having dropped its bombs without effect, it returned to Malta. That forenoon the *Gorizia* and *Bolzano* left Messina and joined the 7th Division and *Trieste*, which had come from the north, at 1900, 12th, at the rendezvous north of Marittimo, setting course to the southward. As already mentioned, they were located soon after this and reported at 1922. When just north of Cape San Vito, orders were received for the 7th Division to proceed to Naples and the 3rd Division to Messina and course was altered to the eastward accordingly.

The reason given in the Italian Official Naval History for this change of plan is that a report of Admiral Vian's force as four cruisers and ten destroyers in the eastern Mediterranean with the diversionary convoy was received from a German submarine, and it was decided that the 8-in. cruisers must reinforce the 6-in. cruisers at Navarino to counter this force. It will be remembered, too, that the attack on " Pedestal " off Pantellaria was subject to air protection for the cruisers being available, and actually there was a shortage of fighters to accompany the bombers for the attacks planned for next day. According to one version, the matter was referred to Mussolini himself, who gave

---

[1] Sunrise 0628, Zone minus 2: Civil Twilight commenced 0601.

precedence to the claims of the aircraft. Probably both considerations had their effect on the Naval Staff in coming to the decision; in any case, it was a welcome one for the British, to whom the cruiser force had become a keen anxiety.

The receipt in Malta of the sighting report at 1922, 12th, had caused no perturbation. In the words of Vice-Admiral Sir Ralph Leatham, " all appeared to be going well with the convoy, and I felt that Force ' X ' would be more than a match for the Italian cruiser force . . . " But before long the picture changed. Reports of the dusk air attack came in, followed by news of the damage to the *Nigeria, Cairo* and *Kenya*, and it became clear that a dawn attack by the Italian cruisers when the convoy was scattered, with its much reduced escort, might well be disastrous. The shadowing aircraft, therefore, was ordered in plain language to illuminate and attack, which it did without causing damage at 0140, 13th August, soon after the cruisers had turned to the eastward. Similar orders were signalled to relief shadowers including an order to report the position for the benefit of imaginary Liberator bombers, lest the Italians should change their minds and turn back.[1]

But they held their easterly course—and ran into trouble. Submarine *P.42* (Lieutenant Mars), which had moved out from her inshore station off Cape Milazzo after being discovered and heavily attacked on 10th August, sighted them a few miles south-westward of Stromboli, steaming about 25 knots. At 0806 she fired her four torpedoes, claiming two hits; she was then attacked by destroyers for more than eight hours, and counted 105 depth charges. She had hit the *Bolzano*, which went north for repairs, and the *Muzio Attendolo*[2] which reached Messina with her bows blown off. The *Gorizia* returned to Messina later in the day and the other cruisers put in to Naples.

67

At 0800, 13th August, just as Lieutenant Mars was having his eminently satisfactory encounter with the Italian cruisers, some two hundred miles to the south-westward Admiral Burrough and the convoy were facing up to the first air attack of the day. About half an hour previously the Rear-Admiral had sent back the *Eskimo* and *Somali* to stand by the *Manchester*[3], of whose sinking he was unaware; he then had left with him the *Kenya* and *Charybdis* and five destroyers, with the merchant ships *Rochester Castle, Waimarama, Melbourne Star* and *Ohio* formed in line ahead, and the *Port Chalmers* and *Dorset* about to rejoin.

The events of the night had delayed the passage, and the force was only a little over 30 miles S.S.E. of Pantellaria, barely within range of the Malta long-range fighters; but the Beaufighters and Spitfires played up magnificently in the fighting which ensued—the latter patrolling above 170 miles from the island[4]—and, despite the serious handicap of lacking fighter direction, inflicted considerable losses on the enemy aircraft, though at times outnumbered by enemy fighters, as was admitted by the Italians.

The attack came in at 0810, when about twelve Ju. 88s made a shallow diving attack, coming down from about 6,000 to 2,000 ft. to drop their bombs. Two dived on the *Waimarama*, making several hits, and she blew up immediately, one of the bombers being destroyed in the explosion. Her next astern, the

---

[1] The torpedo striking force was held back in case the Italian battleships should leave Taranto.
[2] It is not clear why the *Attendolo*, which had been ordered to Naples with the 7th Division, was with the *Bolzano* at this time.
[3] See Section 69 *postea*.
[4] As opposed to 120 miles for which they had planned.

Melbourne Star, could not avoid passing through the flames which immediately blazed up; this she did at full speed and escaped unscathed. The *Ledbury* (Lieutenant-Commander Hill) was ordered to pick up survivors, though it seemed unlikely that there could be any. Skilfully handled, she rescued no fewer than 45 men from the water which, in the words of Admiral Burrough, " must have entailed great gallantry on the part of all concerned as the sea for some distance round was a blazing inferno ".[1]

Soon after this attack the *Port Chalmers* and *Dorset* joined up and the convoy was then formed in two columns. The next attack came at 0925. It was carried out by Stuka dive bombers and described by Admiral Burrough as " of a most determined nature." Diving to 1,500 or 1,000 ft., they concentrated on the *Ohio*, the last ship but one in the starboard column, which received several near misses. One Stuka failed to pull out of his dive and, damaged by the *Ohio's* guns and those of the *Ashanti*, actually hit the side of the ship; but its bombs fell short and did little damage. The *Ohio's* main steering gear was put out of action, however. The *Kenya*, leading the port column, was " near-missed. " The Malta fighters brought down a bomber in this attack, but lost a Spitfire, possibly by the ships' gunfire.

At 1017, and again at 1050, further dive bombing attacks were made, accompanied by Italian aircraft which dropped parachute mines or circling torpedoes ahead and on the flanks of the convoy. In the latter attack, carried out by about 20 bombers (mostly Ju. 88s, with a few Ju. 87s), the *Ohio* suffered again from four or five near misses and her engines were disabled. At the same time the *Rochester Castle* in the other column was near-missed and set on fire but continued with the convoy; and the *Dorset* astern of her was hit and brought to a standstill.

The convoy went on, leaving the *Penn* and *Bramham* with the cripples. They were joined by the *Ledbury*, overtaking with the *Waimarama's* survivors on board, but shortly afterwards, as the result of a signal from the Vice-Admiral, Malta, she proceeded to look for the *Manchester*[2], believed to be moving south along the Tunisian coast.

At 1125 the main body suffered its last air attack. This was a torpedo attack by five S.79s, accompanied by more parachute mine dropping by other aircraft. The torpedoes were dropped at long range and no tracks were observed; but the *Port Chalmers*, which so far had " experienced extraordinary good fortune in just missing the bombs time after time,"[3] had a narrow escape, a torpedo being caught by her paravane.[4]

During these attacks the Beaufighters and Spitfires had been seen to shoot down at least four enemy aircraft in the distance; and at about 1240 the

---

[1] Lieut.-Commander Hill in his report remarked, " I cannot speak too highly of the sheer guts of these men. They were singing and encouraging each other, and as I went through them explaining . . . that I must get the ones nearest the flames first, I received cheerful answers of 'That's all right, Sir. Go and get the other chaps.' The flames were spreading outward all the time . . ." Some time later it was discovered that 23 of the survivors came from the *Melbourne Star.* As she steamed through the flames, those aft—" quite understandably," said Lieut-Commander Hill, who had seen what it looked like—thought their own ship had blown up and jumped over the side.

[2] Actually, it was the *Brisbane Star,* using a peculiar call-sign.

[3] Report by Commander Venables, in R.O. Case W.H.S. 8269.

[4] ". . . The first torpedo passed underneath and the second passed close along the starboard side. Later starboard paravane wire commenced to vibrate violently; ship was stopped and on paravane being hoisted out of water, the torpedo was found fixed firmly along the paravane body, the fins of the torpedo having caught in the guard of the paravane tail. The clump chain forward was unshackled and let go, and the derrick purchase holding paravane was then let go. The torpedo exploded on bottom in 400 fathoms, but the uplift was tremendous, though the ship was clear."—Commander Venables' report.

convoy came within range of the short-range Spitfires, which, flying up to 70 or 80 miles from their base, provided " such excellent protection "[1] that no further attacks against it developed, though large formations were frequently detected coming in, only to be dispersed and driven off.

At 1430, 13th, the Malta escort force—four minesweepers and seven motor launches under Commander Jerome—joined the convoy. He had swept the approach channel in the morning, and then prepared to take over the three merchant vessels remaining in company, sending on the *Rye* and two motor launches to assist the disabled tanker *Ohio*, whose cargo of 12,000 tons of oil was " vital to Malta ".[2] After an exchange of signals with Commander Jerome, Admiral Burrough decided to withdraw to the westward and with his two cruisers and five remaining destroyers parted company at 1600, signalling a rendezvous at which the *Penn*, *Bramham* and *Ledbury* were to rejoin him at 2030 that evening.[3]

68

After the departure of Force " X ", the *Port Chalmers*, *Melbourne Star* and *Rochester Castle*—the last ship " lying very low in the water "—stood on with Commander Jerome, arriving in Grand Harbour two hours or so later, 13th August.

There were still the *Dorset*, *Ohio* and *Brisbane Star*. But the *Dorset* was lost the same evening. After being disabled in the morning, she and the *Ohio* had been lying helpless, with the *Penn* and *Bramham* standing by, the destroyers having found them unmanageable in tow. When the *Rye* arrived at 1730, she and the *Penn* got the *Ohio* in tow, while the *Bramham* remained with the *Dorset*. Then German bombers came again, and the ships were attacked repeatedly till dark; both merchantmen were hit at about 1900 and the *Dorset* sank. Strenuous efforts to tow the *Ohio* throughout the night produced little result.

At daylight, 14th, the *Ledbury* arrived, after a fruitless search in the Gulf of Hammamet for the *Manchester*. She had, however, shot down two Italian torpedo bombers which had attacked her the previous afternoon.[4] Attempts to tow the *Ohio* by the three destroyers and the *Rye*, later directed by Commander Jerome who arrived in the *Speedy*, with two motor launches, continued throughout the forenoon. At 1045 enemy aircraft made their last attack, near-missing the *Ledbury* and causing the tow to part, while protecting Spitfires shot down a bomber and one of the many fighters escorting them. Once again the tow was passed. The slow procession went on, with the *Ohio* becoming ever more unwieldy. At last the endeavours of those tired men were rewarded; in the morning of 15th August the " vital " tanker reached Malta.

" Even though the *Ledbury* was leading her," wrote Admiral Leatham, " the passage of *Ohio* through Tunisian waters at high speed without a compass, with extensive damage to the ship and in hand steering, was a remarkable feat of seamanship and tenacity on the part of Captain Mason and his officers and crew . . . . The towage of this unwieldy ship for a distance of nearly

---

[1] Rear-Admiral Burrough's report.
[2] Signal, Commander Jerome to Rear-Admiral Burrough.
[3] Owing to the urgency of the duty on which they were employed and further directions from the Vice-Admiral, Malta, these three destroyers did not keep the rendezvous.
[4] " Two three-engined Italian bombers approached on the port beam. Four-inch Cease Fire bells were rung in order not to discourage them, and short bursts from Oerlikon and pom-pom shot them both down in flames . . . This success came at a very apt time, as the ship's company were showing signs of great fatigue, and the survivors were, most understandably, jumpy. The whole ship was cheering hard and everything after this went with a swing."—Lieutenant-Commander Hill's report.

100 miles from a position in sight of an Italian island and within easy range of his aerodromes was a feat of seamanship, courage and endurance of the highest order . . .   In particular, the highest praise is due to the Master of the *Ohio*[1] for his courageous handling of the ship until she was immobilised, the Captain of H.M.S. *Penn*, who bore the responsibility during the first desperate day and night, and to Commander M/S, who brought her safely to port through many difficulties."[2]

Meanwhile the *Brisbane Star* had arrived at Malta the day before.   After being torpedoed in the dusk air attack on the 12th, she could not make more than 10 knots.   Rather than saddle Force " X " with a lame duck, Captain Riley decided to leave the convoy and hug the Tunisian coast till off Monastir, striking across to Malta during the night of 13th/14th.   The 13th August was spent fencing with French signal stations and French boarding officers; the latter he handled so firmly and tactfully that they (somewhat reluctantly) allowed the ship to proceed, and were helpful in landing a seriously wounded man for him at Susa.   The *Brisbane Star* shaped course for Malta at dusk, 13th; soon after daylight, 14th, she was twice attacked by single aircraft, one of which was damaged by her gunfire and the other shot down by a Beaufighter.   She reached harbour without further incident at 1530 that afternoon.

69

After leaving the convoy off Malta, Rear-Admiral Burrough with his depleted Force " X " steered to pass 12 miles south of Linosa, and thence for position " R ", about seven miles south of Kelibia.   Led by the *Intrepid*—the only destroyer with a T.S.D. sweep remaining, the others having parted theirs on the outward passage—the force passed through position " R " at 0012, 14th August.   A few minutes later an E-boat was sighted to seaward; the *Kenya* opened fire very promptly and, it was thought, blew her up.[3]

At 0450, near the Fratelli Rocks, the Italian submarine *Granito* fired five torpedoes at the *Ashanti* from the surface, and was nearly rammed by the *Kenya*, next astern of the flagship.

By daylight Force " X " had reached a position S.S.E. of Galita, and soon afterwards the inevitable shadowers appeared, heralding air attacks that began at 0730 and continued till 1315.   German bombers started the business with three attacks by a few Ju. 88s, followed by a severe attack by 30 aircraft —Ju. 88 and Ju. 87—between 1030 and 1050.   An hour later, 15 Savoia high-level bombers attacked, and from then until 1315 the force was vexed by torpedo-carrying Savoias, about 20 aircraft attacking in ones and twos, while others flying very low dropped mines ahead.   Several ships were nearly hit in these attacks, both by bombs and torpedoes, but none was seriously damaged.   Three aircraft were shot down.

After this, Force " X " was left alone.   At 1530 a Catalina flying-boat made contact as A/S escort, and at 1800 Force " X " joined Vice-Admiral Syfret's flag in position 37° 29′ N., 3° 25′ E.

The Vice-Admiral, after parting company with the convoy in the evening of 12th August, had continued to the westward, apparently unobserved by the enemy, till 2300 on the 13th, when, having detached the damaged *Indomitable* with the *Rodney* and five destroyers to Gibraltar, he altered course to the

---

[1] H.M. The King approved the award of the George Cross to Captain D. W. Mason for his conduct on this occasion.
[2] Vice-Admiral Sir R. Leatham's report.
[3] This is not substantiated by Italian sources.

eastward and cruised to the northward of Algiers in order to be in a position to support Force " X " should that prove necessary. After effecting their junction, the two forces headed for Gibraltar, arriving 1800, 15th August.

Most of the remainder of Force " X, " proceeding independently, had already arrived. The *Nigeria*, down about 11 ft. by the head, with the *Derwent*, *Bicester*, *Wilton* and latterly the *Tartar* (after sinking the *Foresight*) had been able to steam from 14 to 16 knots and reached harbour at 0010, 15th. She was fortunate in experiencing calm weather the whole way, and apart from an ineffective attack by three torpedo bombers on the 13th and a couple of submarine alarms, the passage was uneventful. Some hours later the *Eskimo* and *Somali* arrived. After leaving Force " X " in the morning of the 13th to succour the *Manchester*, they fell in with the sinking *Almeria Lykes* and *Wairangi*, whose survivors they picked up from their boats. During the forenoon they recovered about 150 of the *Manchester's* survivors from Carley floats. They were only about half a mile from the coast and were able to see the melancholy spectacle of several hundreds of her ship's company, who had reached the shore, being marched away for internment. They then shaped course for Gibraltar in accordance with their orders, and except for an attack by a single Ju. 88 which narrowly missed the *Somali*, their passage was without incident.

Force " R " (the fuelling force), which had remained cruising in the western basin till it was certain none of Force " X " 's destroyers would require oil arrived back at Gibraltar on the 16th; and the *Penn*, *Ledbury* and *Bramham*, which had put in to Malta after their fine efforts on the *Ohio's* behalf, reached Gibraltar safely on 21st August.

70

Such was Operation " Pedestal ". Five arrivals out of a convoy of fourteen ships with a powerful escort is not a high score, especially at the cost to the escort of an aircraft carrier, a cruiser, an anti-aircraft ship, and a destroyer lost, besides a carrier and two cruisers damaged. But they had to meet attacks by some 240 bombers and 90 torpedo aircraft, all in the space of three days, with the enemy supported by fighters in much greater strength than those which the carriers and Malta could provide; magnificent as the naval and Royal Air Force fighters were, the scales were too heavily weighted. The convoy had also to contend with 20 submarines which had the aid of air reconnaissance, and with minefields and E-boats during the passage at night along the Tunisian coast. Despite the losses, 15,000 tons of fuel and 32,000 tons of general cargo were delivered to Malta.

The spirit in which the operation was carried out appears in Vice-Admiral Syfret's report.

" Tribute has been paid to the personnel of His Majesty's ships; but both officers and men will desire to give first place to the conduct, courage and determination of the masters, officers and men of the merchant ships. The steadfast manner in which these ships pressed on their way to Malta through all attacks, answering every manœuvring order like a well-trained fleet unit, was a most inspiring sight. Many of these fine men and their ships were lost. But the memory of their conduct will remain an inspiration to all who were privileged to sail with them."

CHAPTER VIII

Comment and Reflections

71

THE convoys to Malta in 1941 and 1942 had to face a heavier scale of attack under conditions more favourable to the enemy than was ever before developed in history. The geographical position of Malta—roughly a thousand miles alike from Alexandria and Gibraltar, and within 50 miles of Sicily—conferred on the enemy immeasurable advantage. Whether the convoy came from the east or from the west, it had to pass through waters where the enemy held all the cards.

To recapitulate, the convoys were liable to attack by submarines (of which in 1942 the enemy were always able to dispose at least 20 against them) throughout the length of their routes, which for geographical and other reasons allowed of little variation. In any case, air reconnaissance invariably gave the enemy early intelligence of their movements. The efforts of the U-boats were reinforced by M.T.B.s, based in Crete and Pantellaria, which on more than one occasion were used with considerable effect. The powerful Italian fleet, with its bases situated within a few hundred miles of the convoy routes, was a constant menace. Lack of sea-room and the danger of mines in the Sicilian Narrows made it imprudent for capital ships to accompany the convoys from Gibraltar beyond Skerki Bank, and for the last 250 miles of the passage they had to rely on relatively weak forces of cruisers and destroyers for protection. In the eastern Mediterranean there were no British capital ships during the critical first nine months of 1942. Though no Italian heavy ship ever actually got within sight of a convoy, on two occasions its intervention was sufficient to render abortive operations to replenish Malta from the east, and it was the existence of this fleet " in being " which put an end to such attempts after the failure of operation " Vigorous " in June 1942.

But the chief danger came from the air. Convoys from Gibralter had to spend the last 400 miles (26 hours at 15 knots) of their passage within 150 miles of the Sardinian and Sicilian airfields, exposed to air attack of every variety covered by enemy shore-based fighters. Convoys from Alexandria had to pass through the 300-mile stretch known as " Bomb Alley " between Cyrenaica[1] and Crete, only 180 miles apart, a few hours after putting to sea, and again had to face heavy attack from Tripoli and Sicily as they neared Malta. The fighters to counter these air attacks either had to accompany the convoys in carriers or to come from Malta, where they were urgently needed for the defence of the island itself, or from distant bases in Egypt.

---

[1] Conditions in this area varied with the fighting on shore in North Africa; but during most of the period under consideration, Cyrenaica was in the hands of the enemy.

72

A comparison with the convoys to North Russia[1] is of interest. The weather conditions which in the Arctic imposed such a prolonged and unique strain on ships and crews were of course entirely different; nor were the complications due to perpetual daylight in summer and perpetual darkness in winter present in the Mediterranean. The Arctic passage was about twice as long as the passages to Malta; in each case the routes were severely restricted by land (in the Arctic by ice as well); in each case, too, the convoys were liable to submarine attack throughout their whole voyages, and to a heavy scale of both surface and air attack at a considerable distance from their own bases by forces conveniently placed on the flank of the route. But in the Arctic attacking aircraft had much further to fly to reach their targets, and so lacked the support of the fighter escorts which usually accompanied the enemy striking forces in the Mediteranean. True, the Malta convoys had some air protection, whereas in 1942, except on one occasion, the Arctic convoys had none; but the carrier-borne aircraft were inferior in performance to the enemy's aircraft, and our shore-based fighters from Malta, Libya or Egypt often had to work at their extreme range. It is remarkable that in the circumstances the Fleet Air Arm and Royal Air Force fighters accompanished as much as they did.

As regards heavy surface forces, both the Germans in the Arctic and the Italians[2] in the Mediterranean showed extreme discretion in their employment, and though opportunity offered more than once, they never really pressed home an attack on a convoy; but in both cases (for somewhat different reasons) their potentiality presented the defence with a well-nigh insoluble problem. Their mere existence led to the virtual annihilation of Convoy PQ 17 in the Barents Sea (though they were never within 300 miles of the convoy), and if no comparable disaster occurred in the Mediterranean, it frustrated the attempts to replenish Malta on certainly two occasions.

Two forms of attack not practised against the Arctic convoys had to be met in the Mediterranean, viz. M.T.B.s and minefields laid in the easily mineable waters of the Sicilian Narrows and approaches to Malta.

The Mediterranean convoys enjoyed certain advantages over those in the Arctic. Only ships of 13–15 knots were included, as against the 8–9 knot ships of the latter; the convoys were much smaller and therefore handier; and the comparative shortness of sea time, the generally better weather conditions and absence of the bitter cold and ice left the crews of both merchant ships and escorts fresher when called upon to face attack. But the risks from enemy action—owing mainly to the weight and variety of the attacks which geographical features enabled them to stage at times and places where they would be most effective—were even greater than in the Arctic. Figures not fully qualified by *all* the factors governing them are apt to be misleading; the following percentages are, however, of interest.

In the four operations in 1942 (M.G.I., " Harpoon ", " Vigorous " and " Pedestal ") 35 merchant ships sailed. Of these 45 per cent were sunk on passage, 25 per cent were obliged to turn back,[3] and 30 per cent—more or less damaged—arrived at Malta.[4] During the corresponding period (March–

---

[1] See Naval Staff History, Battle Summary No. 22: *Arctic Convoys*.
[2] The Italian heavy ships laboured under the disadvantage that they had not been trained in night fighting, and they were determined (especially after the Battle of Matapan) to give no opportunity of being brought to action after sunset.
[3] Owing to enemy action.
[4] Of those which arrived at Malta about 30 per cent were destroyed after arrival.

September, 1942), which also happened to be the peak period of the attacks in the Arctic, out of 179 ships which sailed in six convoys to North Russia 29 per cent were sunk on passage, 11 per cent turned back,[1] and 60 per cent duly completed their voyage.[2] Air attack proved most deadly in both theatres, 55 per cent of those sunk being from this cause in the Arctic and 81 per cent in the Mediterranean.   Submarines sank 33 per cent in the Arctic and none in the Mediterranean, the remaining 19 per cent there falling to M.T.B.s. Escorting craft during this period, too, suffered more heavily in the Mediterranean; many more ships were damaged than in the Arctic, and one carrier, two cruisers, one A.A. ship and eight destroyers[3] were sunk as against two cruisers, two destroyers and two minesweepers.

73

Naturally, these Mediterranean convoys were carefully studied and analysed as they occurred, and the reports teem with recommendations and suggestions. Many of these were of a topical or technical nature, e.g. the best disposition of escorting vessels to meet the weapons of the day and tactics employed by the enemy in the various forms of attack, suggestions for improvement of the primitive radar and fighter direction organisation, etc.   No attempt is made here to comment on such points; actually, with the march of time, many of them are already out-dated.

But certain broad conclusions emerge from the story which are of more permanent value.   The following remarks are mainly based on Operation " Pedestal ", because on that occasion—the last seriously contested passage— the experience gained in the previous similar operations had been digested and made use of by both sides.

In the first place, the necessity for the most careful planning and preparation to meet every eventuality that could be foreseen is to be stressed.   Early planning *at the Admiralty* by the Commanders concerned was found to be most satisfactory; and verbal explanation of the plan to commanding officers of escorting vessels and the masters of the merchant ships (in addition to the usual " Convoy Conference "), special instruction to the signal ratings in the merchant ships, and the exercising of the convoy in manœuvres, aircraft recognition, etc. before called upon to face the enemy were considered of great importance.

These measures in different ways might compromise security to some extent, but in the opinion of Admiral Syfret the objections to this were outweighed by the advantages.   Intelligence of the passage of these particular convoys through the Strait of Gibraltar, no matter what ruses and precautions were employed, was almost certain to reach the enemy from his efficient organisation on shore in plenty of time for him to organise his attacks for the most vulnerable periods of the passage.   But that did not mean that security in the early stages could be dispensed with, and it was with concern that several officers, on joining the merchant ships before the convoy had left the Clyde, discovered that knowledge of their destination was common property, owing to loose talk, the careless labelling of certain stores, etc.   The last-minute issue of Mediterranean charts to certain ships hitherto unprovided with them also gave a pointer to where they were going.

---

[1] Owing to weather, etc.
[2] The losses in convoys to North Russia for the whole period over which they were running (1941–1945) amounted to 7·2 per cent.   For comparison, the losses in the Atlantic convoys from all causes amounted to 0·7 per cent.
[3] These figures include those sunk by own forces on account of damage, but do not include those sunk after arrival in harbour.

74

As regards the tactical aspect, nothing particularly new emerged: but two great lessons—already in course of assimilation—received ample confirmation:

1. The necessity to keep ships in convoy and the escort in formation and closed up for mutual support. Stragglers and detached ships presented all forms of attack with their opportunities.

2. The necessity for fighter protection and *fighter direction* (it must be remembered that in 1942 few ships were fitted for the latter) against shore-based air attack.

Provided these two conditions could be maintained, the risks from submarines, M.T.B.s, mines and air were acceptable.

Submarines did not accomplish so much against the merchant ships as might have been expected, only hitting one ship in the four convoys in 1942, though the prowess of the German *U.73* in her bold attack on the *Eagle* and of the Italian *Axum* in hitting three ships with a salvo of four torpedoes shews that resolute and skilful commanders were not lacking. M.T.B.s were difficult to see and harder to hit, but they only once managed to damage a ship in convoy, though they had their successes against escorting craft. The five merchant ships they hit in operation " Pedestal " were all stragglers. Mines, though a constant anxiety at certain stages of the passage, were mainly of nuisance value and could be dealt with by destroyers' T.S.D. sweeps and the minesweeping forces.[1]

Air attack on the scale the enemy was able to lay it on was by far the greatest danger that had to be faced, and, combined with the threat of the Italian battle fleet, compelled the cessation of the convoys in the eastern basin, where neither British capital ships nor carriers were available, during the most critical months of 1942. In the western basin it was largely countered by the inclusion of as many carriers as possible in the escort; and in this connection may be noted the great value of carriers for the provision of fighter protection in areas inaccessible to friendly shore-based fighters.

Operation " Pedestal " provides an example of the effectiveness of the fighter protection so provided, and also of the disastrous results accruing from lack of it and the break up of the convoy formation. The very heavy air attacks from Sardinia by over 100 escorted bombers throughout daylight hours of 12th August, when the convoy was protected by a total of 60 carrier-borne fighters, only succeeded in damaging one merchant ship and two of the escorting ships. The fighters attacking at a distance from the convoy were usually able to break up the enemy formations sufficiently for the A.A. guns of escort and convoy to be able to deal with those that got through. That evening, after the carriers had withdrawn and when the convoy, in some disorder after the submarine attack which robbed it of both its fighter direction ships (one of them its A.A. ship), was protected in the air by only six Beaufighters, about 20 Ju. 88s hit three merchant ships with bombs or torpedoes. The convoy then became completely disorganised; five stragglers (in addition to H.M.S. *Manchester*) fell victims to M.T.B.s. Three merchant ships in convoy were hit by bombs next morning while there was still no fighter direction; and ships which had become detached suffered further damage in the course of day (see Plan 14).

No mention has been made of the Italian heavy surface forces, but in fact they exercised a preponderating influence on the conduct of these operations. It may well be considered that for the furtherance of an object of such supreme

---

[1] In 1942 the " Oyster " mine and such types were not yet in use.

importance as was the reduction of Malta, and in view of their numerical superiority, they might have been used with more resolution: unlike a lonely raider far from home in the open ocean, or even the German fleet in the Arctic, which lacked repair facilities in their poorly equipped Norwegian bases, they were operating on the threshold of their homeland with all their metropolitan resources near at hand at their disposal.

In the western basin, their potentiality could be largely offset by the loan of forces from other stations to accompany the convoys as far as the Narrows: thereafter navigational difficulties and the expedient of doing this part of the passage at night were likely to deter them from attack; and the formation of a respectable air striking force at Malta was an insurance for the last stages of the passage. They could never be discounted, however, and their existence on more than one occasion influenced the decision to scuttle damaged ships, which otherwise might perhaps have been saved.

But in the eastern basin the Italian fleet in 1942 tipped the scale. Admiral Vian's brilliant action in March held their superior force off the convoy, but the delay—as the Italian commander had foreseen—enabled the enemy air forces to cut it up before it reached its destination. Operation " Vigorous " proved that " our air striking force had nothing like the weight required to stop a fast and powerful enemy force, and in no way compensated for our lack of heavy ships ".[1] The efficiency of a submarine screen keeping pace with the convoy was never put to the test. No doubt the knowledge that half a dozen submarines were between them and the convoy would have had considerable moral effect on the enemy; but the relatively slow speed of the submarines, especially when submerged, would militate against their doing more than possibly delay a determined attack.

The lesson, of course, is that for all such operations as those under consideration it is essential to be able to confront the heaviest surface force the enemy can muster with a force that can fight it with at least some chance of defeating it.

75

Though perhaps not strictly part of the story of the Malta convoys, it is of interest to note some of their unplanned effects on the general strategical situation in the Mediterranean, as illustrating the inter-reaction between the operations of one Service and those of others under the conditions of modern warfare.

The immediate object of these convoys was to succour Malta, the key to the whole strategical position in the Mediterranean. Enough—but only just enough—was run into Malta to enable the island to hold out and—except for intervals—to stage serious attacks on the Axis vital supply route to North Africa; but the very fact of running even the least successful (from that point of view) of these convoys carried with it most important " by-products."

For example, the convoys in June 1942 (" Harpoon " and " Vigorous "), which between them succeeded in getting only two merchant ships to their destination, had a fortuitous but far reaching effect on the operations on shore in North Africa. The convoys had originally been planned by the War Cabinet and the Middle East Defence Council to coincide with an offensive by the Eighth Army. This was forestalled by the German Field-Marshal Rommel, who launched his own attack on Bir Hakeim on 26th May, 1942. By 14th June he had destroyed a high proportion of the British armour, and the retreat of the Eighth Army from Gazala had already begun. Hundreds

---

[1] C.-in-C., Mediterranean, report in M.013471/42.

of Eighth Army vehicles, packed nose to tail along the coast road during the critical days between 14th–16th June, presented ideal targets for enemy air attack, which might well have turned the well-ordered retreat into a rout. But, in view of the importance attached to Convoy " Harpoon ", the Panzer Army was informed in the morning of 14th June by General von Waldau, A.O.C., Africa, that air support to the *Afrika Corps* " would have to wait ". Actually, on that day a total of 166 German aircraft, bombers and fighters, were diverted from the land targets presented by the retreating Eighth Army against the British shipping. There was a comparable situation the next day; and these intensive operations against the convoy had a marked effect on the general serviceability of the German air force, which, in conjunction with other factors—e.g. the orderly retreat of the British Western Desert Air Force, which left airfields stripped of useful stores and equipment and yet managed to maintain a high level of aggressive operations—resulted in the Panzer Army being forced to advance into Egypt without adequate air support.

The arrival of the *Welshman* and the two ships from the " Harpoon " Convoy at Malta enabled Malta to recommence offensive operations, and on 24th June Mussolini informed the German Army General Staff that difficulties after the collapse of the Eighth Army lay less in the battle on the ground than in the transport situation at sea. " Owing to Malta's active revival, supply of the Panzer Army in Africa has once more entered a critical phase . . ."

A further interesting side-issue of the June convoys to Malta is provided by the German Admiral Weichold, which shows how intricate and unexpected the effects of an apparently straightforward operation can be under the conditions of modern warfare. In these operations the Italian Fleet expended 15,000 tons of fuel, and this left them with insufficient to maintain their extensive convoy protection commitments. This contributed to a further drop in supplies to North Africa, at a time when extra quantities were urgently required to make good the heavy drain on stocks caused by the fighting.

Much the same, though not so important, were the repercussions of " Pedestal " on the operations on shore. This convoy coincided with a period when the strength, and especially the serviceability, of the German Air Force were being rigidly conserved in preparation for Rommel's last attempt to break through the El Alamein positions and to proceed with the occupation of Egypt. In order to deal with the convoy, about 220 German bombers and fighters were detailed to reinforce the Italian air forces. The result of these operations was to reduce the potentiality of the enemy air force to such an extent that it was unable to provide effective escort for their convoys, and this at a time when the replenishment of the island's fuel made possible a resumption of air strikes from Malta.

As for the fighting on shore, at the Battle of Alam el Halfa (31st August– 4th September)—according to the enemy commander—" The R.A.F.'s command of the air had been virtually complete." This was undoubtedly due in part to the fact that the enemy air force had been stretched to the limit for some time, and the additional burden on both crews and machines demanded by the heavy attacks on " Pedestal " had a directly adverse effect on the efficiency of the air force.

Viewed from this angle, the whole story of the Malta convoys is a good illustration of the inexorable effect of sea power.[1] Sea power enabled the aircraft on which Malta so largely depended to be flown in from carriers. Sea power provided fuel for these aircraft, and the munitions which sustained the

---

[1] The term " sea power " of course includes the air component, without which sea power cannot be efficiently exercised in modern warfare.

island itself, and made possible the attacks thence which so seriously disturbed the Axis line of communications with North Africa.   Sea power, too, frequently compelled the diversion of the enemy air effort from the tactical support of their army in North Africa to the paramount need of denying supplies to Malta, and thereby exercised an important influence on the operations ashore at critical periods; and finally, before the end of 1942, sea power made possible the Allied landings in Algeria, which, combined with the advance of the Eighth Army (itself dependent on sea power for its supplies by the Cape of Good Hope route) transformed the whole situation in the Mediterranean in favour of the Allies.   The most conspicuous contribution of sea power in the Mediterranean, perhaps, was the periodical reinforcement of Malta by the convoys, in the teeth of all that the Italian Navy and the apparently overwhelming shore-based air forces of the Axis could do to prevent it.

76

The story of the Malta convoys may well be regarded with pride by the Royal Navy and the Mercantile Marines which took part.   As in all operations of war, their success ultimately hinged on the human element.   This never faltered; grievous though the losses were; and thanks to the morale engendered and nourished by the leaders, they won through in the end.   Heavy though the strain was on capital ships, carriers and cruisers, it was even heavier on the destroyers—often steaming for days on end, with no let-up on the necessity for their vigilance and with frequent encounters with the enemy—on the F.A.A., both ship-borne and shore-based, pitted against aircraft superior in performance and numbers, and on the R.A.F., working often at extreme range in support of the operations.

But to the merchant ships must go the highest credit, as was stressed in the reports of the Flag Officers conducting the operations.   As another admiral wrote about this time in connection with the Arctic convoys, " We in the Navy are paid to do this sort of job, but it is beginning to ask too much of the men of the Merchant Navy.   We may be able to avoid bombs and torpedoes with our speed . . . "[1]

But in the Mediterranean, as in the Arctic, it was *not* asking too much; and it is good to read the comments of those best able to judge on the skill and determination of the masters and officers and the fortitude of the ships' companies of those sorely-tried ships.   Nor must the work of the Naval Liaison Officers and guns' crews embarked in them be forgotten.

The disappointment of the masters of the ships in the diversionary convoy from the east when they found they were not actually going through to Malta, as noted by Admiral Harwood, will be remembered; and the spirit in which these dangerous ventures were carried through may well be epitomised in the last sentence of Admiral Syfret's report on " Pedestal ":—

" In conclusion I think I am speaking for all in saying that we are disappointed at not doing better, but we should like to try again."   Without that spirit, it is hardly possible that the Malta convoys could have succeeded against the material forces arrayed against them: with such spirit, it is difficult to set a limit to the operations of war which can be undertaken with success.

---

[1] Rear-Admiral Bonham-Carter.

EPILOGUE

On 20th June, 1943—a year almost to the day after the arrival of the battle-scarred remnant of the " Harpoon " convoy—Malta, her sore ordeal now a thing of the past, was en fête. The Baraccas and all other vantage-points were thick with cheering people, as the *Aurora*, flying the Royal Standard, passed through the breakwater and took up her buoys.

On a special platform in front of the bridge stood His Majesty King George VI, come from a visit to the fighting men in North Africa, to mark his admiration for the achievement of the island.

" I have witnessed many memorable spectacles," writes Admiral of the Fleet Lord Cunningham of Hyndhope, " but this was the most impressive of them all. The dense throngs of loyal Maltese, men, women and children, were wild with enthusiasm. I have never heard such cheering and all the bells in the many churches started ringing when he landed.

" The King made an extensive tour of the island . . . and the effect on the inhabitants was tremendous."[1]

The Malta convoys had been justified.

Forces: Operation "Excess", January 1941

Notes—1. The "Forces" are shown in the order in which they appear in the text, which is not always in the alphabetical order of their distinguishing letters.

2. Group II consisted of the *Bonaventure, Duncan, Hasty, Hero* and *Hereward* and the four escorted ships. The remainder of Forces "H" and "F" formed Group I.

I. FROM GIBRALTAR

NAME	TYPE	ARMAMENT	COMMANDING OFFICER
		FORCE "H"	
Renown	Battle cruiser	Six 15-in. Twenty 4·5-in.	Captain C. E. B. Simeon (flag of Vice-Admiral Sir J. F. Somerville, K.C.B., D.S.O.)
Malaya	Battleship	Eight 15-in. Twelve 6-in. Eight 4-in.	Captain A. F. E. Palliser, D.S.C.
Ark Royal	Aircraft carrier (30 Swordfish aircraft, 24 Fulmar aircraft)	Sixteen 4·5-in.	Captain C. S. Holland
Sheffield	Cruiser	Twelve 6-in. Eight 4-in.	Captain C. A. A. Larcom
Faulknor	Destroyer	Five 4·7-in. One 3-in.	Captain A. F. De Salis
Forester	Destroyer	Four 4·7-in.	Lieut.-Cdr. E. B. Tancock, D.S.C.
Fury	Destroyer	Four 4·7-in. One 3-in.	Lieut.-Cdr. T. C. Robinson
Foxhound	Destroyer	Four 4·7-in. One 3-in.	Cdr. G. H. Peters, D.S.C.
Firedrake	Destroyer	Four 4·7-in. One 3-in.	Lieut.-Cdr. S. H. Norris, D.S.O., D.S.C.
Fortune	Destroyer	Four 4·7-in. One 3-in.	Lieut.-Cdr. E. N. Sinclair
Duncan	Destroyer	Four 4·7-in. One 3-in.	Captain F. S. W. de Winton
		FORCE "F"	
Bonaventure	Cruiser	Eight 5·25-in.	Captain H. J. Egerton
Hasty	Destroyer	Four 4·7-in.	Lieut.-Cdr. L. R. K. Tyrwhitt
Hero	Destroyer	Four 4·7-in.	Cdr. H. W. Biggs, D.S.O.
Hereward	Destroyer	Four 4·7-in.	Cdr. C. W. Greening
Jaguar	Destroyer	Six 4·7-in. One 4-in.	Lieut.-Cdr. J. F. W. Hine
		FORCE "G": SUBMARINES	
Triumph	Submarine	Eight torp. tubes	Lieut.-Cdr. W. J. W. Woods
Upholder	Submarine	Four torp. tubes	Lieut. M. D. Wanklyn

II. MEDITERRANEAN FLEET

Name	Type	Armament	Commanding Officer
		FORCE "B"	
Gloucester[1]	Cruiser	Twelve 6-in. Eight 4-in.	Captain H. A. Rowley (flag of Rear-Admiral E. de F. Renouf, C.V.O.)
Southampton[2]	Cruiser	Twelve 6-in. Eight 4-in.	Captain B. C. B. Brooke
Ilex	Destroyer	Four 4·7-in.	Captain H. St. L. Nicolson, D.S.O.
		FORCE "A"	
Warspite	Battleship	Eight 15-in. Eight 6-in. Eight 4-in.	Captain D. B. Fisher, C.B.E. (flag of C.-in-C., Admiral Sir A. B. Cunningham, K.C.B., D.S.O.)
Valiant	Battleship	Eight 15-in. Twenty 4·5-in.	Captain C. E. Morgan, D.S.O.
Illustrious[3]	Aircraft carrier (21 Swordfish aircraft, 12 Fulmar aircraft)	Sixteen 4·5-in.	Captain D. W. Boyd, C.B.E., D.S.C. (flag of Rear-Admiral A. L. St. G. Lyster, C.B., C.V.O., D.S.O.)
Jervis	Destroyer	Six 4·7-in. One 4-in.	Captain P. J. Mack, D.S.O.
Juno	Destroyer	Six 4·7-in.	Cdr. St. J. R. J. Tyrwhitt
Janus	Destroyer	Six 4·7-in.	Cdr. J. A. W. Tothill
Nubian	Destroyer	Eight 4·7-in.	Cdr. R. W. Ravenhill
Mohawk	Destroyer	Eight 4·7-in.	Cdr. J. W. M. Eaton
Greyhound	Destroyer	Four 4·7-in. One 3-in.	Cdr. W. R. Marshall-A'Deane, D.S.O.
Gallant[4]	Destroyer	Four 4·7-in. One 3-in.	Lieut.-Cdr. C. P. F. Brown, D.S.C.
Griffin	Destroyer	Four 4·7-in. One 3-in.	Cdr. J. Lee-Barber, D.S.O.
Dainty	Destroyer	Four 4·7-in. One 3-in.	Cdr. M. S. Thomas, D.S.O.
		FORCE "C": CONVOY ESCORTS	
Calcutta	Anti-aircraft ship	Eight 4-in.	Captain D. M. Lees, D.S.O.
Diamond	Destroyer	Four 4·7-in. One 3-in.	Lieut.-Cdr. P. A. Cartwright
Defender	Destroyer	Four 4·7-in. One 3-in.	Lieut.-Cdr. G. L. Farnfield
Peony	Corvette	One 4-in.	Lieut.-Cdr. M. B. Sherwood, D.S.O.
Salvia	Corvette	One 4-in.	Lieut.-Cdr. J. I. Miller, D.S.O., R.D., R.N.R.
Hyacinth	Corvette	One 4-in.	Lieut.-Cdr. F. C. Hopkins, R.N.R.
Gloxinia	Corvette	One 4-in.	Lieut.-Cdr. A. J. C. Pomeroy, R.N.V.R.
		FORCE "D"	
Orion	Cruiser	Eight 6-in. Eight 4-in.	Captain G. R. B. Back (flag of Vice-Admiral H. D. Pridham-Wippell, C.B., C.V.O.)
Ajax	Cruiser	Eight 6-in. Eight 4-in.	Captain E. D. B. McCarthy.
Perth	Cruiser	Eight 6-in. Eight 4-in.	Captain Sir P. W. Bowyer-Smyth, Bt.
York	Cruiser	Six 8-in. Four 4-in.	Captain R. H. Portal, D.S.C.
Pandora	Submarine	Eight torp. tubes	Lieut.-Cdr. J. W. Linton

[1] Hit by bomb, 11th January—damaged.
[2] Hit by bombs, 11th January—caught fire, sunk by own forces.
[3] Hit by bombs, 10th January—severely damaged.
[4] Hit by mine, 10th January—damaged.

III. CONVOYS

NAME	TONNAGE		DESTINATION
	"EXCESS" (16 knots)		
Clan Cumming	7,500	⎫	
Clan Macdonald	9,500	⎬	Piraeus
Empire Song	9,000	⎭	
Essex	13,500		Malta
	M.W.5½ (15 knots)		
H.M.S. Breconshire	10,000	⎫	
Clan Macaulay	10,500	⎬	Malta
	M.E.5½ (15 knots)		
Lanarkshire	10,000	⎫	
Waiwera	12,500	⎬	Alexandria
	M.E.6 (11 knots)		
Volo	1,500	⎫	
Pontfield	8,500		
Rodi	3,500	⎬	Port Said
Trocas	7,500		
Hoegh Hood	9,500	⎭	
Devis	6,000		Alexandria

Note. Tonnage is "gross registered tonnage," shown to the nearest 500 tons.
Speeds of convoys are those given in the operation orders.
H.M.S. Breconshire was a commissioned auxiliary supply ship.
All ships arrived safely.

APPENDIX B

Particulars of Attacks from the Air,
10th January 1941

EXTRACT FROM A SIGNAL FROM THE COMMANDER-IN-CHIEF, MEDITERRANEAN, TO THE ADMIRALTY, 1916 OF 8TH FEBRUARY 1941

1. Torpedo-bomber attack at 1223 was of usual Italian type with steady level approach from six miles on a bearing abaft destroyer screen at height 150 ft. to drop torpedoes at 2,500 yd. from battle fleet.

Fighters gave chase, damaging one aircraft: no apparent damage from gunfire.

2. Relief fighters were being flown off at 1235, when dive-bombing aircraft were sighted at long range at height 12,000 ft. in two very loose and flexible formations. On being engaged they worked round into positions on each quarter of battle fleet, where they circled while waiting their turn to attack.

Dive attack started at 1240, concentrated mainly on *Illustrious* (18 to 24 aircraft); but *Warspite* and *Valiant* were also attacked (3 to 6 aircraft each); both Junkers 87B and Junkers 88 were employed.

The attack on *Illustrious* developed in three main waves, in each of which at least two sub-flights of three each carried out synchronised attacks in different sectors. Aircraft of each sub-flight attacked in succession from bearings 5 to 10 degrees apart. The main weight of the attack came from astern; and it appeared that in each wave one or two sub-flights attacked from astern and one from either beam. Each wave lasted about a minute and a half, and the interval between waves about thirty seconds.

Some aircraft dived straight from 12,000 ft. to release bombs at 1,500 ft., but most spiralled down to about 5,000 ft. before turning into aiming dive; bomb release in some cases was as low as 800 ft. Many aircraft continued their dive across the ship to flatten out at 100 ft. and zigzag away, flying low. Angle of dive varied between 50 and 80 degrees.

Confirmed three aircraft shot down and two damaged by gunfire, and three unconfirmed. Fulmars, engaging retiring aircraft, shot down five certain, two probable, and damaged two.

3. High-level bombing at 1330 by seven aircraft each on *Illustrious* and battle fleet and three on Convoy " Excess " was ineffectual. Aircraft variously reported as Savoia 79, Heinkel III, and Junkers 88. One damaged by gunfire from *Calcutta*, escorting convoy.

4. Dive-bombing attacks at 1615 on *Illustrious* and at 1715 on battle fleet were small-scale repetitions of 1240 attack. That on *Illustrious* was markedly less determined and less synchronised: that on battle fleet was comparable in skill and determination, but bomb release was at or above 1,500 ft.

At least one aircraft in each attack was damaged by gunfire, and three by Fulmars, which intercepted after the attack.

5. Probable moonlight torpedo-bomber attack on *Illustrious* in Malta searched channel by two aircraft, which were heard and seen. No torpedoes or tracks observed.

APPENDIX C

Remarks on Operation " Excess ", January 1941, by Admiral Sir Andrew Cunningham, Commander-in-Chief, Mediterranean

" These operations marked the advent of the German Air Force in strength in the Mediterranean, and included the damaging of H.M.S. *Illustrious* on 10th January and the loss of H.M.S. *Southampton* on 11th January . . .

" The dive-bombing attacks by German aircraft were most efficiently performed, and came as an unpleasant surprise. The results of short-range anti-aircraft fire were disappointing, though it has been subsequently learned that this fire was in fact more effective than it appeared, and the Germans suffered considerable loss. Nevertheless, it is a potent new factor in Mediterranean war, and will undoubtedly deny us that free access to the waters immediately surrounding Malta and Sicily which we have previously enjoyed, until our own air forces have been built up to a scale adequate to meet it.

" The dive-bombing attacks on the 3rd Cruiser Squadron in the afternoon of 11th January—resulting in the loss of the *Southampton*—were a complete surprise, delivered at a time when the ships concerned believed themselves to have drawn clear of the threat of air attack, and when officers and men were doubtless relaxing the vigilance to some extent after a very strenuous four days. This damaging attack served to emphasize the importance of including a radio-direction-finder in detached units whenever possible.

" The remarks of the commanding officer, H.M.S. *Jaguar*[1], are of considerable interest, in particular his practice of firing 4·7-inch barrage over the stern of a ship attacked by dive-bombers. The idea is now under development in the Mediterranean Fleet with a view to the destroyer screen's putting an umbrella barrage over the fleet . . .

" It is satisfactory to record that convoy ' Excess ', whose safe passage had been the main object of the operation, reached its destination safely."

---

[1] The following is an extract from the report of Lieutenant-Commander Hine, H.M.S. *Jaguar*:—

" In the first attack [1240 on 10th January] *Jaguar*, which was on port side of screen, commenced in controlled fire, and later fired barrage abaft *Illustrious* with 4·7-inch and 4-inch. Aircraft were engaged when pulling out of dive or retiring within range of pom-pom, 0·5-inch, and military Bren . . .

" In waters where dive-bombing is likely . . . it is suggested that modern destroyers with six guns . . . should be put on the wings of the screen. It is the German practice to dive bomb from astern; and the controlled fire from these destroyers could be employed on formation as it prepares to attack, shifting to long-range barrage over carrier's stern as dive bombing developed, and employing close-range armament on them as they pull out and retire."

(The *Jaguar* had on board her some soldier passengers who engaged the enemy aircraft with their Bren guns.)

(2) From the Mediterranean War Diary for January, 1941: part of the general summary of the month's work

" The arrival of German air units in the central Mediterranean early in January had a profound effect upon the whole strategical position. By the end of December, 1940, the fleet had achieved a degree of supremacy over the large-scale Italian air attacks sufficient to give it complete freedom of movement in the eastern Mediterranean and a large measure of immunity in the central Mediterranean. But the disablement of the *Illustrious*, the loss of the *Southampton*, and the heavy air attacks on Malta quickly made it clear that until adequate fighter protection was available not only must the through-Mediterranean convoys be suspended, but the fleet itself would operate by day within range of the dive-bombers only at considerable risk. In the absence of a modern aircraft carrier, it therefore became necessary to abandon any idea of offensive operations against the enemy's coasts. It seemed, however, that the acquisition of aerodromes in Libya would enable the Royal Air Force to provide a high degree of immunity to shipping all along the Libyan coast. This would simplify the running of convoys to Malta and the Aegean, and enable light forces to operate from these advanced bases; but in spite of the rapid advance of the army to beyond Derna by the end of the month there was still little security gained to compensate for the enormously increased supply requirements. Previously, a fair proportion of supplies could reach the advanced units of the army and air force by road and rail; but now, owing to the rapidly lengthening lines of communication, everything had to be transported by sea. The air force was fully extended in maintaining pressure on the retreating enemy, and had no fighters to spare for protection of shipping.

" In these circumstances, it was to be expected that the enemy light forces known to be based at Brindisi and Taranto would attempt to interfere with our extended lines of communication in the Aegean and along the Libyan coast; but apparently the German influence had not yet reached the Italian Navy, for no attacks developed . . .

" There was a decided slowing up in the rate of advance of the Greek Army. At the beginning of the month, it seemed that Valona and the line of high land to the eastward would fall into Greek hands; but the advance was checked by the arrival of heavy Italian reinforcements and the difficulties of mountain transport in winter. The Greek supply problems were eased by the arrival at Piraeus of the three remaining ships of ' Excess ' convoy; but the most important of all, the *Northern Prince*, with ammunition and essential supplies for the Greek powder factories, had been left at Gibraltar, having grounded there."

Forces: Operation "Substance", July 1941

NAME	TYPE	ARMAMENT	COMMANDING OFFICER
		FORCE "H"	
Renown	Battle-cruiser	Six 15-in. Twenty 4·5-in.	Rear-Admiral R. R. McGrigor (as Captain) (flag of Vice-Admiral Sir J. F. Somerville, K.C.B., D.S.O.)
Nelson	Battleship	Nine 16-in. Twelve 6-in. Six 4·7-in.	Captain T. H. Troubridge
Ark Royal	Aircraft carrier (30 Swordfish aircraft, 24 Fulmar aircraft)	Sixteen 4·5-in.	Captain L. E. H. Maund
Hermione	Cruiser	Ten 5·25-in.	Captain G. N. Oliver
Faulknor	Destroyer	Five 4·7-in. One 3-in.	Captain A. F. De Salis
Foresight	Destroyer	Four 4·7-in. One 3-in.	Commander J. S. C. Salter
Forester	Destroyer	Four 4·7-in.	Lieut.-Cdr. E. B. Tancock, D.S.C.
Fury	Destroyer	Four 4·7-in. One 3-in.	Lieut.-Cdr. T. C. Robinson
Lightning	Destroyer	Six 4·7-in. One 4-in.	Cdr. R. G. Stewart
Duncan	Destroyer	Four 4·7-in. One 3-in.	Lieut.-Cdr. A. N. Rowell
		FORCE "X"	
Edinburgh	Cruiser	Twelve 6-in. Twelve 4-in.	Captain H. W. Faulkner (flag of Rear-Admiral E. N. Syfret)
Manchester[1]	Cruiser	Twelve 6-in. Eight 4-in.	Captain H. Drew, D.S.C.
Arethusa	Cruiser	Six 6-in. Four 4-in.	Captain A. C. Chapman
Manxman	Minelayer	Six 4-in.	Captain R. K. Dickson
Cossack	Destroyer	Six 4·7-in. Two 4-in.	Captain E. L. Berthon, D.S.C.
Maori	Destroyer	Six 4·7-in. Two 4-in.	Cdr. R. E. Courage, D.S.O., D.S.C.
Sikh	Destroyer	Six 4·7-in. Two 4-in.	Cdr. G. H. Stokes
Nestor	Destroyer	Six 4·7-in. One 4-in.	Cdr. A. S. Rosenthal, R.A.N.
Fearless[2]	Destroyer	Four 4·7-in.	Cdr. A. F. Pugsley
Foxhound	Destroyer	Four 4·7-in. One 3-in.	Cdr. G. H. Peters, D.S.O.
Firedrake[3]	Destroyer	Four 4·7-in. One 3-in.	Lieut.-Cdr. S. H. Norris, D.S.O., D.S.C.
Farndale	Destroyer	Six 4-in.	Cdr. S. H. Carlill
Avon Vale	Destroyer	Six 4-in.	Lieut. R. G. Dreyer
Eridge	Destroyer	Six 4-in.	Lieut.-Cdr. W. F. N. Gregory-Smith

[1] Torpedoed by aircraft, 23rd July—damaged.
[2] Torpedoed by aircraft, 23rd July—sunk.
[3] Damaged by near miss, 23rd July.

FORCE "S"

NAME	TYPE	ARMAMENT	COMMANDING OFFICER
Brown Ranger	Oiler		
Beverley	Destroyer	Three 4-in. One 12-pdr.	Lieut.-Cdr. J. Grant

SUBMARINES

NAME	TYPE	ARMAMENT	COMMANDING OFFICER
O.21 (Dutch)	Submarine	8 torp. tubes	Lieut.-Cdr. J. F. van Dulm, R.N.N.
Olympus	Submarine	8 torp. tubes	Lieut.-Cdr. H. G. Dymott
P. 32	Submarine	4 torp. tubes	Lieut. D. A. B. Abdy
Unique	Submarine	4 torp. tubes	Lieut. A. F. Collett
Upholder	Submarine	4 torp. tubes	Lieut.-Cdr. M. D. Wanklyn, D.S.O.
Upright	Submarine	4 torp. tubes	Lieut. J. S. Wraith, D.S.C.
Urge	Submarine	4 torp. tubes	Lieut. E. P. Tomkinson
Utmost	Submarine	4 torp. tubes	Lieut.-Cdr. R. D. Cayley, D.S.O.

ESCORT CONVOY M.G.1

NAME	TYPE	ARMAMENT	COMMANDING OFFICER
Encounter	Destroyer	Four 4·7-in. One 3-in.	Lieut.-Cdr. E. V. St. J. Morgan

CONVOYS

NAME	TONNAGE	REMARKS

GIBRALTAR TO MALTA (G.M.1)

NAME	TONNAGE	REMARKS
Melbourne Star	11,000	
Sydney Star[1]	12,500	
City of Pretoria	8,000	Speed of convoy: 14 knots
Port Chalmers	8,500	
Durham	13,000	
Deucalion	7,500	

MALTA TO GIBRALTAR (M.G.1)

NAME	TONNAGE	REMARKS
H.M.S. *Breconshire*	10,000	Speed of group: 17 knots.
Talabot	7,000	
Thermopylae	6,500	Speed of group: 14 knots.
Amerika	10,000	
Settler	6,000	Speed of group: 12 knots.
Svenor	7,500	
Hoegh Hood[2]	9,500	

---

[1] Torpedoed by motor torpedo-boat, 24th July—reached Malta.
[2] Torpedoed by aircraft, 24th July—reached Gibraltar.

Forces: Operation "Halberd", September 1941

NAME	TYPE	ARMAMENT	COMMANDING OFFICER
		FORCE "A"	
Nelson[1]	Battleship	Nine 16-in. Twelve 6-in. Six 4·7-in.	Captain T. H. Troubridge (flag of Vice-Admiral Sir J. F. Somerville, K.C.B., D.S.O.)
Rodney	Battleship	Nine 16-in. Twelve 6-in. Six 4·7-in.	Captain J. W. Rivett-Carnac, D.S.O.
Prince of Wales	Battleship	Ten 14-in. Sixteen 4·25-in.	Captain J. C. Leach, M.V.O. (flag of Vice-Admiral A. T. B. Curteis, C.B.)
Ark Royal	Aircraft carrier	Sixteen 4·5-in. (30 Swordfish aircraft, 24 Fulmar aircraft)	Captain L. E. H. Maund
Duncan	Destroyer	Four 4·7-in. One 3-in.	Captain H. W. Williams
Gurkha	Destroyer	Eight 4-in.	Cdr. C. N. Lentaigne
Legion	Destroyer	Eight 4-in.	Cdr. R. F. Jessel
Lance	Destroyer	Eight 4-in.	Lieut.-Cdr. R. W. F. Northcott
Lively	Destroyer	Eight 4-in.	Lieut.-Cdr. W. F. E. Hussey, D.S.C.
Fury	Destroyer	Four 4·7-in. One 3-in.	Lieut.-Cdr. T. C. Robinson
Isaac Sweers (Dutch)	Destroyer	Six 4-in.	Cdr. J. Houtsmuller, R.N.N.
Piorun (Polish)	Destroyer	Six 4·7-in. One 4-in.	—
Garland (Polish)	Destroyer	Four 4·7-in. One 3-in.	—
		FORCE "X"	
Kenya	Cruiser	Twelve 6-in. Twelve 4-in.	Captain M. M. Denny, C.B. (flag of Rear-Admiral H. M. Burrough, C.B.)
Edinburgh	Cruiser	Twelve 6-in. Twelve 4-in.	Captain H. W. Faulkner (flag of Rear-Admiral E. N. Syfret)
Sheffield	Cruiser	Twelve 6-in. Eight 4-in.	Captain A. W. Clarke
Hermione	Cruiser	Ten 5·25-in.	Captain G. N. Oliver
Euryalus	Cruiser	Ten 5·25-in.	Captain E. W. Bush, D.S.O., D.S.C.
Cossack	Destroyer	Six 4·7-in. Two 4-in.	Captain E. L. Berthon, D.S.C.
Zulu	Destroyer	Six 4·7-in. Two 4-in.	Commander H. R. Graham, D.S.O.
Foresight	Destroyer	Four 4·7-in. One 3-in.	Commander J. S. C. Salter
Forester	Destroyer	Four 4·7-in.	Lieut.-Cdr. E. B. Tancock, D.S.C.
Farndale	Destroyer	Six 4-in.	Cdr. S. H. Carlill
Heythrop	Destroyer	Six 4-in.	Lieut.-Cdr. R. S. Stafford
Laforey	Destroyer	Six 4·7-in. One 4-in.	Captain R. M. J. Hutton
Lightning	Destroyer	Six 4·7-in. One 4-in.	Cdr. R. G. Stewart
Oribi	Destroyer	Four 4·7-in. One 4-in.	Lieut.-Cdr. J. E. H. McBeath, D.S.O.

[1] Torpedoed by aircraft, 27th September—damaged.

NAME	TYPE	ARMAMENT	COMMANDING OFFICER

FORCE "S"

Brown Ranger	Oiler		
Fleur de Lys	Corvette	One 4-in.	Lieut. A. Collins, R.N.R.

SUBMARINES

O.21 (Dutch)	Submarine	8 torp. tubes	Lieut.-Cdr. J. F. van Dulm, R.N.N.
Upholder	Submarine	4 torp. tubes	Lieut.-Cdr. M. D. Wanklyn, D.S.O.
Trusty	Submarine	10 torp. tubes	Lieut.-Cdr. W. D. A. King, D.S.O., D.S.C.
Sokol (Polish)	Submarine	4 torp. tubes	Lieut.-Cdr. B. Karnicki, Polish Navy
Urge	Submarine	4 torp. tubes	Lieut.-Cdr. E. P. Tomkinson
Upright	Submarine	4 torp. tubes	Lieut.-Cdr. J. S. Wraith, D.S.C.
Utmost	Submarine	4 torp. tubes	Lieut.-Cdr. R. D. Cayley, D.S.O.
Ursula	Submarine	6 torp. tubes	Lieut. I. L. M. McGeoch
Unbeaten	Submarine	4 torp. tubes	Lieut. C. P. Norman

CONVOYS

NAME	TONNAGE	REMARKS

GIBRALTAR TO MALTA (G.M.2)

Clan Macdonald	9,500	
Clan Ferguson	7,500	
Ajax	7,500	
Imperial Star[1]	12,500	
City of Lincoln	8,000	Speed of convoy: 15 knots
Rowallan Castle	8,000	
Dunedin Star	14,000	
City of Calcutta	8,000	
H.M.S. Breconshire	10,000	

MALTA TO GIBRALTAR (M.G.2)

Melbourne Star	11,000	Part 1
City of Pretoria	8,000	Part 2
Port Chalmers	8,500	

[1] Torpedoed by aircraft, 27th September—sunk.

APPENDIX F

Remarks on Operation "Halberd", September 1941

(From M.016621/41 and M.04385/42)

(1) By Vice-Admiral Somerville

" The rough handling which the enemy torpedo aircraft received whilst passing over the destroyer screen may have accounted for the tendency of the later attacks to be delivered from abaft the beam. Should this direction of attack be adopted, it will be necessary to station additional destroyers on after bearings at the expense of anti-submarine protection. Deliberate attacks by torpedo aircraft against destroyers on the screen may force the latter to take drastic avoiding action; this will have the effect of disturbing gunfire and distracting attention, thereby opening a gap in the screen through which successive attackers could pass. Destroyers on the screen adjacent to the vessel attacked, and close escorts on the threatened bearing, must maintain a careful watch in order to frustrate such manœuvres.

" Cruising Disposition No. 17, adopted for the passage of the Narrows, was a compromise designed to give protection against E-Boat and torpedo-bomber attack at night. It did not prove satisfactory, and amendments are under consideration."

(The need was to increase arcs of fire.)

(2) By Rear-Admiral Burrough

" The air torpedo attack at dusk in bright moonlight presented a most difficult problem. With the exception of one or two individuals in *Kenya*, the aircraft were neither seen nor heard, and it was only by alarm signals from the destroyers on the flank and on one occasion by *Kenya's* [radio direction-finder] that the direction of attack could be gauged; in spite of this, ships put up a very good anti-aircraft barrage on the three occasions that the attack appeared to be pressed home.

" I feel very strongly that in any future operation of this nature success will be gravely jeopardized unless a moonless night is selected for the passage through the Sicilian Channel. The final air torpedo attack took place thirty minutes after official dusk, and the invisible enemy had the whole convoy clearly silhouetted against a bright moon in a cloudless sky. Had the enemy sent reconnaissance machines, they would have had no difficulty in maintaining touch until moonset at 0010, thus enabling continuous attacks to be carried out up to this hour, by which time the evasive route of the convoy would have been entirely compromised and air and surface attacks could have been planned for dawn. I do not consider that this unseen attack could have taken place on a moonless night, and am strongly of the opinion that, had the night [of the 27th–28th] been moonless, the convoy would have reached Malta intact. The cruising disposition adopted under these circumstances proved its efficiency."

(3) By Rear-Admiral Syfret

" It is easy to criticize the disposition of our own forces, both before and after Force " X " parted company, if only one form of attack by the enemy

117

is envisaged. But regarded from all points of view, viz., evasion, attack by surface vessels or submarines or E-Boats, various forms of attack by aircraft, and protection against mines, I find it difficult to suggest any improvements on the disposition used.

" Every commanding officer would like his ship stationed so that its clear arcs for gunfire were the maximum possible. Unfortunately, the greater the number of escorting ships, the less the clear arcs; and a particularly strong escort was provided. In my view, a ' square ' formation provides the best all-round defence; and I can find no fault in the dispositions adopted for heavy ships, cruisers, and ships of the convoy, except that I think it would have been better if the heavy ships had kept abaft the beam of the cruisers leading the convoy columns.

" I consider the positioning of the destroyers both by day and night to have been the best possible, except that I think it would have been better to station the destroyers at night so that they were abaft the beam of the leading escorting cruisers and before the beam of the rear escorting cruisers."[1]

(4) BY CAPTAIN TROUBRIDGE, H.M.S. *Nelson*

" Italian tactics have hitherto been the same. The formations approach within about 20 to 30 miles at heights up to 5,000 ft., and then commence to lose height, being usually lost on the radio-direction-finder screen at about 15 miles. Shortly afterwards the machines are sighted low over the water on relative bearings of Red or Green 70 degrees to the mean line of advance, when they maintain a steady course and a height of approximately 100 ft., coming on until they either fire, are shot down, or turn away without attacking —a few press on with commendable gallantry.

" To counter those tactics, it has been the practice in Force ' H ' to fire two barrages successively, long at 4,000 yd. and short at 2,000 yd. In order that this may be done without endangering our own ships, the destroyer screen is moved out with the wings thrown back at such an angle that there is a distance of 6,000 yd. clear space for big ships to fire the long barrage. In both operations [July and September] there were sufficient destroyers to ensure that the attacks caused through the wings of the screen, where the destroyers' fire and the long barrage caused the faint-hearted (some 50 per cent or more) to turn away.

" It seems probable that these tactics are forced on the enemy for two reasons: (1) because the large machines they use are not so manoeuvrable as Swordfish or Albacores, and hence are committed to a long straight approach; (2) the low height at the early stages of the approach is probably accounted for by the need for security from our fighters. In future attacks the enemy may well come in from further aft with a view to avoiding the fire of the screen.

" The chief difficulty, in firing both long and short barrages, encountered in the *Nelson* has been target selection. This is due principally to the smoke of bursting shell from the destroyer screen intermittently obscuring the enemy planes; and [in September] some interference in addition was caused by the *Ark Royal* and her cruiser escort, at the critical moment, fouling the range.

" It is emphasized that the above is the experience of action in Mediterranean summer visibility. In thick weather, target selection for the long barrage would be very much more difficult, and barrage would in all probability be confined to the short variety, possibly even fired in sectors."

---

[1] In another letter, Admiral Syfret said that the *Rodney* and *Nelson* sometimes fouled the lines of fire of the *Kenya* and *Edinburgh* respectively, and that at night the *Edinburgh's* line of fire was " severely restricted " by the positions of the *Cossack* and *Laforey*.

APPENDIX G

Vice-Admiral Sir James Somerville's orders for action against enemy surface ships

Note. The paragraph numbers are those in the respective operation orders, of which these are extracts.

1. THE ORDERS FOR JANUARY, 1941

54. " The enemy may attempt to interfere with the passage of the convoy by (i) a concentration of force superior to the British forces with the object of direct attack on the escort and convoy, (ii) a feint with a smaller force to draw off the escort from the convoy and thus provide an opportunity for attack on the latter by cruiser and destroyer forces."

55. " To deal with (i): If air reconnaissance indicates that the enemy is concentrated, and there is a prospect of engaging him within a reasonable distance, i.e. about 30–40 miles, it is my intention to move out and attack with all forces, less *Bonaventure* and two destroyers, who will remain as anti-aircraft and anti-submarine escort for the convoy. Early disablement and if possible destruction of enemy vessels at this stage may exercise a deterrent effect to further attempts by the enemy to interfere with the passage of the convoy."

56. " To deal with (ii): It is my intention to act as in paragraph 55, but to maintain a position on interior lines, from which I can frustrate any such attempts."

57. " Should there be reasonable prospects of destroying one or more enemy capital ships, it is my intention to accept a certain degree of risk to the convoy: but unless I am satisfied that the destruction of enemy capital ships can probably be effected, the safety of the convoy will remain my primary object."

58. " I intend that capital ships, cruisers, and destroyers shall remain in close support of one another during the approach with a view to bringing concentrated fire to bear on any enemy encountered within range."

Ships to follow the Admiral's motions " should communications fail or be delayed."

59. Two destroyers to screen the *Ark Royal*, when she is detached, the remaining destroyers screening the *Renown* and *Malaya* until required " for attack or counter-attack."

60. Ships " may be ordered to make smoke " to cover movements or to hide the convoy.

61. The *Bonaventure* and the convoy to endeavour to go on to the eastward. Should this prove impossible, the convoy " may be ordered to retire to the west." The convoy would then separate, if necessary, to give the escort freedom of action to engage the enemy.

2. THE ORDERS FOR JULY, 1941

47. Similar to paragraph 57 in the January orders.

48. *Action by day*. The *Manxman* and the three ' Hunt '-class destroyers to stay with the convoy.

The *Ark Royal* and two destroyers " to operate under cover of our main force, remaining as close to the convoy as is practicable."

Other ships " to concentrate on *Renown*. If effective air reconnaissance is available, cruisers should normally remain close to *Renown*, and destroyers continue to screen *Renown* and *Nelson* until contact with the enemy is made."

The *Ark Royal* to provide spotting aircraft for the capital ships and a torpedo striking force—both to be flown off when ordered by the Admiral.

49. *Action by night*. The capital ships, and the destroyers on the disengaged side of the screen, to turn away until the nature of the enemy is determined.

Cruisers and destroyers on the side making contact to close and engage.

50. " As our policy is evasion," searchlight rather than star-shell to be used.

3. THE ORDERS FOR SEPTEMBER, 1941

43. " To judge from previous experience, it is unlikely that the enemy will seek action with his main fleet. He may, however, arrange a concentration of his main units to the south of Sardinia, but under cover of his shore-based aircraft, with a view to drawing off our escorting forces and thus opening the way for attack on the convoy by light surface forces and aircraft.

" *Our primary object is the safe passage of the convoy to its destination*. This object must be constantly borne in mind; and action taken by our escorting forces. must in consequence be related to the achievement of this object."

44. " Unless the enemy main forces close the convoy, or the speed of an enemy capital ship is reduced materially as the result of torpedo attack, and in a position which renders interception by our forces practicable, or some other very favourable opportunity arises to bring the enemy's main forces to action, it is not my intention to part company from the convoy until forced to do so by near approach to the Skerki Channel."

45. " Should I decide to engage the enemy ":—

The *Hermione*, *Euryalus*, and four destroyers to stay with the convoy.

The *Ark Royal* and two destroyers to work independently near the convoy— the convoy to have first claim on fighter protection.

Other ships " to join my flag as ordered, *Prince of Wales* and cruisers in the van, destroyers screening the capital ships until ordered otherwise "—five destroyers to screen the *Prince of Wales*, seven to screen the *Nelson* and *Rodney*.

The ships in the van (under the Vice-Admiral in the *Prince of Wales*) " are to be manœuvred so that, if the enemy continues to close, fire can be opened by the van and main body simultaneously. The van must be prepared to fall back on the main body immediately, should the situation become obscure by reason of smoke, and a danger arise of the van's becoming heavily engaged without the support of the main body."

Note. An Appendix contains the orders for action against surface ships after the convoy parted company with the capital ships, and proceeded with an escort of cruisers and destroyers only. The escort was to be organized in three divisions as follows:—

    1st Division: *Kenya, Sheffield*, and four destroyers.
    2nd Division: *Edinburgh, Hermione, Euryalus*, and four destroyers.
    3rd Division: Two destroyers.

When ordered to engage the enemy, " the 1st and 2nd Divisions will move out as necessary to interpose themselves between the convoy and the enemy, and will attack the enemy from either bow with torpedoes, making the fullest use of smoke for this purpose." The 3rd Division was to take charge of the convoy, and both escort and convoy were to make smoke. " The convoy should not be diverged from its direct course for Malta until ordered to do so: in the last resort, the convoy should be ordered to scatter."

APPENDIX H

Vice-Admiral Somerville's orders for action during air attacks

1. THE ORDERS FOR JANUARY, 1941

" When air attack is expected, the screen may be ordered to close by the signal flag 9. If an attack develops without warning, destroyers are to close the battle fleet without further orders during day or night.

" A good look-out for torpedo-bomber attacks is to be maintained, particularly at dusk, during moonlight, and during high-level bombing attacks. Experience in the eastern Mediterranean indicates that high-level bombing, especially at or after dusk, is used to provide cover for torpedo-bomber attack.

" Reliance is placed on the destroyers to protect the fleet from torpedo-bomber attack over the arcs covered by the destroyer screen."[1]

2. THE ORDERS FOR JULY, 1941

" If our fighters are in hot pursuit of any enemy who is under fire from the fleet, or is about to come under fire from the fleet, *Ark Royal* may order ' Cease fire . . .' On receipt of this signal, which is to remain operative for one minute, all ships are immediately to check fire on the bearing ordered. The order to cease fire is only to be given when there is a good chance of our fighters either destroying the enemy or preventing an attack on the fleet: it is not to be given while dive-bombers are in the near vicinity of the ships.

" It must be borne in mind that all forces may be engaged with enemy aircraft throughout Day 3, Day 4, and a part of Day 5; and a careful control must therefore be kept on the expenditure of anti-aircraft ammunition. A heavy concentration is required against the first bombing attack, as this will probably affect the morale of the enemy in subsequent attacks—in subsequent attacks, fire should not be opened until the target is within range, and should cease when the target passes overhead."

3. THE ORDERS FOR SEPTEMBER, 1941

" The best defence against enemy air attack is (*a*) interception by our fighters before the enemy can reach their target; and subsequently (*b*) the development of the maximum volume of anti-aircraft fire.

" (*b*) requires that ships shall not become scattered, but keep locked up in their assigned stations, except when torpedo-bomber attack renders it desirable to increase speed to obtain greater manœuvrability.

" Synchronized high-level bombing and torpedo-bomber attack must be expected. Of these, the latter is the more serious danger.

" Destroyers on the screen must consider it their first duty to sight, report and ward off such attacks by opening fire on the approaching low-flying aircraft directly they are within range. Destroyers must also be careful not to drop inside their assigned distance from the fleet, in order that the latter can develop barrage fire to the fullest extent, if the torpedo aircraft succeed in passing the destroyer screen.

" A careful watch must be maintained by all ships for torpedo tracks, and immediate action taken to comb, if these approach on bearings which may result in a hit."

---

[1] Compare Admiral Cunningham's remarks and the report of the *Jaguar* in Appendix C.

APPENDIX I

Forces and Convoy: Operation M.G.1, March 1942

NAME	TYPE	ARMAMENT	COMMANDING OFFICER

FORCE "B" (*from Alexandria*)

15TH CRUISER SQUADRON

Cleopatra	Cruiser	Ten 5·25-in. 6 torp. tubes	Captain G. Grantham, D.S.O. (flag of Rear-Admiral P. L. Vian, D.S.O.)
Dido	Cruiser	Eight 5·25-in. One 4-in. 6 torp. tubes	Captain H. W. U. McCall
Euryalus	Cruiser	As *Cleopatra*	Captain E. W. Bush, D.S.O., D.S.C.

14TH DESTROYER FLOTILLA

Jervis	Destroyer	Six 4·7-in. 9 torp. tubes	Captain A. L. Poland, D.S.O., D.S.C.
Kipling	Destroyer	Six 4·7-in. One 4-in. 5 torp. tubes	Cdr. A. St. Clair-Ford, D.S.O.
Kelvin	Destroyer	As *Kipling*	Cdr. J. H. Allison, D.S.O.
Kingston	Destroyer	As *Kipling*	Cdr. P. Somerville, D.S.O., D.S.C.

22ND DESTROYER FLOTILLA

Sikh	Destroyer	Six 4·7-in. Two 4-in. 4 torp. tubes	Captain St. J. A. Micklethwait, D.S.O.
Lively	Destroyer	Eight 4-in. 8 torp. tubes	Lieut.-Cdr. W. F. E. Hussey, D.S.O., D.S.C.
Hero	Destroyer	Four 4·7-in. 8 torp. tubes	Cdr. R. L. Fisher, D.S.O., O.B.E.
Havock	Destroyer	Four 4·7in. One 3-in. 4 torp. tubes	Lieut.-Cdr. G. R. G. Watkins, D.S.C.
Zulu	Destroyer	As *Sikh*	Cdr. H. R. Graham, D.S.O., D.S.C.
Hasty	Destroyer	As *Havock*	Lieut.-Cdr. N. H. G. Austen

FORCE "K" (*from Malta*)

Penelope	Cruiser	Six 6-in. Eight 4-in. 6 torp. tubes	Captain A. D. Nicholl, D.S.O.
Legion	Destroyer	Eight 4-in. 8 torp. tubes	Cdr. R. F. Jessel

CLOSE ESCORT FOR CONVOY

Carlisle	Anti-aircraft ship	Eight 4-in.	Captain D. M. L. Neame, D.S.O.

5TH DESTROYER FLOTILLA

Southwold	Destroyer	Six 4-in.	Cdr. C. T. Jellicoe, D.S.C.
Beaufort	Destroyer	As *Southwold*	Lieut.-Cdr. Sir O. G. Roche, Bart.
Dulverton	Destroyer	do.	Lieut.-Cdr. W. N. Petch, O.B.E.
Hurworth	Destroyer	do.	Lieut.-Cdr. J. T. B. Birch
Avon Vale	Destroyer	do.	Lieut.-Cdr. P. A. R. Withers, D.S.C.
Eridge	Destroyer	do.	Lieut.-Cdr. W. F. N. Gregory-Smith, D.S.C.
Heythrop[1]	Destroyer	do.	Lieut.-Cdr. R. S. Stafford

[1] Torpedoed by submarine and later sank, 20th March.

NAME	TYPE	ARMAMENT	COMMANDING OFFICER

SUBMARINES

IN SOUTHERN APPROACHES TO MESSINA

Unbeaten	Submarine	4 torp. tubes	Lieut.-Cdr. E. A. Woodward, D.S.O.
P.34	Submarine	4 torp. tubes	Lieut. P. R. Harrison, D.S.C.

IN APPROACHES TO TARANTO

Proteus	Submarine	8 torp. tubes	Lieut.-Cdr. P. S. Francis
Upholder	Submarine	4 torp. tubes	Lieut.-Cdr. M. D. Wanklyn, V.C., D.S.O.
P. 36	Submarine	4 torp. tubes	Lieut. H. N. Edmonds, D.S.C.

CONVOY M.W.10

NAME	TONNAGE[1]	REMARKS
H.M.S. Breconshire[2]	10,000	Captain C. A. G. Hutchison (Commodore). Disabled by bombs 23rd March, and anchored outside Malta; towed into Marsaxlokk, 25th; damaged again by bombs, 26th; and sank, 27th.
Clan Campbell	7,500	Sunk by bombs on way into Malta, 23rd March.
Pampas	5,500	Arrived Malta, 23rd March; damaged by bombs and aground with all holds except two flooded, 26th.
Talabot (Norwegian)	7,000	Arrived Malta, 23rd March; damaged by bombs, 26th, and had to be scuttled.

---

[1] Tonnage is gross registered tonnage to the nearest 500 tons.

[2] *H.M.S. Breconshire* was a commissioned auxiliary supply ship.

APPENDIX J
Forces and Convoys: June 1942

1. OPERATION "HARPOON"

NAME	TYPE	ARMAMENT	COMMANDING OFFICER
		FORCE "W"	
Malaya	Battleship	Eight 15-in. Twelve 6-in. Eight 4-in.	Captain J. W. A. Waller
Eagle	Aircraft carrier	Nine 6-in. Four 4-in. (16 Hurricane and 4 Fulmar aircraft)	Captain E. G. N. Rushbrooke, D.S.C.
Argus	Aircraft carrier	Four 4-in. (2 Fulmar and 18 Swordfish aircraft)	Captain G. T. Philip, D.S.C.
Kenya	Cruiser	Twelve 6-in.	Captain A. S. Russell (flag of Vice-Admiral A. T. B. Curteis, C.B.)
Liverpool	Cruiser	Twelve 6-in. Eight 4-in.	Captain W. R. Slayter, D.S.C.
Charybdis	Cruiser	Eight 4·5-in.	Captain L. D. Mackintosh, D.S.C.
Onslow	Destroyer	Four 4·7-in. One 4-in.	Captain H. T. Armstrong, D.S.C.
Icarus	Destroyer	Four 4·7-in. One 3-in.	Lieut.-Cdr. C. D. Maud, D.S.C.
Escapade	Destroyer	As *Icarus*	Lieut.-Cdr. E. N. V. Currey, D.S.C.
Wishart	Destroyer	Three 4·7-in. One 12-pdr.	Cdr. H. G. Scott
Westcott	Destroyer	Four 4-in. One 12-pdr.	Cdr. I. H. Bockett-Pugh, D.S.O.
Wrestler	Destroyer	Three 4-in. One 12-pdr.	Lieut. R. W. B. Lacon
Vidette	Destroyer	As *Wrestler*	Lieut.-Cdr. E. N. Walmsley
Antelope	Destroyer	Three 4·7-in. One 3-in.	Lieut.-Cdr. E. N. Sinclair
		FORCE "X"	
Cairo	Anti-aircraft ship	Eight 4-in.	Act. Captain C. C. Hardy, D.S.O.
Bedouin	Destroyer	Six 4·7-in. Two 4-in.	Cdr. B. G. Scurfield, O.B.E., A.M.
Marne	Destroyer	Six 4·7-in.	Lieut.-Cdr. N. H. A. Richardson, D.S.C.
Matchless	Destroyer	As *Marne*	Lieut.-Cdr. J. Mowlam
Ithuriel	Destroyer	Four 4·7-in.	Lieut.-Cdr. D. H. Maitland-Makgill-Crichton, D.S.C.
Partridge	Destroyer	Five 4-in.	Lieut.-Cdr. W. A. F. Hawkins, O.B.E., D.S.C.
Blankney	Destroyer	Six 4-in.	Lieut.-Cdr. P. F. Powlett, D.S.C.
Middleton	Destroyer	As *Blankney*	Lieut.-Cdr. D. C. Kinloch
Badsworth	Destroyer	do.	Lieut. G. T. S. Gray, D.S.C.
Kujawiak (Polish)	Destroyer	do.	Cdr. L. Lichodziejewski
Speedy	Minesweeper	One 4-in.	Lieut.-Cdr. A. E. Doran
Hebe	Minesweeper	As *Speedy*	Lieut.-Cdr. G. Mowatt, R.D., R.N.R.
Rye	Minesweeper	One 3-in.	Lieut. J. A. Pearson, R.N.R.
Hythe	Minesweeper	One 3-in. One 12-pdr.	Lieut.-Cdr. L. B. Miller
No. 121 134 135 168 459 462	Motor launch	One 3-pdr. One 2-pdr. or Two 2-pdr. Two 0·5-in. 2 Lewis	Lieut.-Cdr. E. J. Strowlger, R.N.V.R., in No. 121, S.O.

APPENDIX J

NAME	TYPE	ARMAMENT	COMMANDING OFFICER

FORCE "Y"

NAME	TYPE	ARMAMENT	COMMANDING OFFICER
Geranium	Corvette	One 4-in.	Lieut.-Cdr. A. Foxall, R.N.R.
Coltsfoot	Corvette	As *Geranium*	Lieut. Hon. W. K. Rous, R.N.V.R.
Brown Ranger	Oiler		

SPECIAL SERVICE

Welshman	Minelayer	Six 4-in.	Captain W. H. D. Friedberger

SUBMARINES

P.211	Submarine	7 torpedo tubes	Cdr. B. Bryant, D.S.O.
P.42	Submarine	4 do.	Lieut. A. C. G. Mars
P.43	Submarine	4 do.	Lieut. A. C. Halliday
P.44	Submarine	4 do.	Lieut. T. E. Barlow

CONVOY

COMMODORE: Commander J. P. W. Pilditch, O.B.E.

NAME	TONNAGE	REMARKS
Troilus	7,500	Arrived Malta, 16th June.
Burdwan	6,000	Damaged by near miss, 15th June; torpedoed and sunk by aircraft later same day.
Chant (U.S.)	5,500	Sunk by bombs, 15th June.
Orari	10,500	Damaged by mine, 16th June; arrived Malta same day.
Tanimbar (Dutch)	8,000	Torpedoed and sunk by aircraft, 14th June.
Kentucky (U.S.)	5,500	As *Burdwan*.

2. OPERATION "VIGOROUS"

(*Note.* The 4th Cruiser Squadron and the 7th, 12th and 2nd Destroyer Flotillas and *Centurion* were lent from the Eastern Fleet for the occasion.)

NAME	TYPE	ARMAMENT	COMMANDING OFFICER
15TH CRUISER SQUADRON			
Cleopatra	Cruiser	Ten 5·25-in.	Captain G. Grantham, D.S.O. (flag of Rear-Admiral P. L. Vian, K.B.E. D.S.O.)
Dido	Cruiser	As *Cleopatra*	Captain H. W. U. McCall
Hermione	Cruiser	do.	Captain G. N. Oliver, D.S.O.
Euryalus	Cruiser	do.	Captain E. W. Bush, D.S.O., D.S.C.
Arethusa	Cruiser	Six 6-in. Four 4-in.	Captain A. C. Chapman
Coventry	Anti-aircraft ship	Eight 4-in.	Captain R. J. R. Dendy
4TH CRUISER SQUADRON			
Newcastle	Cruiser	Twelve 6-in. Eight 4-in.	Captain P. B. R. W. William-Powlett, D.S.O. (flag of Rear-Admiral W. G. Tennant, C.B., M.V.O.)
Birmingham	Cruiser	As *Newcastle*	Captain H. B. Crane
7th DESTROYER FLOTILLA			
Napier	Destroyer	Six 4·7-in. One 4-in.	Captain S. H. T. Arliss, D.S.O.
Nestor	Destroyer	As *Napier*	Cdr. A. S. Rosenthal, D.S.O., R.A.N.
Norman	Destroyer	do.	Cdr. H. M. Burrell, R.A.N.
Nizam	Destroyer	do.	Lieut.-Cdr. M. J. Clark, D.S.C., R.A.N.
14TH DESTROYER FLOTILLA			
Jervis	Destroyer	As *Napier*	Captain A. L. Poland, D.S.O., D.S.C.
Kelvin	Destroyer	do.	Cdr. M. S. Townsend, O.B.E., D.S.C.
Javelin	Destroyer	do.	Lieut.-Cdr. H. C. Simms, D.S.O.

NAME	TYPE	ARMAMENT	COMMANDING OFFICER
12TH DESTROYER FLOTILLA			
Pakenham	Destroyer	Five 4-in.	Captain E. B. K. Stevens, D.S.O., D.S.C.
Paladin	Destroyer	As *Pakenham*	Cdr. A. F. Pugsley
Inconstant	Destroyer	Four 4·7-in.	Lieut.-Cdr. W. S. Clouston
22nd DESTROYER FLOTILLA			
Sikh	Destroyer	Six 4·7-in. Two 4-in.	Captain St. J. A. Micklethwait, D.S.O.
Zulu	Destroyer	As *Sikh*	Cdr. R. T. White, D.S.O.
Hasty	Destroyer	Four 4·7-in. One 3-in.	Lieut.-Cdr. N. H. G. Austen
Hero	Destroyer	Four 4·7-in.	Lieut. W. Scott
5TH DESTROYER FLOTILLA			
Dulverton	Destroyer	Six 4-in.	Lieut.-Cdr. W. N. Petch, O.B.E.
Exmoor	Destroyer	As *Dulverton*	Lieut.-Cdr. L. St. G. Rich
Croome	Destroyer	do.	Lieut.-Cdr. J. D. Hayes, D.S.O.
Eridge	Destroyer	do.	Lieut.-Cdr. W. F. N. Gregory-Smith, D.S.C.
Airedale	Destroyer	Four 4-in.	Lieut.-Cdr. A. G. Forman
Beaufort	Destroyer	As *Dulverton*	Lieut.-Cdr. Sir S. O'G. Roche, Bart.
Hurworth	Destroyer	do.	Lieut.-Cdr. J. T. B. Birch
Tetcott	Destroyer	do.	Lieut. H. R. Rycroft
Aldenham	Destroyer	Four 4-in.	Lieut. H. A. Stuart-Menteth
2ND DESTROYER FLOTILLA			
Fortune	Destroyer	Three 4·7-in. One 3-in.	Lieut.-Cdr. R. D. H. S. Pankhurst
Griffin	Destroyer	Four 4·7-in. One 3-in.	Lieut.-Cdr. A. N. Rowell
Hotspur	Destroyer	As *Griffin*	Lieut. T. D. Herrick, D.S.C.
OTHER VESSELS¹ IN COMPANY			
Delphinium	Corvette	One 4-in.	Cdr. R. L. Spalding
Primula	Corvette	As *Delphinium*	Lieut.-Cdr. J. H. Fuller, R.N.R.
Erica	Corvette	do.	Lieut.-Cdr. W. C. Riley, R.N.V.R.
Snapdragon	Corvette	do.	Lieut. P. H. Potter, R.N.R.
Boston	Minesweeper	One 3-in.	Lieut. D. H. G. Coughlan, R.N.R.
Seaham	Minesweeper	As *Boston*	Lieut. R. E. Brett, R.N.R.
Centurion	Unarmed special service		Cdr. A. H. Alexander
Antwerp	Unarmed rescue ship		Lieut.-Cdr. J. N. Hulse, R.N.R.
Malines	do. do.		Lieut. J. R. Freeman, R.N.R.

SUBMARINES

Proteus	Submarine	8 torp. tubes	Lieut.-Cdr. P. S. Francis
Thorn	do.	11 do.	Lieut.-Cdr. R. G. Norfolk
Taku	do.	11 do.	Lieut.-Cdr. J. G. Hopkins
Thrasher	do.	11 do.	Lieut. H. S. Mackenzie
Porpoise	do.	6 do.	Lieut. L. W. A. Bennington, D.S.C.
Una	do.	4 do.	Lieut. C. P. Norman
P.31	do.	4 do.	Lieut. J. B. Kershaw
P.34	do.	4 do.	Lieut. P. R. Harrison, D.S.C.
P.35	do.	4 do.	Lieut. S. L. C. Maydon

¹ Four motor torpedo boats were to have accompanied the convoy for its protection. They joined p.m. 13th June and were taken in tow by merchant ships. Owing to the bad weather, they had to be sent back the same night, and M.T.B. No. 259 was so much damaged that she foundered; the rest arrived at Alexandria again on the 14th.

CONVOY M.W.11

COMMODORE: Rear-Admiral H. T. England (Ret.)

NAME	TONNAGE	REMARKS
City of Pretoria	8,000	
City of Calcutta	8,000	Damage by near miss, 12th June; detached to Tobruk.
Bhutan	6,000	Sunk by bombs, 14th June.
Potaro	5,500	Damaged by near miss, 14th June; returned to Alexandria with the convoy.
Bulkoil	8,000	
Rembrandt (Dutch)	8,000	
Aagtekirk (Dutch)	7,000	Detached to Tobruk, 14th June, being too slow; sunk by bombs the same day.
City of Edinburgh	8,000	
City of Lincoln	8,000	
Elizabeth Bakke (Norwegian)	5,500	Detached to Alexandria, 13th June, being too slow.
Ajax	7,500	

Forces and Convoys: August 1942

OPERATION " PEDESTAL "

NAME	TYPE	ARMAMENT	COMMANDING OFFICER
		FORCE " Z "	
Nelson	Battleship	Nine 16-in. Twelve 6-in. Six 4·7-in.	Captain H. B. Jacomb (flag of Acting Vice-Admiral E. N. Syfret, c.b.)
Rodney	Battleship	As *Nelson*	Captain J. W. Rivett-Carnac, d.s.c.
Victorious	Aircraft carrier	Sixteen 4·5-in. (6 Hurricane, 16 Fulmar and 12 Albacore aircraft)	Captain H. C. Bovell, o.b.e. (flag of Rear-Admiral A. L. St. G. Lyster, c.b., c.v.o., d.s.o.)
Indomitable	Aircraft carrier	As *Victorious* (10 Martlet, 24 Hurricane and 16 Albacore aircraft)	Captain T. H. Troubridge
Eagle[1]	Aircraft carrier	Nine 6-in. Four 4-in. (16 Hurricane aircraft)	Captain L. D. Mackintosh, d.s.c.
Sirius	Cruiser	Ten 5·25-in.	Captain P. W. B. Brooking
Phoebe	Cruiser	Eight 5·25-in. One 4-in.	Captain C. P. Frend
Charybdis	Cruiser	Eight 4·5-in.	Captain G. A. W. Voelcker
Laforey	Destroyer	Six 4·7-in. One 4-in.	Captain R. M. J. Hutton
Lightning	Destroyer	As *Laforey*	Cdr. H. G. Walters, d.s.c.
Lookout	Destroyer	do.	Cdr. C. P. F. Brown, d.s.c.
Quentin	Destroyer	Four 4·7-in.	Lieut.-Cdr. A. H. P. Noble, d.s.c.
Tartar	Destroyer	Six 4·7-in. Two 4-in.	Cdr. St. J. R. J. Tyrwhitt, d.s.c.
Eskimo	Destroyer	As *Tartar*	Cdr. E. G. le Geyt
Somali	Destroyer	do.	Cdr. E. N. V. Currey, d.s.c.
Wishart	Destroyer	Three 4·7-in. One 12-pdr.	Cdr. H. G. Scott
Zetland	Destroyer	Six 4-in.	Lieut. J. V. Wilkinson
Ithuriel	Destroyer	Four 4·7-in.	Lieut.-Cdr. D. H. Maitland-Makgill- Crichton, d.s.c.
Antelope	Destroyer	Three 4·7-in. One 3-in.	Lieut.-Cdr. E. N. Sinclair.
Vansittart	Destroyer	As *Wishart*	Lieut.-Cdr. T. Johnston, d.s.c.

ADDITIONAL SHIPS FOR DETACHED ESCORTS

NAME	TYPE	ARMAMENT	COMMANDING OFFICER
Keppel	Destroyer	Two 4·7-in. One 3-in.	Cdr. J. E. Broome
Westcott	Destroyer	Four 4-in. One 12-pdr.	Cdr. I. H. Bockett-Pugh, d.s.o.
Venomous	Destroyer	As *Wishart*	Cdr. H. W. Falcon-Steward
Malcolm	Destroyer	As *Keppel*	Acting Cdr. A. B. Russell
Wolverine	Destroyer	Two 4·7-in. One 12-pdr.	Lieut.-Cdr. P. W. Gretton, o.b.e., d.s.c.
Amazon	Destroyer	As *Keppel*	Lieut.-Cdr. Lord Teynham
Wrestler	Destroyer	Three 4-in.	Lieut. R. W. B. Lacon, d.s.c.
Vidette	Destroyer	As *Wrestler*	Lieut.-Cdr. E. N. Walmsley, d.s.c.

[1] The *Eagle* was sunk on 11th August, before the convoy came under air attack.

NAME	TYPE	ARMAMENT	COMMANDING OFFICER
		FORCE " R "	
Jonquil	Corvette	One 4-in.	Lieut.-Cdr. R. E. H. Partington, R.D., R.N.R.
Spirea	Corvette	As *Jonquil*	Lieut.-Cdr. R. S. Miller, D.S.C., R.D., R.N.R.
Geranium	Corvette	do.	Lieut.-Cdr. A. Foxhall, R.N.R.
Coltsfoot	Corvette	do.	Lieut. the Hon. W. K. Rouse, R.N.V.R.
Salvonia	Tug		
Brown Ranger	Fleet oiler		
Dingledale	Fleet oiler		
		FORCE " X "	
Nigeria	Cruiser	Twelve 6-in. Eight 4-in.	Captain S. H. Paton (flag of Rear-Admiral H. M. Burrough, C.B., D.S.O.)
Kenya	Cruiser	As *Nigeria*	Captain A. S. Russell
Manchester	Cruiser	do.	Captain H. Drew, D.S.C.
Cairo	Anti-aircraft ship	Eight 4-in.	Acting Captain C. C. Hardy, D.S.O.
Ashanti	Destroyer	Eight 4·7-in. Two 4-in.	Acting Captain R. G. Onslow, D.S.O.
Intrepid	Destroyer	Four 4·7-in. One 3-in.	Commander C. A. de W. Kitcat
Icarus	Destroyer	As *Intrepid*	Lieut.-Cdr. C. D. Maud, D.S.C.
Foresight[1]	Destroyer	do.	Lieut.-Cdr. R. A. Fell
Fury	Destroyer	do.	Lieut.-Cdr. C. H. Campbell, D.S.C.
Derwent	Destroyer	Four 4-in.	Cdr. R. H. Wright, D.S.C.
Bramham	Destroyer	Six 4-in.	Lieut. E. F. Baines
Bicester	Destroyer	As *Bramham*	Lieut.-Cdr. S. W. F. Bennetts
Ledbury	Destroyer	do.	Lieut.-Cdr. R. P. Hill
Pathfinder	Destroyer	Five 4-in.	Cdr. E. A. Gibbs, D.S.O.
Penn	Destroyer	As *Pathfinder*	Lieut.-Cdr. J. H. Swain
Wilton	Destroyer	As *Bramham*	Lieut. A. P. Northey, D.S.C.
Jaunty	Tug	One 12-pdr.	Lieut.-Cdr. H. Osburn, O.B.E., R.N.R.

MALTA ESCORT FORCE

(Acting Commander H. J. A. S. Jerome, Senior Officer, in *Speedy*)

NAME	TYPE	ARMAMENT	COMMANDING OFFICER
Speedy	Minesweeper	One 4-in.	Lieut.-Cdr. A. E. Doran
Hebe	Minesweeper	As *Speedy*	Lieut.-Cdr. G. Mowatt, R.D., R.N.R.
Hythe	Minesweeper	One 3-in. One 12-pdr.	Lieut.-Cdr. L. B. Miller
Rye	Minesweeper	One 3-in.	Lieut. J. A. Pearson, D.S.C., R.N.R.
No. 121 126 134 135 168 459 462	Motor launch	One 3-pdr. One 2-pdr. or Two 2-pdr. Two 0·5-in. 2 Lewis	Lieut.-Cdr. E. J. Strowlger, R.N.V.R., in No. 121, S.O.

OPERATION " BELLOWS "

NAME	TYPE	ARMAMENT	COMMANDING OFFICER
Furious	Aircraft carrier	Twelve 4-in. (4 Albacore aircraft); 40 Spitfires for Malta	Captain T. O. Bulteel

FORCE " Y " (OPERATION "ASCENDANT ")

NAME	TYPE	ARMAMENT	COMMANDING OFFICER
Matchless	Destroyer	Six 4·7-in. One 4-in.	Lieut.-Cdr. J. Mowlam
Badsworth	Destroyer	Six 4-in.	Lieut. G. T. S. Gray, D.S.C.

[1] The *Foresight* was disabled before the separation on 12th August, and did not continue with Force " X ".

NAME	TYPE	ARMAMENT	COMMANDING OFFICER

SUBMARINES

NORTH OF SICILY

NAME	TYPE	ARMAMENT	COMMANDING OFFICER
P.211	Submarine	7 torp. tubes	Cdr. B. Bryant, D.S.C.
P.42	Submarine	4 do.	Lieut. A. C. G. Mars

BETWEEN MALTA AND TUNISIA

NAME	TYPE	ARMAMENT	COMMANDING OFFICER
P.44	Submarine	4 torp. tubes	Lieut. T. E. Barlow
P.222	Submarine	7 do.	Lieut.-Cdr. A. J. Mackenzie
P.31	Submarine	4 do.	Lieut. J. B. Kershaw, D.S.O.
P.34	Submarine	4 do.	Lieut. P. R. Harrison, D.S.C.
P.46	Submarine	4 do.	Lieut. J. Stevens
Utmost	Submarine	4 do.	Lieut. A. W. Langridge

CONVOYS

CONVOY W.S.21.S: TO MALTA

COMMODORE: Commander A. G. Venables

NAME	TONNAGE	REMARKS
Port Chalmers	8,500	Arrived Malta, 13th August.
Clan Ferguson	7,500	Sunk by air torpedo, 12th August.
Melbourne Star	11,000	Arrived Malta, 13th August.
Brisbane Star	13,000	Damaged by air torpedo, 12th August; arrived Malta 14th.
Almeria Lykes (U.S.)	8,000	Torpedoed by motor torpedo boat, 13th August, and abandoned.
Santa Elisa (U.S.)	8,500	Torpedoed by motor torpedo boat, 13th August, and abandoned; sunk by bombs later same day.
Rochester Castle	8,000	Torpedoed by motor torpedo boat, 13th August; arrived Malta with the convoy same day.
Empire Hope	12,500	Disabled by bombs, 12th August; sunk by Penn.
Glenorchy	9,000	Sunk 13th August; cause uncertain.
Dorset	13,000	Disabled by bombs, 13th August; sunk by bombs later same day.
Deucalion	7,500	Damaged by near misses, 12th August; sunk by air torpedo later same day.
Wairangi	12,500	Torpedoed by motor torpedo boat and abandoned, 13th August.
Waimarama	13,000	Sunk by bombs, 13th August.
Ohio	10,000	Torpedoed by submarine, 12th August; disabled by near misses, 13th, and damaged again by bombs that day; towed to Malta, arriving 15th.

CONVOY "ASCENDANT": MALTA TO GIBRALTAR

NAME	TONNAGE	REMARKS
Troilus	7,500	} Sailed 10th August; arrived at Gibraltar 14th.
Orari	10,500	

APPENDIX L

Report on planning Operation "Pedestal"

(R.O. Case W.H.S.8268)

The following recommendations with regard to planning an operation similar to " Pedestal " in the future were made:—

" We understand that the planning of this operation was far better than in any of its predecessors, because it was started earlier and was done more thoroughly because the facilities at, and the resources of, the Admiralty were placed at the disposal of the Flag Officer concerned.

" We strongly recommend that a similar procedure should be carried out in future operations, with certain modifications as suggested below:—

(A) It would greatly assist the officers who carry out the planning if there was a permanent officer appointed to Operations Division who would attend during the planning of all such operations and would analyse the results, in the same manner as we are doing now. This officer would know all the Admiralty Departments, and he would insure that details, which are liable to be over-looked by the planning officers and their operational staffs, are raised at an early stage, and that lessons learnt are not forgotten. It is understood that the present staff of Operations Division does not allow of one officer specialising in this duty.

(B) We strongly recommend that where possible a Senior Officer, or officers, as representatives from the place or station affected should be sent home by air to take part in the planning In this operation certainly the Malta Command, and also possibly Gibraltar, should have been represented, thereby making for closer contact and obviating excessive signalling.

(C) In a ' Fleet ' the various communication orders are cut-and-dried, and are continually being used and exercised, but this is not the case with a Command, as was Force ' F ' on this occasion. Therefore for any special operation of this nature we recommend that the Senior Officer, or Officers, conducting the operation should bring their Signal Officers as well as their Operations Officers to the Admiralty during the planning stage."[1]

---

[1] These recommendations were approved in principle by the Board, but events in North Africa rendered the further running of convoys to Malta under such adverse conditions unnecessary.

Operations "M.G.1," "Harpoon," "Vigorous," "Pedestal": Analysis of ships lost and damaged

(Ships sunk are shown in capitals)

I. WARSHIPS

METHOD OF ATTACK	NAME	CLASS	REMARKS	OPERATION
Aircraft (bombs)	*Indomitable*	Carrier	Damaged	" Pedestal "
	Victorious	,,	Slightly damaged	,,
	Birmingham	Cruiser	Damaged	" Vigorous "
	Arethusa	,,	Damaged	,,
	LEGION	Destroyer	Damaged: later sunk, Malta	M.G.1
	KINGSTON	,,	Sunk, Malta	,,
	AIREDALE	,,	Damaged: sunk by own forces	" Vigorous "
	NESTOR	,,	Damaged: sunk by own forces	,,
	Primula	Corvette	Damaged	,,
	P.36	S/M	Sunk, Malta	M.G.1
	Centurion	Sp. service	Slightly damaged	" Vigorous "
Aircraft (torpedoes)	*Liverpool*	Cruiser	Damaged	" Harpoon "
	BEDOUIN	Destroyer	Sunk	,,
	FORESIGHT	,,	Damaged: sunk by own forces	" Pedestal "
Surface ships	*Cleopatra*	Cruiser	Damaged	M.G.1
	Havock	Destroyer	Damaged	,,
	Kingston	,,	Damaged	,,
	Lively	,,	Damaged	,,
	Bedouin	,,	Damaged	" Harpoon "
	Partridge	,,	Damaged	,,
	Hebe	Minesweeper	Damaged	,,
Motor torpedo boats	*MANCHESTER*	Cruiser	Damaged: scuttled	" Pedestal "
	Newcastle	,,	Damaged	" Vigorous "
	HASTY	Destroyer	Damaged: sunk by own forces	,,
Submarines	*EAGLE*	Carrier	Sunk	" Pedestal "
	Nigeria	Cruiser	Damaged	,,
	HERMIONE	,,	Sunk	" Vigorous "
	Kenya	,,	Damaged	" Pedestal "
	CAIRO	A.A. ship	Damaged: sunk by own forces	,,
Mines	*HEYTHROP*	Destroyer	Sunk	M.G.1
	SOUTHWOLD	,,	Sunk	,,
	KUJAWIAK	,,	Sunk	" Harpoon "
	Badsworth	,,	Damaged	,,
	Matchless	,,	Damaged	,,
	Hebe	Minesweeper	Damaged	,,

II. MERCHANT SHIPS

METHOD OF ATTACK	NAME	TONNAGE	REMARKS	OPERATION
Aircraft (bombs)	*H.M.S. BRECONSHIRE*	10,000	Damaged: later sunk, Malta	M.G.1
	CLAN CAMPBELL	7,500	Sunk	,,
	TALABOT	7,000	Sunk, Malta	,,
	PAMPAS	5,500	Damaged: later sunk, Malta	,,
	CHANT	5,500	Sunk	" Harpoon "
	KENTUCKY	5,500	Damaged: sunk by own forces	,,
	BURDWAN	6,000	Damaged: sunk by own forces	,,
	City of Calcutta	8,000	Damaged	" Vigorous "
	AAGTEKIRK[1]	7,000	Sunk	,,
	BHUTAN	6,000	Sunk	,,
	Potaro	5,500	Damaged	,,
	Deucalion	7,500	Damaged	" Pedestal "
	EMPIRE HOPE	12,500	Damaged: sunk by own forces	,,
	WAIMARAMA	13,000	Sunk	,,
	Rochester Castle	8,000	Damaged	,,
	SANTA ELISA [1]	8,500	Sunk	,,
	Ohio[1]	10,000	Damaged	,,
	DORSET[1]	13,000	Sunk	,,
Aircraft (torpedoes)	*TANIMBAR*	8,000	Sunk	" Harpoon "
	CLAN FERGUSON	7,500	Sunk	" Pedestal "
	Brisbane Star	13,000	Damaged	,,
	DEUCALION [1]	7,500	Sunk	,,
Surface ships	—	—		
Motor torpedo boats	*GLENORCHY*[1]	9,000	Sunk	" Pedestal "
	WAIRANGI[1]	12,500	Sunk	,,
	ALMERIA LYKES[1]	8,000	Sunk	,,
	Rochester Castle[1]	8,000	Damaged	,,
	Santa Elisa[1]	8,500	Damaged	,,
Submarines	*Ohio*	10,000	Damaged	" Pedestal "
Mines	*Orari*	10,500	Damaged	" Harpoon "

ABSTRACT

METHOD OF ATTACK	WARSHIPS		MERCHANT SHIPS		TOTAL
	SUNK	DAMAGED	SUNK	DAMAGED	
Aircraft, bombs	5	6	13	5	29
Aircraft, torpedoes	2	1	3	1	7
Surface ships	—	7	—	—	7
Motor torpedo boats ..	2	1	3	2	8
Submarines	4	2	—	1	6
Mines	2	3	—	1	6

[1] Straggling or detached from convoy.

APPENDIX N

Strengths in operations and numbers sunk or damaged

1941

TYPE	JANUARY "Excess" NO.	s.	D.	JULY "Substance" NO.	s.	D.	SEPTEMBER "Halberd" NO.	s.	D.
Capital ships	4	—	—	2	—	—	3	—	1
Aircraft carriers	2	—	1	1	—	—	1	—	—
Cruisers	8	1	1	4	—	1	5	—	—
Anti-aircraft ship	1	—	—	—	—	—	—	—	—
Minelayer	—	—	—	1	—	—	—	—	—
Destroyers	23	—	1	18	1	1	18	—	—
Corvettes	4	—	—	—	—	—	1	—	—
Submarines	3	—	—	8	—	—	9	—	—
Merchant ships	14	—	—	13	—	1	12	1	—

1942

Note. These figures do not necessarily agree with those given in the abstract in Appendix M, since in Appendix M the same ship may appear more than once, e.g. *Bedouin* damaged by *surface craft*, sunk by *A/C torpedoes; Ohio* damaged by *submarine,* and again by *A/C bombs.*

TYPE	MARCH "M.G.1" NO.	s.	D.	JUNE "Harpoon" NO.	s.	D.	JUNE "Vigorous" NO.	s.	D.	AUGUST "Pedestal" NO.	s.	D.
Capital ships	—	—	—	1	—	—	—	—	—	2	—	—
Aircraft carrier	—	—	—	2	—	—	—	—	—	3	1	1
Cruisers	4	—	2	3	—	1	7	1	3	6	1	2
Anti-aircraft ships	1	—	—	1	—	1	1	—	—	1	1	—
Minelayers	—	—	—	1	—	—	—	—	—	—	—	—
Destroyers	18	2	3[1]	17	2	3	26	3	—	34	1	—
Corvettes	—	—	—	2	—	—	4	—	1	4	—	—
Submarines	5	1	—	4	—	—	9	—	—	8	—	—
Minesweepers	—	—	—	4	—	1	2	—	—	4	—	—
Motor launches	—	—	—	6	—	—	—	—	—	7	—	—
Merchant ships[4]	4[2]	1	1	6	4	1	11[3]	2	2	14	9	3

[1] Two sunk in harbour after arrival at Malta.
[2] Three sunk in harbour after arrival.
[3] Survivors returned to Egypt: none arrived at Malta.
[4] Including H.M.S. *Breconshire.*

APPENDIX O

Table of performance of British aircraft, 1941-1942

(a) FIGHTER AIRCRAFT CAPABLE OF DECK LANDING

	BRITISH NAVAL[1]			R.A.F.	
	SEA HURRICANE	MARTLET	FULMAR	HURRICANE	SPITFIRE
Crew	1	1	2	1	1
Armament	8 Browning	4 Colt 0·5	8 ·303F[2] One 500-lb or One 250-lb bomb	8 ·303F	8 ·303F
Whether dive-bomber ..	No	No	No	No	No
Whether fitted for observer navigation, W/T, and folding	No[3]	No[3]	Yes	No[3]	No[3]
Maximum speed (knots)	250	260	230	No	No
Endurance at maximum speed (approx.)	$\frac{3}{4}$ hr	$1\frac{1}{4}$ hr	2 hr	1 hr	$\frac{3}{4}$ hr
Maximum endurance at economical speed	$2\frac{1}{4}$ hr (420 miles approx.)	$4\frac{1}{4}$ hr (720 miles approx.)	6 hr[4] (750 miles approx.)	$4\frac{1}{4}$ hr	$3\frac{1}{4}$ hr

[1] The climb of these aircraft varied from $3\frac{1}{2}$ to $4\frac{1}{2}$ minutes to 10,000 ft.
[2] F = fixed front gun
[3] But with R/T
[4] With extra tank; 8 hours equal about 1,100 miles

(b) RECONNAISSANCE AND STRIKE AIRCRAFT

| | British Naval | | | R.A.F. |
	SWORDFISH	ALBACORE	WALRUS[1]	BATTLE
Crew	3 Recce. 2 for strike	3 Recce. 2 for strike	3 Recce.	2 or 3
Armament	torpedo[2] or bombs: 1,500 lb	torpedo[2] or bombs: 1,500 lb	bombs[2]: 500 lb	bombs[2]: 1,000 lb plus 500 at expense of range
Whether capable of dive-bombing	Yes	Yes	Limited	No
Whether capable of torpedo attack	Yes	Yes	No	No
Maximum speed (knots)..	125	155	110	220
Maximum endurance and range without extra tankage: (i) Recce. ..	5½ hr	6 hr	3½ hr	8 hr
(ii) Strike force ..	550 miles	650 miles	300 miles	1,200 miles
Whether extra tankage ..	Yes	Yes	No	No

[1] Catapult ship aircraft.
[2] With one ·303-in. (or ·3-in.) front gun, and one ·303-in. (or ·3-in.) rear gun.

Performance Table—German

	FIGHTERS				
	GERMAN		**ITALIAN**		**GER**
	Me. 109	Me. 110	C.R. 42	Ju. 87D	Ju. 88
Description	Single-engine monoplane	Twin-engine monoplane	Single-engine biplane; open cockpit	Single-engine monoplane	T/B. recce. fighter; twin-engine monoplane
Crew	1	2	1	2	4
Armament	One 7·9 mm., Two 20 mm. (occasionally) in wings	Four 7·9 mm., One 20 mm.; Dorsal—two or twin 7·9 mm.	No provision for wing guns; Two 12·7 mm. in fuselage	One 2,000-lb. bomb; Wing gun—Two 2·79 mm.; Dorsal—twin 7·9 mm.	Typical bomb or torpedo load two 2,000-lb and two 500-lb; For'd—7·9 and 20 mm.; Dorsal—two 7·9 mm.; Ventral—twin 7·9 mm.
Capable of Dive Bombing	In some forms Glide Bomber	In some forms Glide Bomber	No	Yes	No.
Capable of Torpedo Attack	No	No	No	No	Yes
Maximum Speed ..	317 knots	328 knots	262 knots	204 knots	249 knots
Maximum Range ..	655 miles	1,200 miles	690 miles	670 miles	1,900 miles
Endurance at ..	3·3 hours	7·5 hours	4·5 hours	3·7 hours	10·7 hours
Speed	178 knots	160 knots	132 knots	159 knots	180 knots

[1] Extra fuel in drums for

138

and Italian aircraft, 1940-1942

approximate)

BOMBERS			NAVAL RECONNAISSANCE		
MAN He. 111	F.W. 200[1]	**ITALIAN** S. 79	Do. 18	**GERMAN** Ar. 196	**ITALIAN** Cant. 501
T.B.R. twin-engine monoplane	T.B.R. four-engine monoplane	T.B.R. three-engine monoplane	Twin-engine monoplane flying boat	Fighter-bomber, single-engine monoplane, twin floats	Recce. and light bombing single-engine monoplane flying boat
5—6	5—7	4—5	4	2	4—5
For'd.—One or two 7·9 mm., One 20 mm.; Dorsal—one 7·9 mm.; Lateral—two 7·9 mm.; Ventral—twin 7·9 mm. or one 20 mm.	Three 300-lb (mixed) bombs; Mixed 20 mm. turret and 7·9 mm. in dorsal, lateral and ventral positions (variable)	Five 500-lb bombs; For'd. —one 12·7 mm.; Dorsal—one 12·7 mm.; Lateral—one or two 7·7 mm.; Ventral —one 12·7 mm.	440-lb bomb; One dorsal turret gun 7·9 20 mm.; One for'd. 7·9 13 mm.	Two 112-lb bombs; For'd. —one 7·9 mm.; Wings—two 20 mm.; Dorsal—twin 7·9 mm.	For'd.—one 7·7 mm.; Dorsal—three 7·7 mm.
No	No	No	Yes (Glide only)	Yes	No
Yes	Yes (Not so used)	Yes	No	No	No
218 knots	213 knots	227 knots	130 knots	172 knots	134 knots
1,930 miles	2,700 miles	1,700 miles	2,640 miles	600 miles	2,700 miles
10 hours	16·5 hours	11 hours	24 hours	5·2 hours	38 hours
166 knots	147 knots	136 knots	97 knots	105 knots	72 knots

replenishment in flight in early type.

APPENDIX Q

Italian surface ships in 1942

NAME	ARMAMENT	REMARKS
	BATTLESHIPS (6)	
Littorio	Nine 15-in.	
	Twelve 6-in.	
Vittorio Veneto	Twelve 3·5-in.	
Andrea Doria	Ten 12·6-in.	
	Twelve 5·3-in.	
Caio Duilio	Ten 3·5-in.	
Giulio Cesare	Ten 12·6-in.	
	Twelve 4·7-in.	
Conte di Cavour	Eight 4-in.	*Cavour* under repair.
	8-IN. CRUISERS (4)	
Gorizia		
Bolzano	Eight 8-in.	
Trento	Twelve 4-in.	*Trento* disabled by air torpedo and
Trieste		sunk by *P.35* on 15th June.
	6-IN. CRUISERS (8)	
Luigi de Savoia,	Ten 6-in.	
Duca degli Abruzzi	Eight 4-in.	
Giuseppe Garibaldi		
Raimondo Montecuccoli		
Muzio Attendolo		
Eugenio di Savoia		
Emanuele Filiberto,	Eight 6-in.	
Duca d'Aosta	Six 4-in.	
Luigi Cadorna		
Giovanni delle Bande Nere		*Bande Nere* sunk by *Urge* on
		1st April.
	"FLEET" DESTROYERS (30)	
Twenty-one	Four 4·7-in.	
	6 torpedo tubes	
Nine	Six 4·7-in.	
	4 torpedo tubes	

Notes. (1) There were ten old destroyers and about 40 torpedo boats, mostly armed with three or four 4-in. guns and four torpedo tubes.

    (2) "E-boats" (*motoscafi anti-sommergibili*): there were 40 to 50 with four 21-in. torpedo tubes, and about 35 with two 18-in. tubes.

Index

The numerical references are to pages.

Only the names of individuals and ships that are specifically mentioned in the text of the narrative are included in the index: for other names the appropriate Appendix must be consulted, viz., A, D, E, I, J or K.

(SO 36404) Wt. 37472—P2044 300 5/58 H & S Ltd. Gp. 578

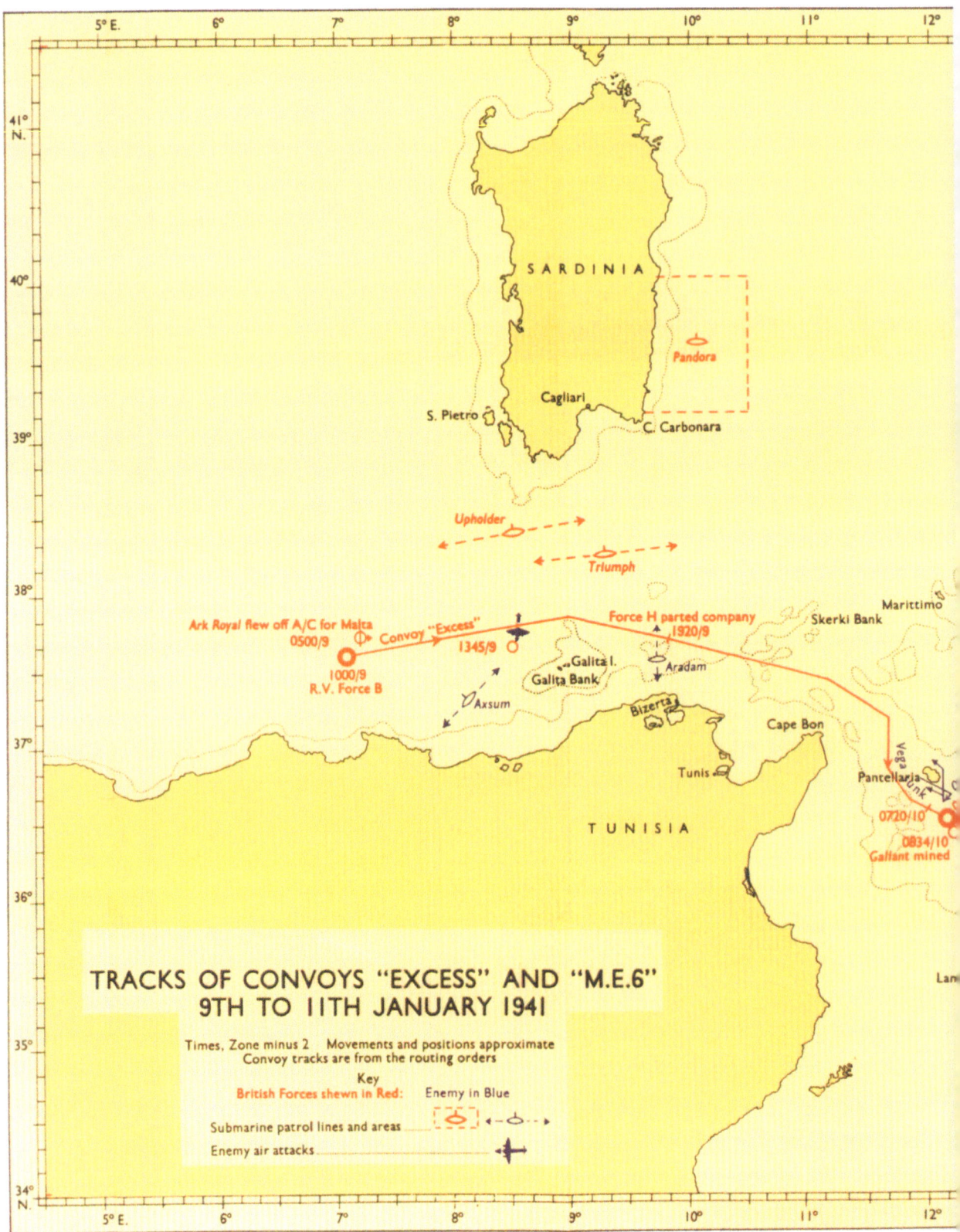

TRACKS OF CONVOYS "EXCESS" AND "M.E.6"
9TH TO 11TH JANUARY 1941

Times, Zone minus 2   Movements and positions approximate
Convoy tracks are from the routing orders

Key

British Forces shewn in Red: Enemy in Blue

Submarine patrol lines and areas

Enemy air attacks

C.B.H.22729

PLAN I

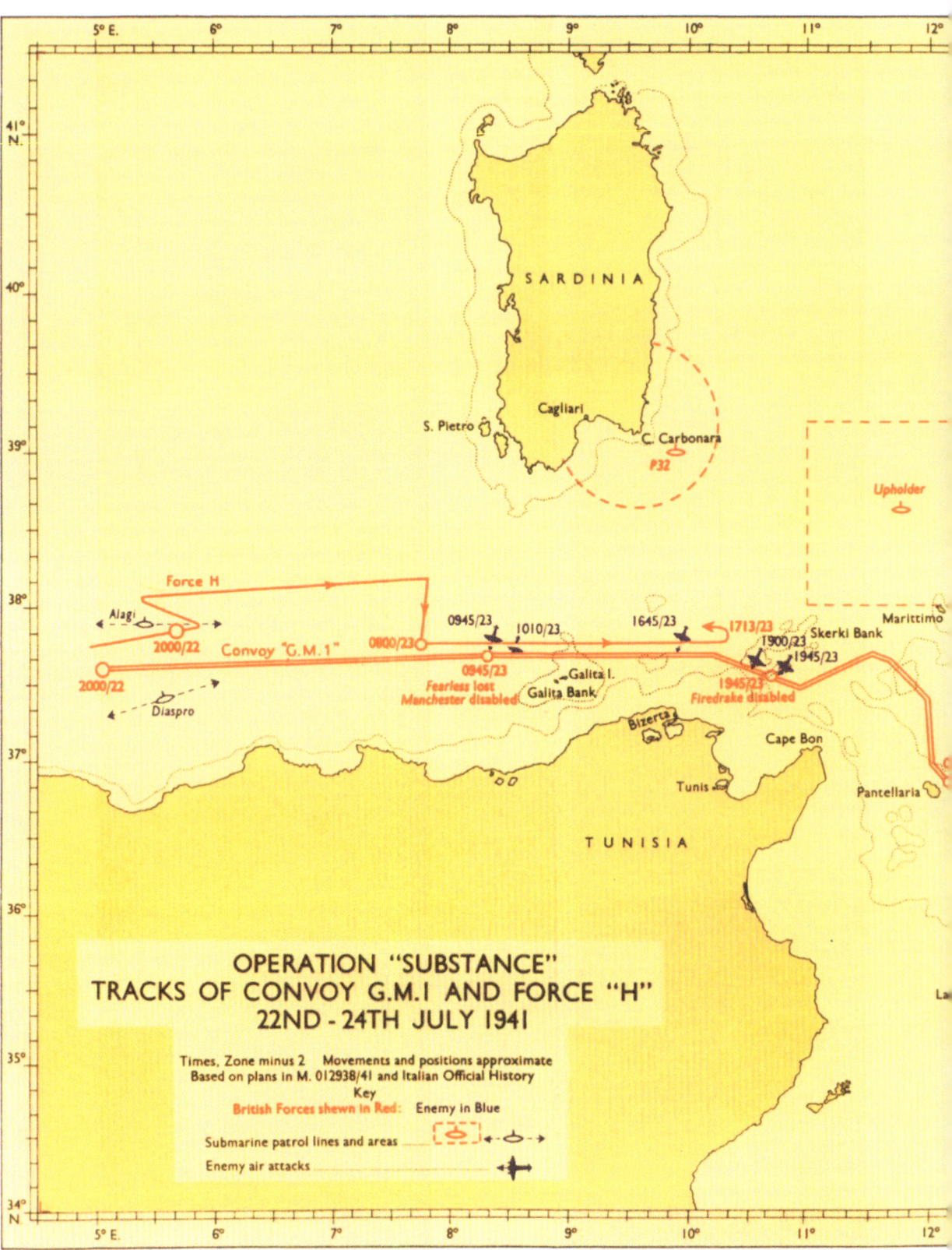

OPERATION "SUBSTANCE"
TRACKS OF CONVOY G.M.I AND FORCE "H"
22ND - 24TH JULY 1941

Times, Zone minus 2   Movements and positions approximate
Based on plans in M. 012938/41 and Italian Official History
Key
British Forces shewn in Red: Enemy in Blue

Submarine patrol lines and areas
Enemy air attacks

C.B.H. 22729

PLAN 2

CRUISING DISPOSITION No. 16
AS USED ON THE 23rd JULY 1941

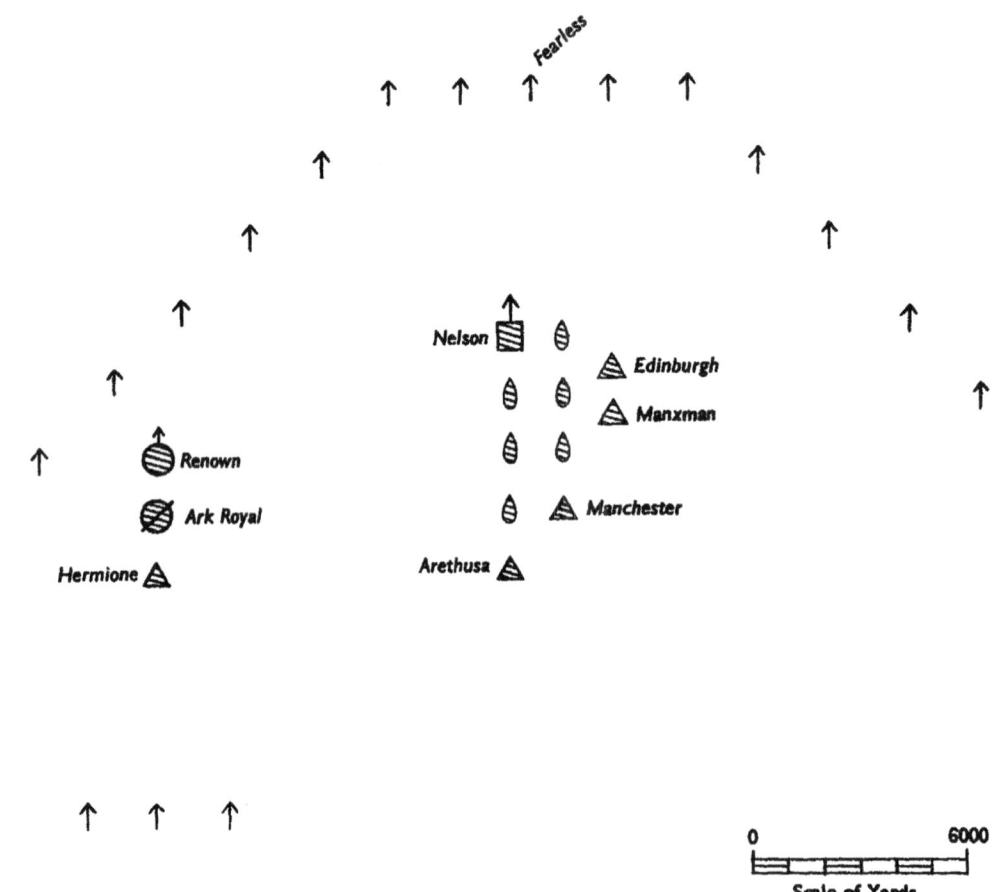

CRUISING DISPOSITION No. 17
FOR THE NIGHT OF 23rd — 24th JULY 1941

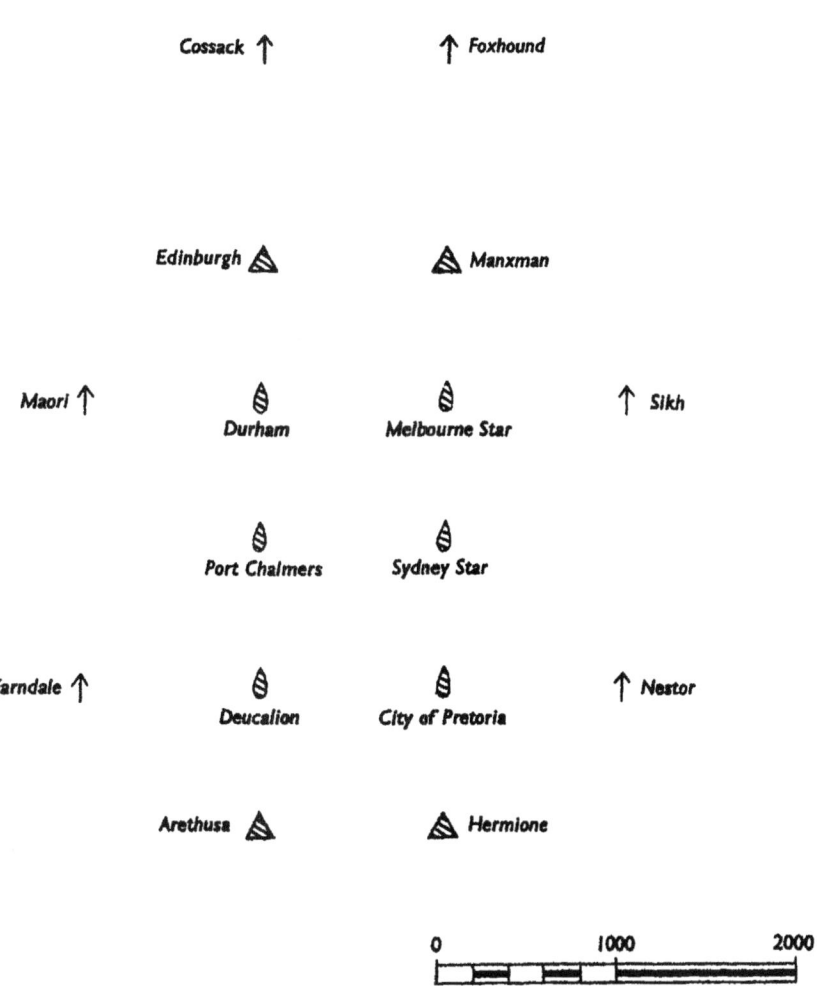

Note:—
Until she was disabled and had to leave the convoy, the *Firedrake* occupied the station in which the *Cossack* is shown. The *Foxhound* and *Firedrake* had sweeps streamed.

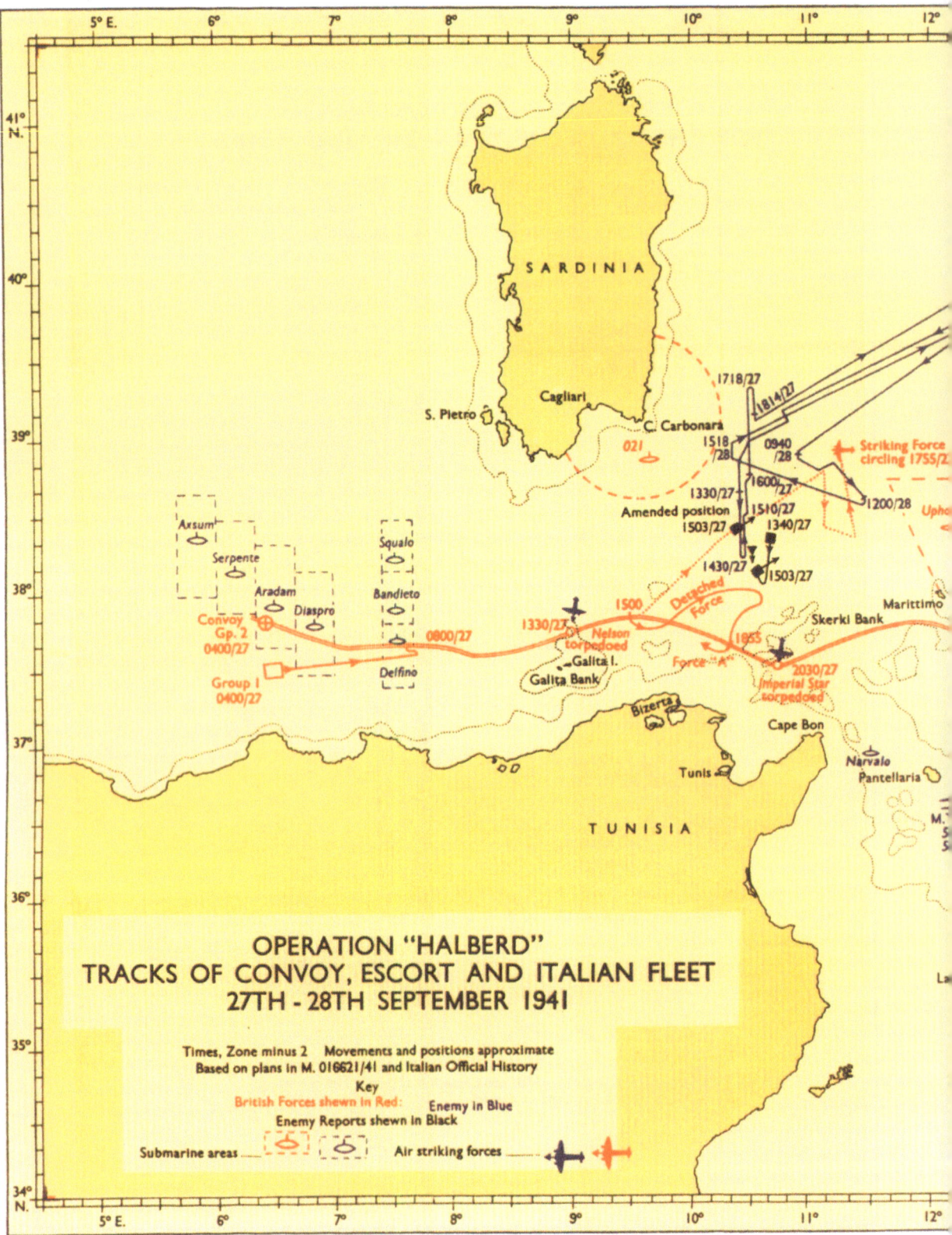

OPERATION "HALBERD"
TRACKS OF CONVOY, ESCORT AND ITALIAN FLEET
27TH - 28TH SEPTEMBER 1941

Times, Zone minus 2   Movements and positions approximate
Based on plans in M. 016621/41 and Italian Official History

Key
British Forces shewn in Red: Enemy in Blue
Enemy Reports shewn in Black

Submarine areas   Air striking forces

SARDINIA

Cagliari

S. Pietro

C. Carbonara

1718/27
1814/27
1518/28
0940/28
Striking Force circling 1755/2...
021
1330/27
1600/27
1200/28
Uph...
Amended position
1510/27
1503/27
1340/27
1430/27
1503/27

Axsum
Serpente
Aradam
Diaspro
Squalo
Bandieto
Convoy Gp. 2
0400/27
0800/27
Delfino
1330/27
Nelson torpedoed
1500
Detached Force
Marittimo
Skerki Bank
1655
Galita I.
Force "A"
2030/27
Imperial Star torpedoed
Group I
0400/27
Galita Bank

Bizerta
Cape Bon
Narvalo
Pantellaria
Tunis
M. ...
S...

TUNISIA

La...

C.B.H.

PLAN 5

41° N.

Naples

Taranto

40° N.

Gulf of Taranto

39°

Utmost

Trusty

Urge   Upright

Sokol

Palermo   Messina

38°

Trapani   Unbeaten

S I C I L Y   Catania

Ursula

37°

Cruisers
0830/28 × part company

Gozo

36°

Linosa   MALTA

pedusa

35°

Medina Bank

34° N.

13°   14°   15°   16°   17°   18°   19°   20° E.

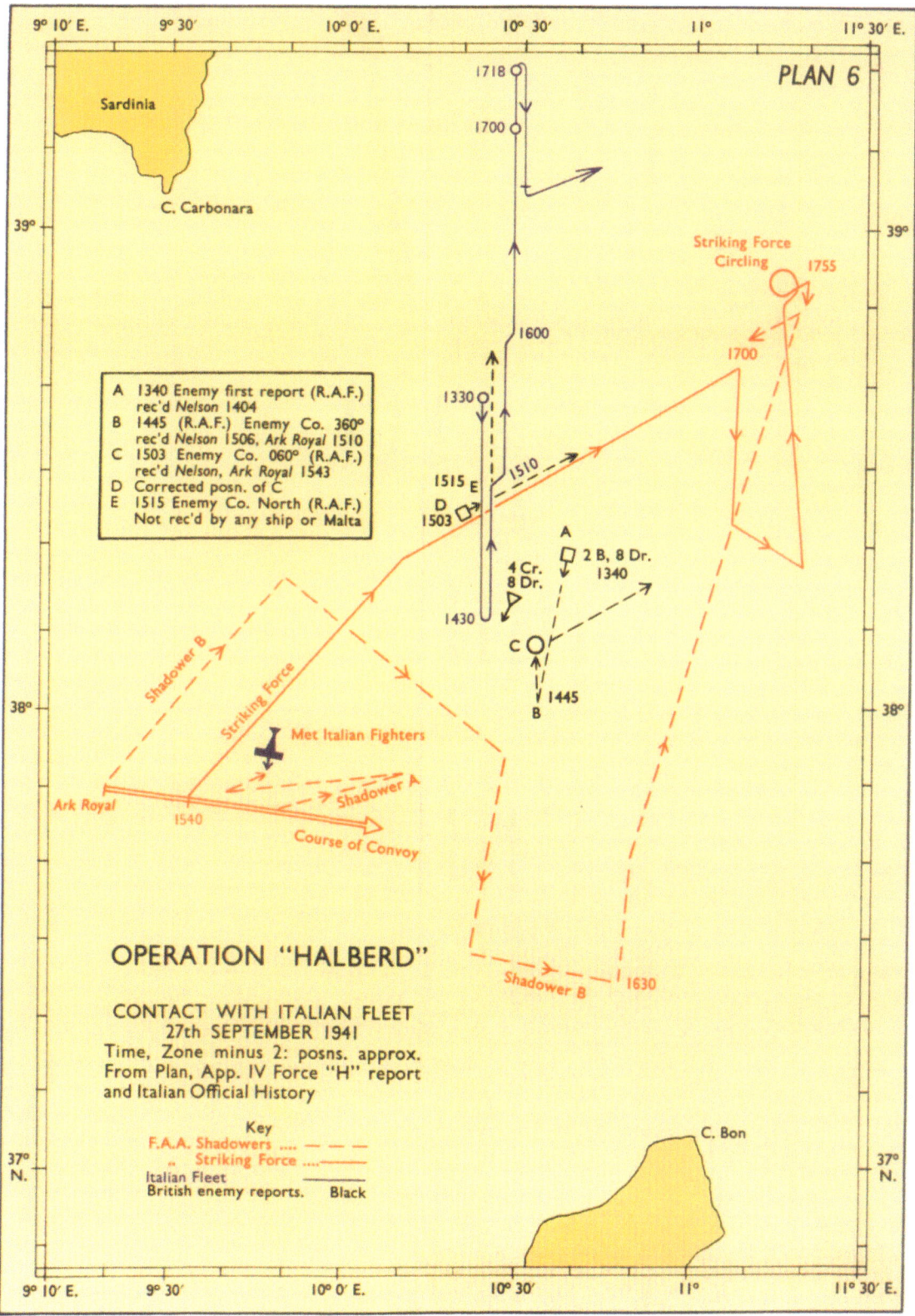

9° 10′ E.   9° 30′   10° 0′ E.   10° 30′   11°   11° 30′ E.

PLAN 6

Sardinia

C. Carbonara

39°

Striking Force Circling

1718

1700

1600

1755

1700

A 1340 Enemy first report (R.A.F.)
   rec'd *Nelson* 1404
B 1445 (R.A.F.) Enemy Co. 360°
   rec'd *Nelson* 1506, *Ark Royal* 1510
C 1503 Enemy Co. 060° (R.A.F.)
   rec'd *Nelson*, *Ark Royal* 1543
D Corrected posn. of C
E 1515 Enemy Co. North (R.A.F.)
   Not rec'd by any ship or Malta

1330

1510

1515 E
D
1503

A
2 B, 8 Dr.
1340

4 Cr.
8 Dr.

1430

C
1445

B

Shadower B

Striking Force

38°

Met Italian Fighters

Ark Royal

Shadower A

1540

Course of Convoy

Shadower B   1630

OPERATION "HALBERD"

CONTACT WITH ITALIAN FLEET
27th SEPTEMBER 1941
Time, Zone minus 2: posns. approx.
From Plan, App. IV Force "H" report
and Italian Official History

C. Bon

37°
N.

Key
F.A.A. Shadowers .... — — —
   „   Striking Force .... ————
Italian Fleet
British enemy reports.   Black

9° 10′ E.   9° 30′   10° 0′ E.   10° 30′   11°   11° 30′ E.

C.B.H. 22729.

CRUISING DISPOSITION No. 16A AS USED ON THE 27th SEPT. 1941

← Lance

← Isaac Sweers

← Gurkha

← Duncan

← Garland

← Lively

← Heythrop

← Fury

← Zulu

← Cosseck

← Foresight

← Forester

← Laforey

← Farndale

← Lightning

← Oribi

← Kenya △

Ajax ◊

Clan MacDonald ◊

Imperial Star ◊

Rowallan Castle ◊

City of Calcutta ◊

Rodney ⬛

Prince of Wales ⬛

← Edinburgh △

Clan Ferguson ◊

Dunedin Star ◊

Brecanshire △

City of Lincoln ◊

Sheffield △

← Nelson ⬛

← Euryalus △

Ark Royal ⬯

△ Hermione

{ Operating
Independently
for flying

← Piorun

← Legion

Scale of Yards

0 — 3000 — 6000

Note:—
If the Ark Royal's group had to move outside the screen to starboard or astern, the Lightning and Oribi, or the Piorun and Legion, respectively, would screen the group.

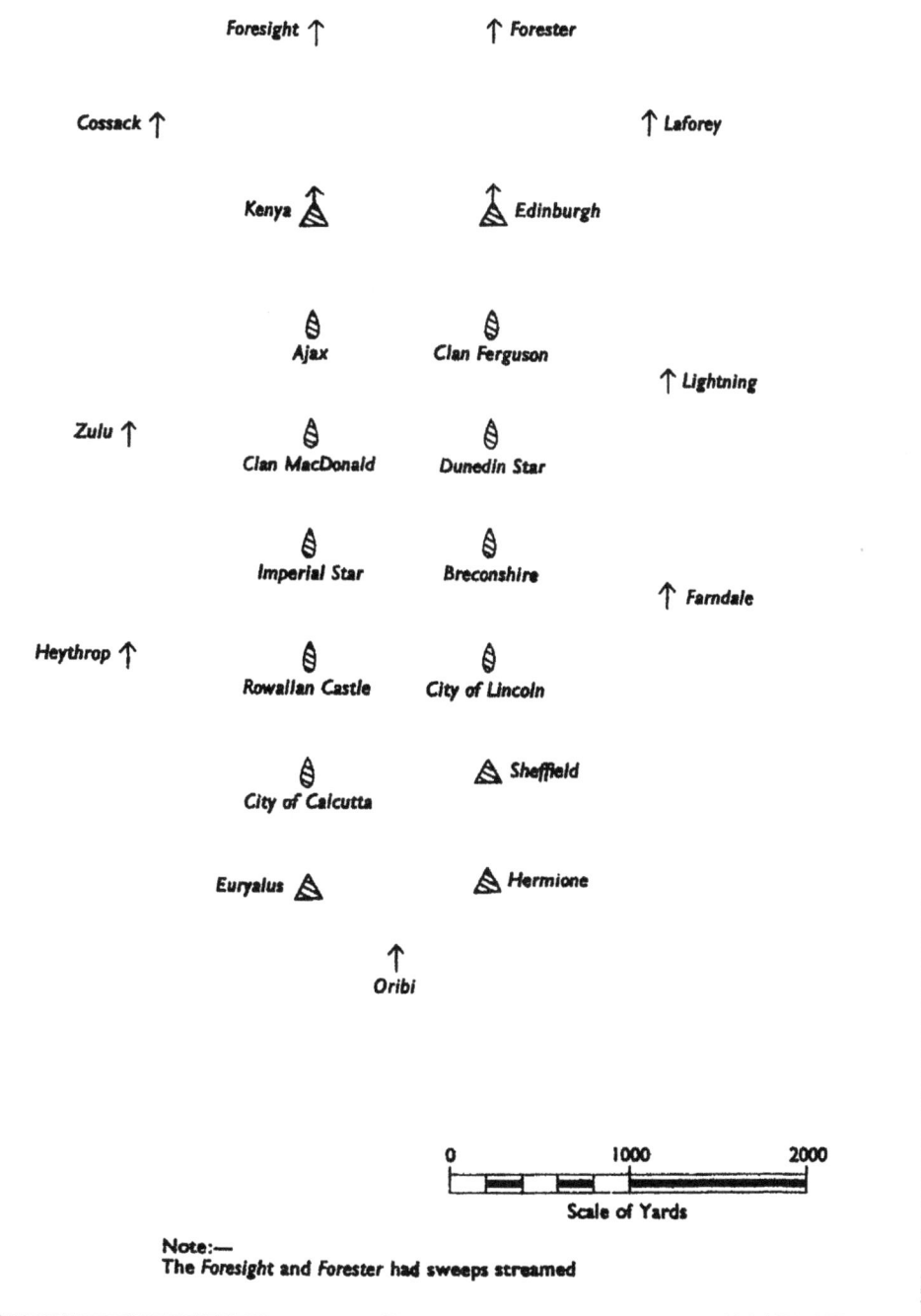

CRUISING DISPOSITION No. 17
AS USED ON THE NIGHT OF 27th — 28th SEPT. 1941

Foresight ↑   ↑ Forester

Cossack ↑   ↑ Laforey

Kenya ▲   ▲ Edinburgh

Ajax   Clan Ferguson

Zulu ↑   ↑ Lightning

Clan MacDonald   Dunedin Star

Imperial Star   Breconshire   ↑ Farndale

Heythrop ↑

Rowallan Castle   City of Lincoln

City of Calcutta   Sheffield

Euryalus   Hermione

↑
Oribi

0   1000   2000

Scale of Yards

Note:—
The *Foresight* and *Forester* had sweeps streamed

C B.H 22729

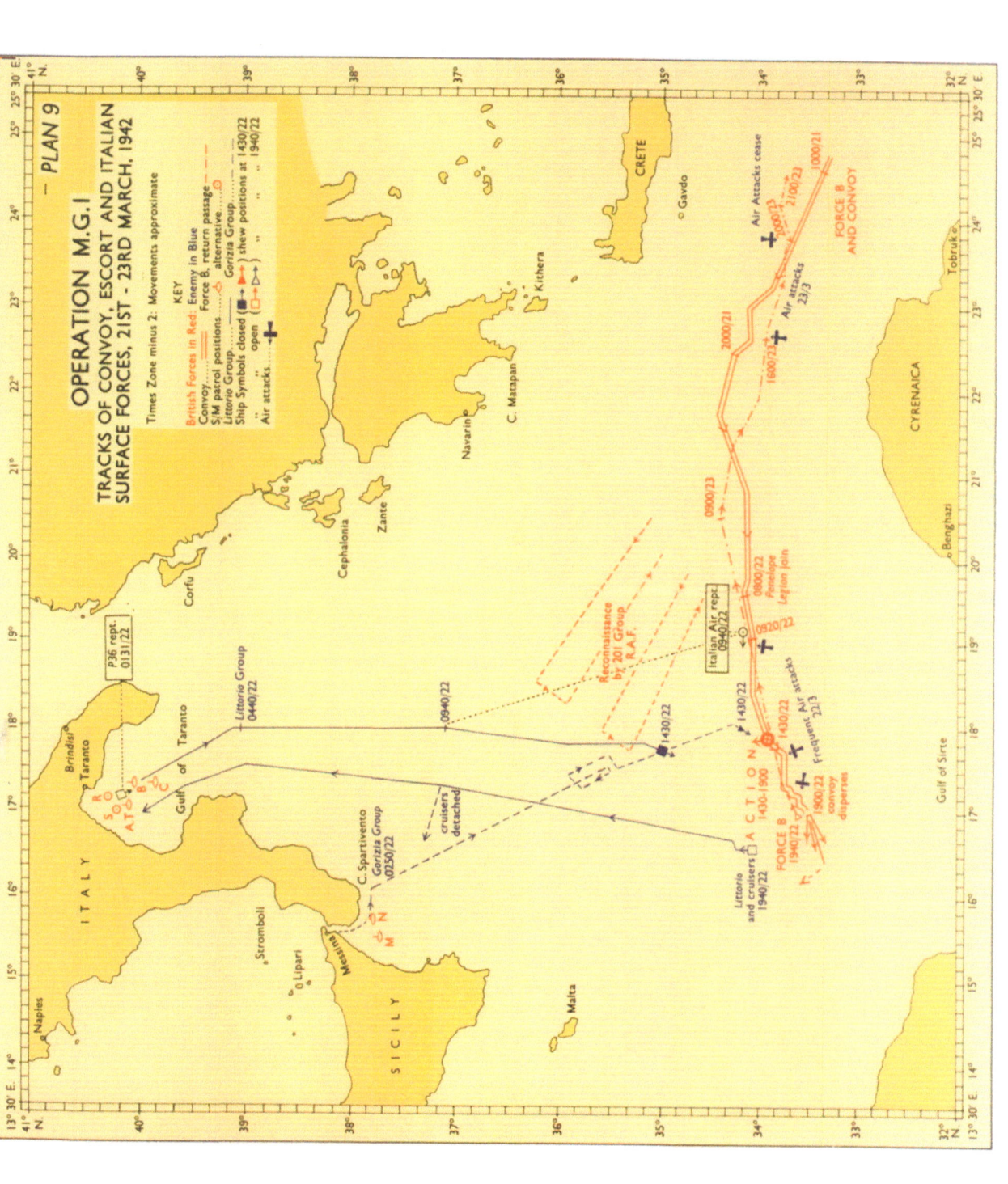

— PLAN 9

OPERATION M.G.I

TRACKS OF CONVOY, ESCORT AND ITALIAN
SURFACE FORCES, 21ST - 23RD MARCH, 1942

Times Zone minus 2: Movements approximate

KEY

British Forces in Red: Enemy in Blue
Convoy................................ Force B, return passage ____
S/M patrol positions .... ○ alternative .... ○
Littorio Group .... ⊙ Gorizia Group ....
Ship Symbols closed (■→▲→) shew positions at 1430/22
open .... (□→□→) 1940/22
Air attacks..... ☩

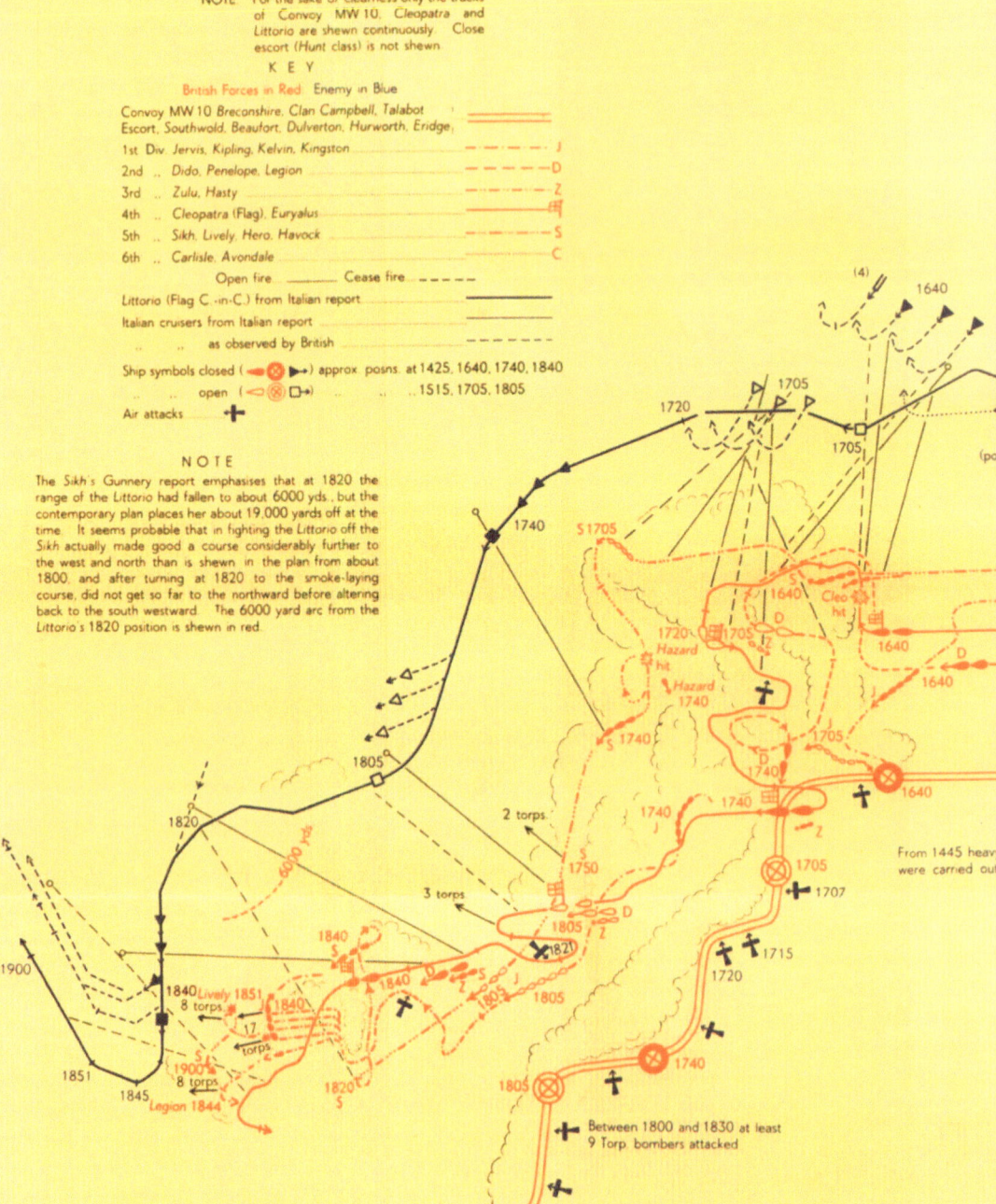

OPERATION M.G.I
SURFACE ACTION, 22 MAR. 1942
BASED ON BRITISH AND ITALIAN PLANS

Times Zone minus 2: movements approximate

NOTE For the sake of clearness only the tracks
of Convoy MW 10, Cleopatra and
Littorio are shewn continuously. Close
escort (Hunt class) is not shewn.

K E Y

British Forces in Red. Enemy in Blue

Convoy MW 10 Breconshire, Clan Campbell, Talbot
Escort, Southwold, Beaufort, Dulverton, Hurworth, Eridge,

1st Div. Jervis, Kipling, Kelvin, Kingston .... J

2nd „ Dido, Penelope, Legion .... D

3rd „ Zulu, Hasty .... Z

4th „ Cleopatra (Flag), Euryalus ....

5th „ Sikh, Lively, Hero, Havock .... S

6th „ Carlisle, Avondale C

Open fire _____ Cease fire _ _ _ _ _

Littorio (Flag C.-in-C.) from Italian report ....

Italian cruisers from Italian report ....

„   „   as observed by British ....

Ship symbols closed (◀⊗▶) approx. posns. at 1425, 1640, 1740, 1840

„   „   open (◁⊗□▶) „   „   1515, 1705, 1805

Air attacks ✛

N O T E

The Sikh's Gunnery report emphasises that at 1820 the
range of the Littorio had fallen to about 6000 yds., but the
contemporary plan places her about 19,000 yards off at the
time. It seems probable that in fighting the Littorio off the
Sikh actually made good a course considerably further to
the west and north than is shewn in the plan from about
1800, and after turning at 1820 to the smoke-laying
course, did not get so far to the northward before altering
back to the south westward. The 6000 yard arc from the
Littorio's 1820 position is shewn in red.

(map annotations)

1640

(4)

1720   1705

1705

1705

(posn.)

C

1740

S 1705

1640   Cleo. hit

1720   1705   D   1640

Hazard hit   1640

Hazard 1740

S 1740   1705

1740   1740   1640

Z

2 torps   1740   1740   1705   1707

1750   S   From 1445 heavy a... were carried out b...

3 torps   1805   D   1715

1840   1840   S   1805   J   1805   1720

1840 Lively 1851   1840   6000 yds

8 torps   17 torps   S   1805   1805   1740

1851   1900 8 torps   1820 S   1805

1845   Legion 1844

1900   Between 1800 and 1830 at least
9 Torp. bombers attacked

1840

1900 convoy disperses

C.B.H. 22729

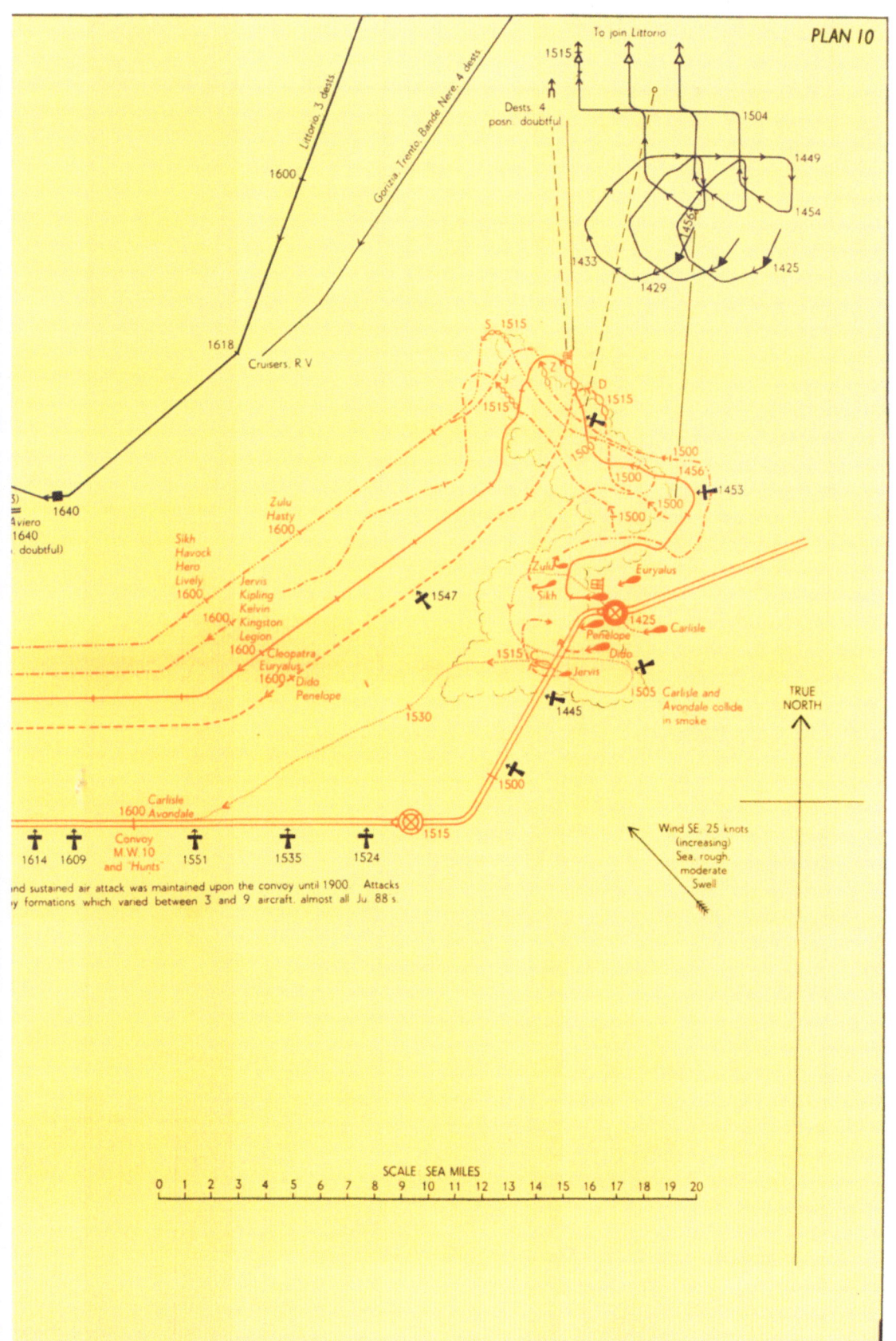

PLAN 10

To join Littorio

1515

1504

1449

1454

Dests. 4
posn. doubtful

1433

1425

1429

1458

Littorio 3 dests

1600

Gorizia, Trento, Bande Nere, 4 dests

1618   Cruisers. R.V

S. 1515

1515

D
1515

1515

1500

1500   1456

1500   1453

1500

1500

1640

Aviero
1640
(doubtful)

Zulu
Hasty
1600

Zulu
Euryalus
Sikh

1425
Penelope   Carlisle
Dido

Sikh
Havock
Hero
Lively
1600

Jervis
Kipling
Kelvin
Kingston
Legion
Cleopatra
Euryalus
Dido
Penelope

1600 x

1600 x

1600 x

1600 x

1547

1515

Jervis

1505 Carlisle and
Avondale collide
in smoke

1445

1530

1500

TRUE
NORTH

Carlisle
1600 Avondale

1614 1609

Convoy
M.W. 10
and "Hunts"

1551

1535

1524

1515

Wind SE. 25 knots
(increasing)
Sea. rough.
moderate
Swell

...nd sustained air attack was maintained upon the convoy until 1900. Attacks
...y formations which varied between 3 and 9 aircraft. almost all Ju 88 s.

SCALE SEA MILES

0 1 2 3 4 5 6 7 8 9 10 11 12 13 14 15 16 17 18 19 20

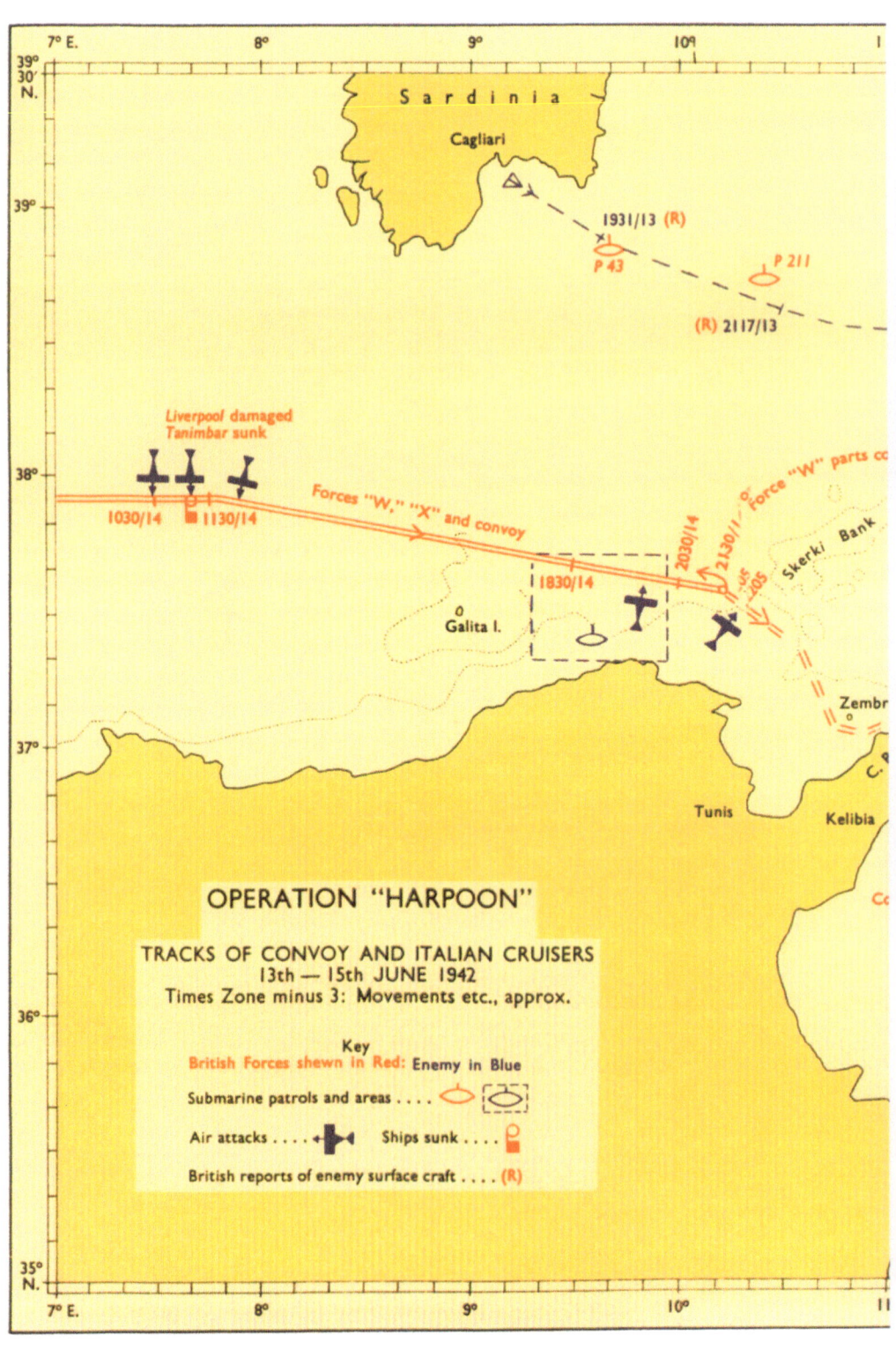

S a r d i n i a

Cagliari

1931/13 (R)

P 43   P 211

(R) 2117/13

Liverpool damaged
Tanimbar sunk

1030/14   1130/14

Forces "W," "X" and convoy   Force "W" parts co

2130/1   Skerki Bank

2030/14

1830/14   Zembr

Galita I.

Tunis   Kelibia

C. P

Co

OPERATION "HARPOON"

TRACKS OF CONVOY AND ITALIAN CRUISERS
13th — 15th JUNE 1942
Times Zone minus 3: Movements etc., approx.

Key
British Forces shewn in Red: Enemy in Blue

Submarine patrols and areas . . . .

Air attacks . . . .   Ships sunk . . . .

British reports of enemy surface craft . . . . (R)

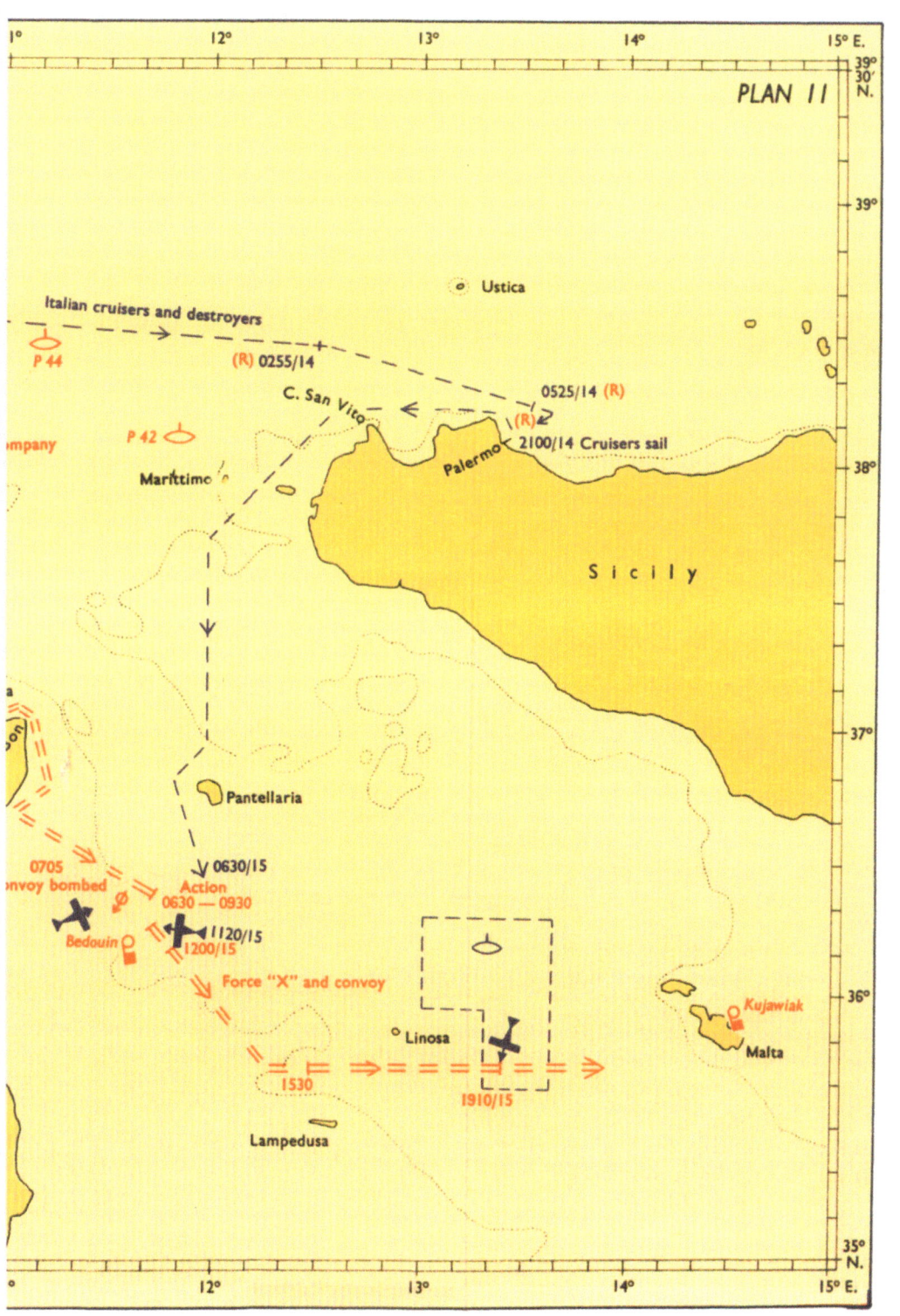

PLAN II

Ustica

Italian cruisers and destroyers

P 44

(R) 0255/14

C. San Vito

0525/14 (R)

(R)

P 42

2100/14 Cruisers sail

ompany

Marittimo

Palermo

Sicily

Pantellaria

0705

nvoy bombed

Bedouin

0630/15

Action
0630 — 0930

1120/15
1200/15

Force "X" and convoy

Linosa

Kujawiak

Malta

1530

1910/15

Lampedusa

OPERATION HARPOON
SURFACE ACTION, 15TH JUNE 1942

Times Zone minus 3 movements approximate

Key

British Forces in Red	Enemy in Blue
Convoy	Cairo
11th Div. (Marne)	12th Div.

Italian cruisers from contemporary British plans.
Italian cruisers after 0740 from Italian Official History.
Italian Destroyers. *Marne's* plan

Air Attack

N O T E

The track of the Italian forces as shewn in the Italian Official History cannot be reconciled with that shewn in contemporary British reports. In this plan the tracks and times shewn up to 0740 are taken from the *Marne's* report. After 0740, when smoke and increasing ranges made accurate observation of enemy movements difficult, the tracks are from the Italian Official History. During this period the Italian cruisers may have been further to the south and west relative to the *Cairo*; but taking all available evidence into consideration, it is believed the action was fought substantially as shewn.

Wind. Force 2

Badsworth
Middleton
Kujawiak
Blankney

Cairo
Convoy (14 knots)
0630

Marne
Matchless
Ithuriel
Partridge

0705
0700
0720
0730
0800
0830
0840
0840
0920
0930
0700

Chant sunk
Kentucky dam'd

0910
0900
0700
0920
0833
0830
0800

Partridge 0700
0710

0910
0900
0810
0810
0720
0730
0740
0800
0800
0810

Enemy Crs. open fire

0720
0717
0710
0710
0701 Bedouin
0700
0930
0920
0700

Marne O.F. on rear Cr.
Marne shift to drs. 12,000 yd.
Marne shift to van Cr.
0728 0857

0640
0700
0710
0720
0728
0720
0730
0830
0840
0850
0900
0910
0920
0930

0745
0740
0800

N (true)

Scale Sea miles
0 1 2 3 4 5 6 7 8 9 10 11 12

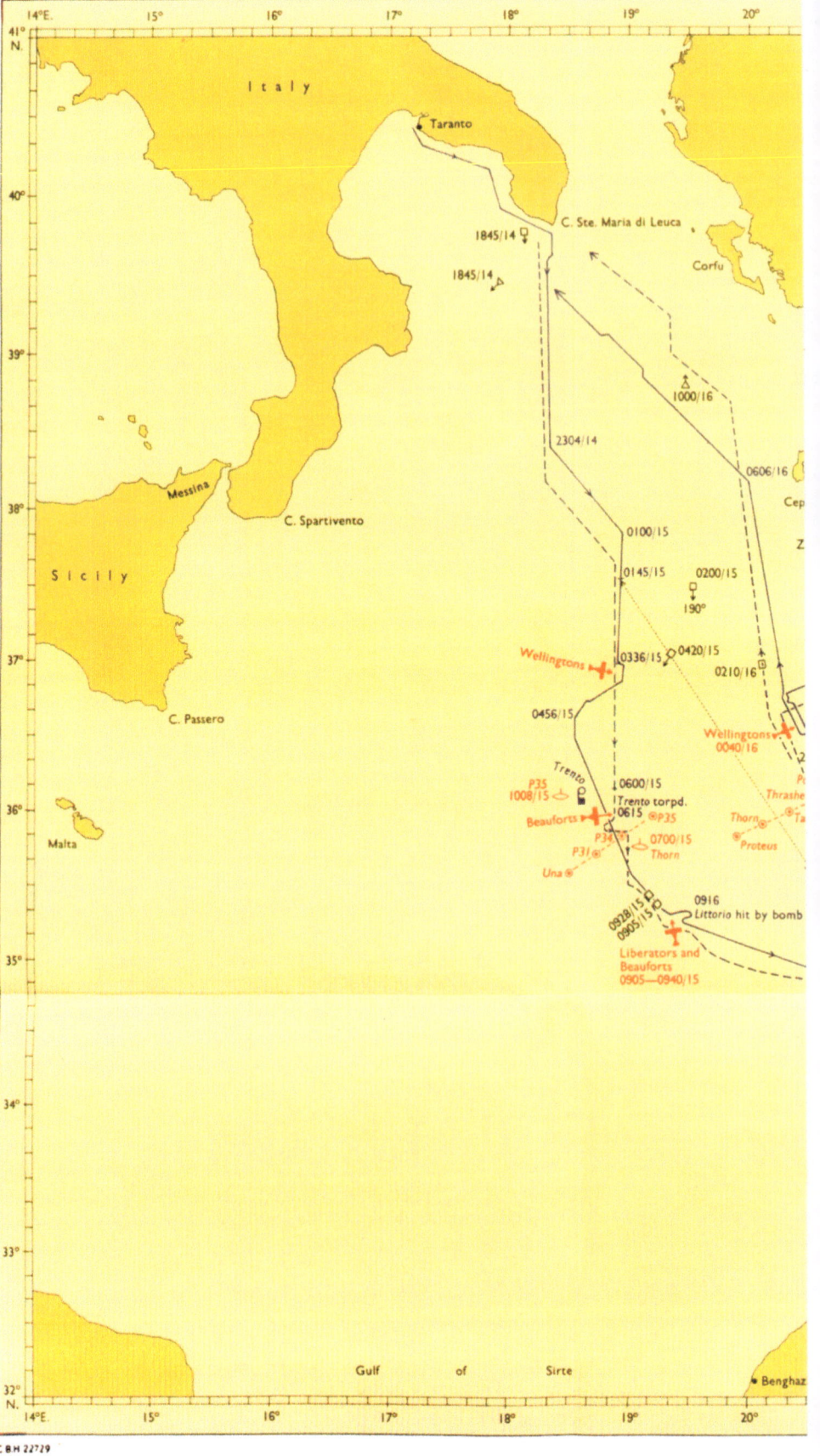

Italy

Taranto

C. Ste. Maria di Leuca

1845/14

1845/14

Corfu

1000/16

0606/16

Cep

2304/14

Messina

C. Spartivento

0100/15

0145/15   0200/15

190°

Sicily

Z

C. Passero

Wellingtons

0336/15   0420/15

0210/16

0456/15

Wellingtons
0040/16

Trento

P35
1008/15

0600/15

Trento torpd.
0615   P35

Thrashe

Thorn

Beauforts

Ta

P34   0700/15
Thorn

Proteus

P31

Una

0916
Littorio hit by bomb

0928/15
0905/15

Malta

Liberators and
Beauforts
0905—0940/15

Gulf   of   Sirte

Benghaz

C.B.H 22729

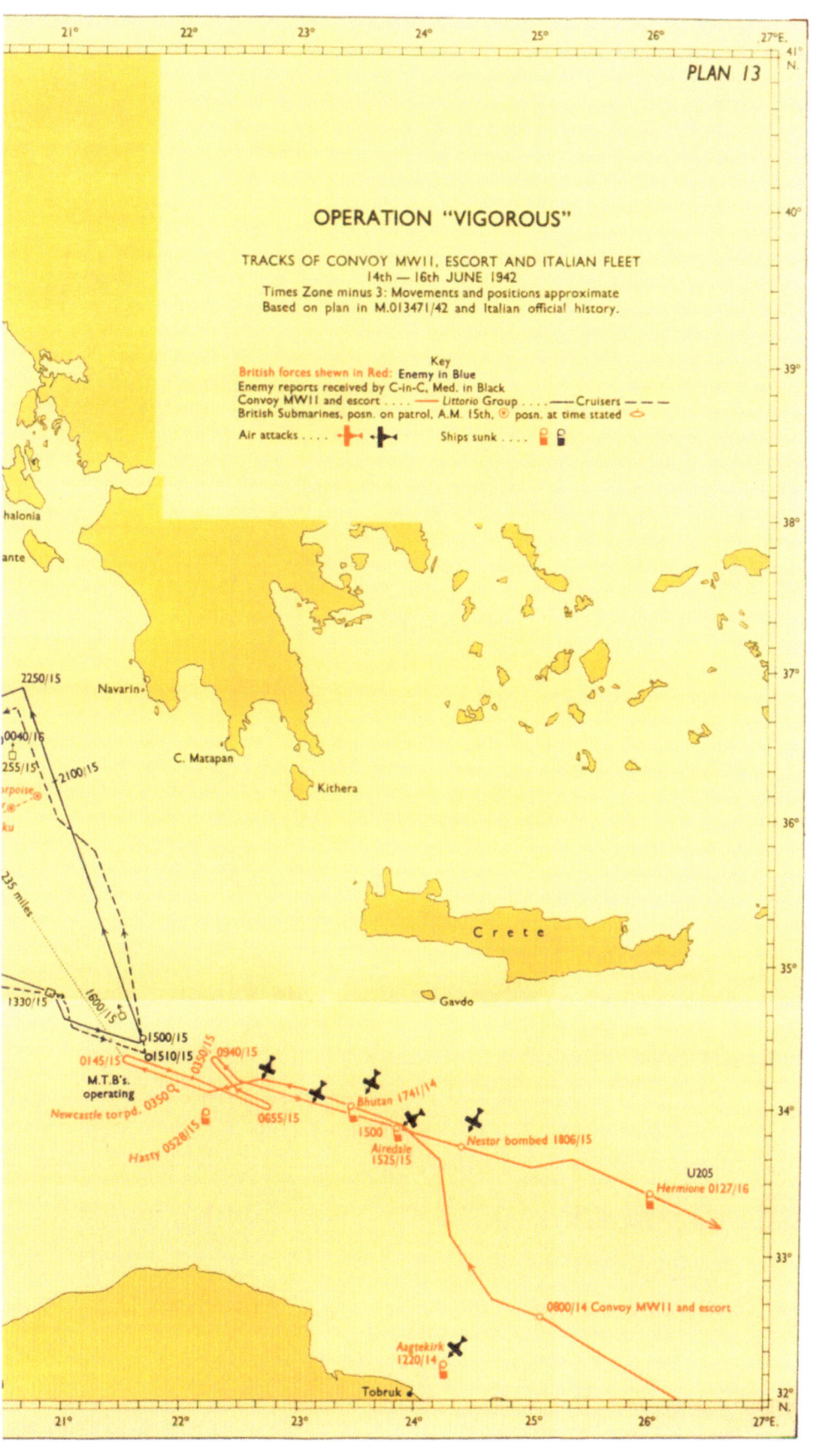

PLAN 13

OPERATION "VIGOROUS"

TRACKS OF CONVOY MWII, ESCORT AND ITALIAN FLEET
14th — 16th JUNE 1942
Times Zone minus 3: Movements and positions approximate
Based on plan in M.013471/42 and Italian official history.

Key
British forces shewn in Red: Enemy in Blue
Enemy reports received by C-in-C, Med. in Black
Convoy MWII and escort . . . . ──── Littorio Group . . . . ──── Cruisers ── ── ──
British Submarines, posn. on patrol, A.M. 15th, ⊗ posn. at time stated ◁▷
Air attacks . . . . ◼▬ ◆   Ships sunk . . . . ⬮ ⬮

2250/15
Navarin
0040/16
255/15
2100/15
orpoise
ku
C. Matapan
Kithera

235 miles

Crete

Gavdo

1330/15
1600/15
1500/15
0145/15   01510/15   0940/15
M.T.B.'s
operating   0330/15
Newcastle torpd. 0350   Bhutan 1741/14
Hasty 0528/15   0655/15
1500
Airedale   Nestor bombed 1806/15
1525/15
U205
Hermione 0127/16

0800/14 Convoy MWII and escort

Aagtekirk
1220/14

Tobruk

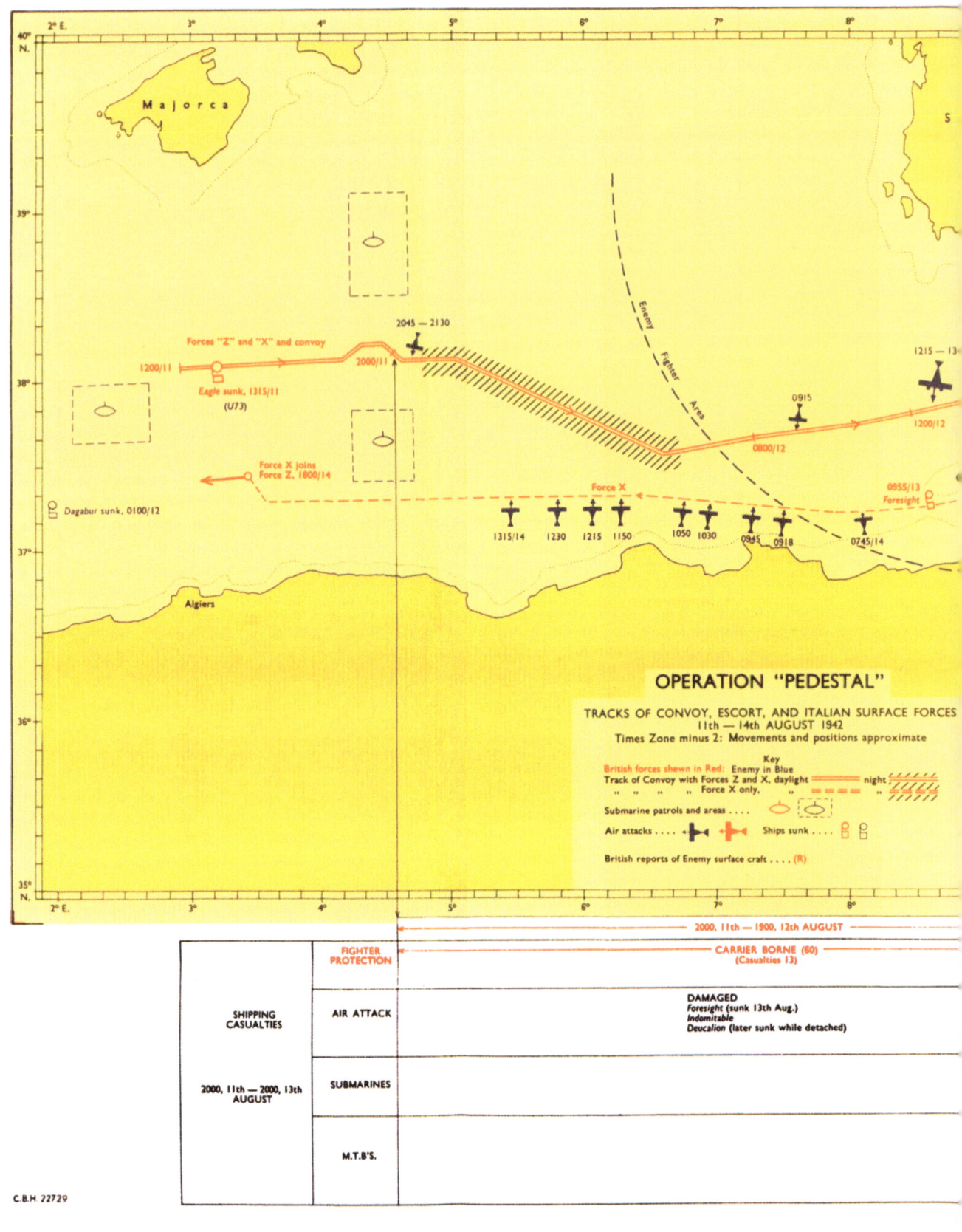

OPERATION "PEDESTAL"

TRACKS OF CONVOY, ESCORT, AND ITALIAN SURFACE FORCES
11th — 14th AUGUST 1942
Times Zone minus 2: Movements and positions approximate

Key

British forces shewn in Red; Enemy in Blue

Track of Convoy with Forces Z and X, daylight ══════ night ╱╱╱╱╱
   "   "   "   "   Force X only, ━━━━━ " ╱╱╱╱╱
Submarine patrols and areas ....
Air attacks ....   Ships sunk ....
British reports of Enemy surface craft .... (R)

		2000, 11th — 1900, 12th AUGUST
SHIPPING CASUALTIES 2000, 11th — 2000, 13th AUGUST	FIGHTER PROTECTION	CARRIER BORNE (60) (Casualties 13)
	AIR ATTACK	DAMAGED *Foresight* (sunk 13th Aug.) *Indomitable* *Deucalion* (later sunk while detached)
	SUBMARINES	
	M.T.B'S.	

C.B.H 22729

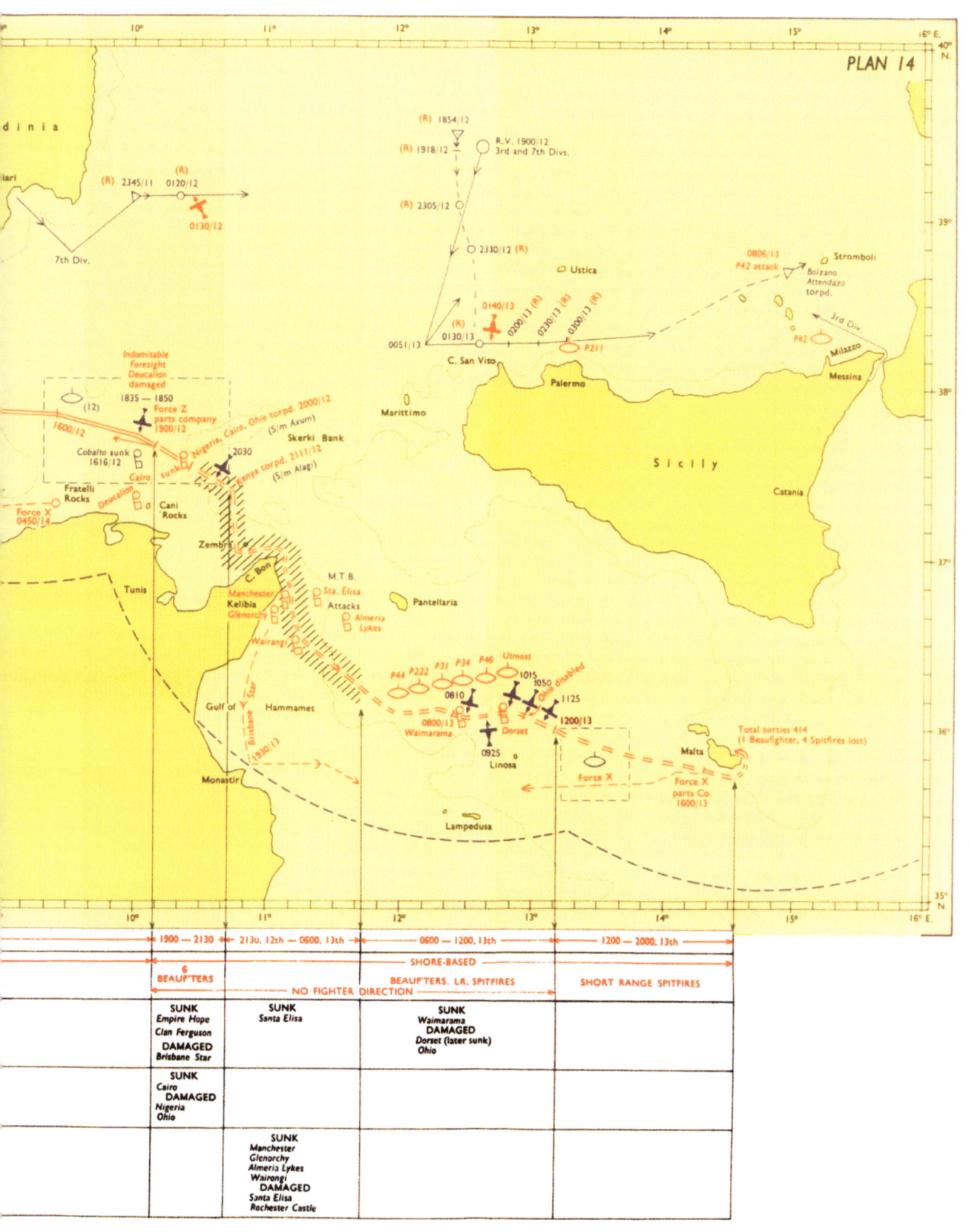

PLAN 14

Sardinia

7th Div.

(R) 2345/11 (R) 0120/12
0130/12

(R) 1854/12
R.V. 1900/12
3rd and 7th Divs.
(R) 1918/12
(R) 2305/12
2330/12 (R)
Ustica
0806/13
P42 attack
Stromboli
Bolzano
Attendazo
torpd.
3rd Div.
0140/13 (R) 0200/13 (R) 0230/13 (R) 0300/13 (R)
P42
Milazzo
0051/13
(R) 0130/13
C. San Vito
P211
Messina
Palermo
Marittimo
Sicily
Catania

Indomitable
Foresight
Deucalion
damaged
1835 – 1850
(12)
1600/12
Force Z
parts company
1900/12
Nigeria, Cairo, Ohio torpd. 2000/12
(S/m Axum)
Skerki Bank
Cobalto sunk
1616/12
2030
Kenya torpd. 2111/12
(S/m Alagi)
Cairo
Deucalion
Fratelli
Rocks
Cani
Rocks
Force X
0450/14
Zembra
C. Bon
M.T.B.
Sta. Elisa
Attacks
Pantellaria
Tunis
Manchester
Glenorchy
Kelibia
Almeria
Lykes
Wairangi

Gulf of Hammamet
Brisbane Star
1830/13
P44 P222 P31 P34 P46 Utmost
0810
1015
1050
Ohio disabled
1125
0800/13
Waimarama
1200/13
Dorset
0925
Linosa
Malta
Total sorties 414
(1 Beaufighter, 4 Spitfires lost)
Force X
Force X
parts Co.
1600/13
Monastir
Lampedusa

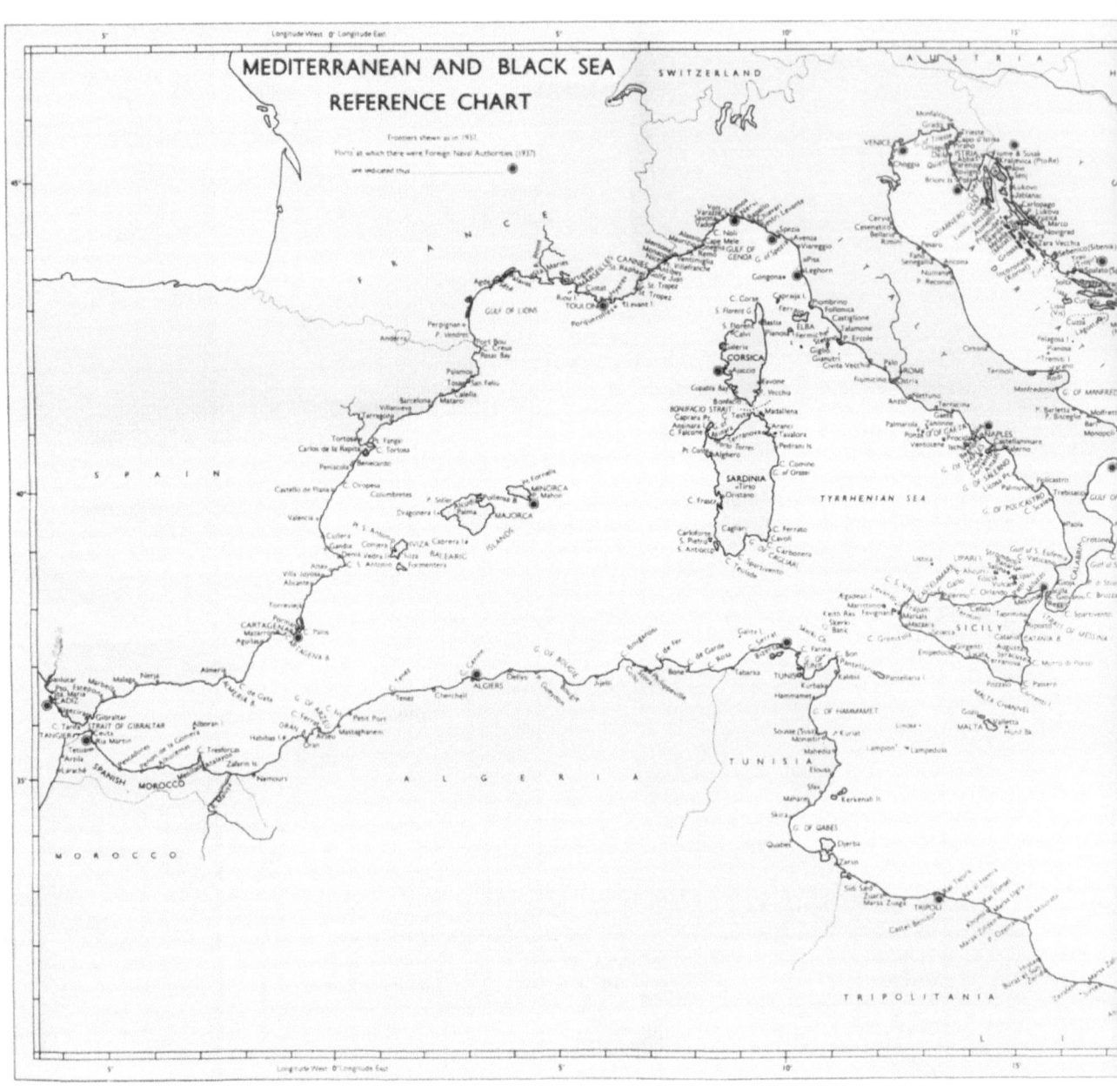

MEDITERRANEAN AND BLACK SEA
REFERENCE CHART

Frontiers shown as in 1937

Ports at which there were Foreign Naval Authorities (1937)
are indicated thus

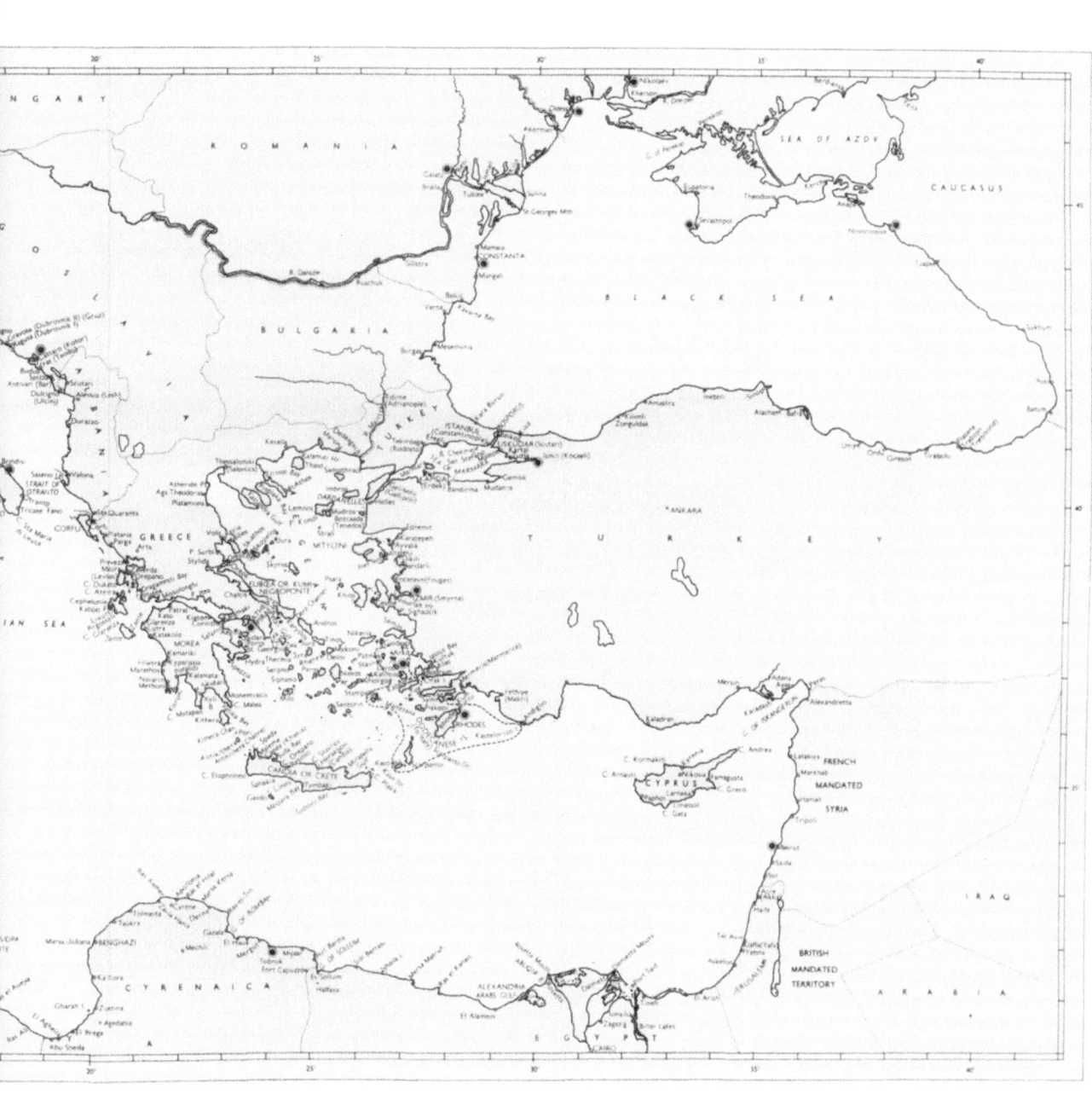